THE
LIFE HISTORY
OF A TEXAS
BIRDWATCHER

THE LIFE HISTORY OF A TEXAS BIRDWATCHER

Connie Hagar of Rockport

KAREN HARDEN MCCRACKEN

Foreword by Roger Tory Peterson

TEXAS A&M UNIVERSITY PRESS   COLLEGE STATION

Previously published as
Connie Hagar: The Life History of a Texas Birdwatcher.

Unless otherwise noted, all photographs are from the Ornithological Archives
of the Texas Cooperative Wildlife Collections, Texas A&M University.

Maps compiled by Amy Koltermann and Suzanne Dilworth,
the Center for Coastal Studies, Texas A&M University–Corpus Christi.

The paper used in this book meets the minimum requirements
of the American National Standard for Permanence
of Paper for Printed Library Materials, Z39.48-1984.
Binding materials have been chosen for durability.

LIBRARY OF CONGRESS CATALOGING-IN-PUBLICATION DATA

McCracken, Karen Harden, 1905–1992
    The life history of a Texas birdwatcher : Connie Hagar of Rockport/
by Karen Harden McCracken ; foreword by Roger Tory Peterson.
    p.cm.
    Rev. ed. of: Connie Hagar. 1986.
    ISBN 1-58544-144-9 (cloth : alk. paper) —ISBN 1-58544-164-3
(pbk : alk. paper)
    1. Hagar, Martha Conger, 1886–1973.   2. Bird watching—
Texas.   3. Bird watchers—Texas—Biography.   I. McCracken,
Karen Harden, 1905–1992. Connie Hagar.   II. Title

QL31.H24.M35 2000
598'.07'234764—dc21
[B]   2001027373

TO THE MEMORY OF MY PARENTS,

Dollie Baggett Harden

&

Thaddeus E. Harden

CONTENTS

ILLUSTRATIONS

[ix]

FOREWORD

Texas boasts the largest avifauna of any of the fifty states. It is number one; California, as might be expected, runs second.

Nearly 800 miles from top to bottom or from east to west, and covering some 267,000 square miles, Texas can claim avian diversity by virtue of size alone. East blends with West, biologically, along the 100th meridian, which runs through the Edwards Plateau, and North meets South, especially along the Rio Grande, where birds from the northern plains meet Mexican species. But nowhere else in the state do more birds pass during migration than the central and upper coast, which draws birdwatchers from far and near to witness the annual pageant.

For many years the aficionados of birding converged on the small seaside town of Rockport, just north of Corpus Christi, because of a trim ninety-seven pound wren of a woman, Martha Conger Hagar, who monitored the migrations. Over a period of more than thirty years she seldom missed a day in the field.

Born in north Texas in the town of Corsicana, where her father was mayor, she had all the advantages of a genteel aristocratic upbringing. Music, literature, and a love of nature were part of her parental heritage. But social life in Corsicana, in which she played an active role, was not as fulfilling to her as birdwatching.

After spending a month with her sister at the coastal resort village of Rockport in 1934 (the year that my first *Field Guide* saw the light of day), she made the decision to pull up stakes in her hometown, move to Rockport, and simply enjoy the birds.

Her husband Jack, a Bostonian who had adopted Texas ways, went along with the idea, but inasmuch as he had no intention of retiring at the age of fifty-seven, he bought the Rockport Cottages—a motel-like complex of eight small one-room white dwellings—which he remodeled. They soon became filled with birders, especially during the spring and fall migrations.

Connie had already made a name for herself as the number-one field birder in Texas when I met her in 1948 at my very first Audubon Screen Tour lecture in Corpus Christi. My film, *The Riddle of Migration* was spliced together from spare footage taken by other screen tour lecturers. Inasmuch as I was inexperienced on the platform, and the film was not really my own, I suspect my debut was a near-disaster, but Connie seemed to enjoy it.

Guy Emerson, a New York banker who at the time was treasurer of the National Audubon Society, had told me about Connie, and he was to become one of her most constant visitors and admirers, coming almost yearly for a stint of birding at Rockport. The Hagars always put him in Cottage no. 2, the best one.

Guy, twenty years older than I, was perhaps the most civilized man I have ever known, a friend whom I loved dearly. He had learned about Connie through Dr. Harry Oberholser, senior biologist of the Bureau of Biological Survey, who was preparing his monumental *Birds of Texas*. Oberholser, a specimen-tray museum man of the old school, had questioned some of Connie's published reports and had gone to Rockport to see for himself and to quiz Connie. Putting her through relentless grillings he became satisfied that she knew what she was talking about. Her sight records were convincing and met his academic standards.

Connie Hagar kept daily notes in her "calendar" over a period of more than thirty-five years, but there was another dimension that could be filled in only by a biographer. It is my belief that unless events are put in writing and eventually published, they are lost; almost as though they had never happened. Connie was fortunate to have as a close friend Kay McCracken, a reporter with the *Caller-Times* of Corpus Christi. Kay, a good birder herself, became the Boswell to Connie's Johnson. Starting the interviews when Connie was seventy-six, Kay talked with her for many hours, often day after day, bringing to the surface happenings that were only hinted at in the "calendar."

I first met Mrs. McCracken, then Kay Bynum, in 1953 when James Fisher of England and I were on our hundred-day odyssey around the perimeter of the continent, which we recounted in *Wild America*. We had reached Rockport during the third week in May, a little late for the big spring fallouts. Connie knew that we would be driving through Corpus Christi on our way to the Rio Grande, so she alerted Kay, who, being an opportunistic reporter, requested an interview. I remember it well. She observed that James Fisher's fair English skin was taking a beating under the Texas sun. At one point she stopped jotting down her notes and directed our attention to a hooded oriole, a bird we had not yet seen. James Fisher shouted "Tallyho!"—his ritual response whenever he saw a new bird.

After the publication of *Wild America* others followed our trail, stopping at the Rockport Cottages. Stuart Keith, a young Englishman who later became president of the newly formed American Birding Association, was one of the first. He topped our record by seeing more birds north of the Mexican border than we did. A few years later a couple of British colonials from far-away Malaya—Mr. and Mrs. F. G. H. Allen—followed the *Wild America* itinerary. They also stopped to see Connie Hagar.

But it was Guy Emerson more than any other person who spread the word about the wonder-woman of Rockport. At his urging Ludlow Griscom, the dean of American birdwatchers, flew down from Boston to see if the reports were true, half expecting they were not. As Ludlow sat in Connie's living room examining her field journal, he turned to her and said, "Surely, Mrs. Hagar, you don't mean that Wied's crested [brown-crested] flycatchers are present this far north in Texas. Are you sure?"

"Mr. Griscom," she replied, "if you will move your chair back a bit and look out the window, you will see a pair building their nest."

Ludlow was further chastened when he expressed doubt about the numbers of buff-breasted sandpipers she claimed to see. She directed him to a field where in a single flock he saw three times as many buffbreasts as he had spotted in all his years of birding.

The list of ornithological stars who signed in at the Rockport Cottages is impressive. Many of New England's top birders soon followed Griscom: George and Annette Cottrell, Dr. Norman Hill, Dorothy Snyder of the Peabody Museum, and Ruth Emery, to name a few.

From the New York City area came Richard Pough, author of the *Audubon Bird Guides*; Edwin Way Teale, the revered nature writer, and his wife Nellie; and Robert Cushman Murphy of the American Museum. The National Audubon crowd—both staff and members of the board—flocked in: presidents John Baker and Carl Buchheister; vice-presidents Roland Clement and Charles Callison; editor Eleanor King; sanctuary and research directors Robert Porter Allen, Charlie Brookfield, Alexander Sprunt, Jr., and his son Sandy; as well as Allan and Helen Cruickshank.

From our nation's capital came John Aldrich of the National Museum; Fred Packard of the National Parks Association; Clarence Cottam of the Fish and Wildlife Service; and Dillon Ripley, who was to become secretary of the Smithsonian. Academia was further represented by Cornell's Professor Arthur Allen, the first U.S. professor of ornithology; George Lowery and Bob Newman of Louisiana State University; Harold Mayfield, a president of the American Ornithologists' Union; and Jim Baillie of the Toronto Museum. The Hagars also hosted artists Richard Grossenheider and John Henry Dick; *Life* photographer Alfred Eisenstadt; Henry Hill Collins, who published the first field checklist; Don Bleitz; Edward Chalif; Karen and Whitney Eastman; Locke Mackenzie; Burt Monroe; Frank Watson; Dale Zimmerman; Milton Trautman; Ivan Sanderson; Leonard Hall; and many other well-known field ornithologists.

Two of New Jersey's top birders, Lee Edwards and Clarence Brown of the Urner Ornithological Club, became so obsessed with the excellent birding at Rockport that after their retirement they booked in at the cottages each year for weeks at a time. In fact, "Brownie" and Connie tallied 204 species in a single day during a fallout, thereby exceeding the record of 200 for the first time in the United States.

Closer to home, the ornithological elite of Texas became Connie's intimates: J. Frank Dobie; George Williams; Roy Bedichek; Jerry Stillwell; Irby Davis; Fred Webster; and Edgar Kincaid, who edited Oberholser's great work.

To today's younger crowd of birders many of these names may not be meaningful, but they represented the state-of-the-art as it was during the generation from the mid-thirties through the 1960s. Although I knew nearly every one of the men and women mentioned by Kay McCracken in her biography of Connie, I realize, sadly, that two-thirds of them are now gone. On a more positive note, the foundations they laid and their legacy of field work remain as a baseline with which to compare today's trends and those of the future.

To Kay McCracken we owe a debt of gratitude for putting on record the life story of a remarkable woman who had many friends.

ROGER TORY PETERSON

PREFACE

Connie and Jack Hagar had lived in Rockport eight years when I arrived to work on the weekly newspaper. We were cordial friends, but at that time I shared the then widely prevalent opinion that birdwatchers were harmless but definitely quirky people. It's an opinion I still hold, and I am now pleased to be included in that category. Nobody gets more out of life and travel than we birders do. However, not until nearly two decades after I had joined the quirky fraternity did it occur to me that someone, not necessarily I, should write Connie's life story. It's a good story, and as a newspaper reporter I think all good stories should be in print.

Ornithology benefited greatly from Connie Hagar's contributions. Her discoveries were known to many individuals, but no individual knew them all. They were not contained in any single, written source. Would Connie document her life and work? Certainly not—nor would anyone else I sought. So in the summer of 1962 I began interviewing her for about two hours daily, five days a week. I am the Kay Bynum, later Kay Mc-Cracken, who surfaces in the narrative in 1953.

Not until I got into these interviews did I realize that Connie was an exceptional person quite aside from her knowledge of birds. Hers was the most phenomenal memory I have ever encountered. I was constantly amazed by her vivid recollections of events, people, details, even dialogue—she could remember what was said and who said it. Imagine a mere toddler remembering her mother's exact words, "Get up off the floor, Mr.

Neblett. You're spoiling the child." It was that way all through the interviews: details, scenes, and comments so explicit that I had a sense of having been there.

Connie gave me her "Nature Calendars"—twenty-five volumes of notes on her daily observations—as well as dozens of letters, photographs, hundreds of clippings about herself, and other documents. (These sources have been given to the Texas A&M University Archives.)

Then, too, I was on the scene, either at Rockport or Corpus Christi; I met and birded with—and interviewed—many of the people who figure in this book. They described many of the episodes that I had already heard from Connie. I wish I could relate every story I heard, but space forbade. Many of these people also gave me letters she'd written, photographs, and clippings they had saved.

The names of many birds have been changed over the years. For clarity I have used the 1983 AOU Checklist designations except when the name appears in a quotation. These older names are listed in an appendix along with the new terms.

To the many who shared their reminiscences with me and gave other assistance, I am immensely grateful; the list would require pages, and I dare not try lest some be omitted. But I must mention Thomas P. Harrison, Jr., of the University of Texas, and Frank Wardlaw, director of the University of Texas Press and later of Texas A&M University Press, who gave me encouragement and from time to time, when I had abandoned this project, set me to work again. I cannot thank them enough.

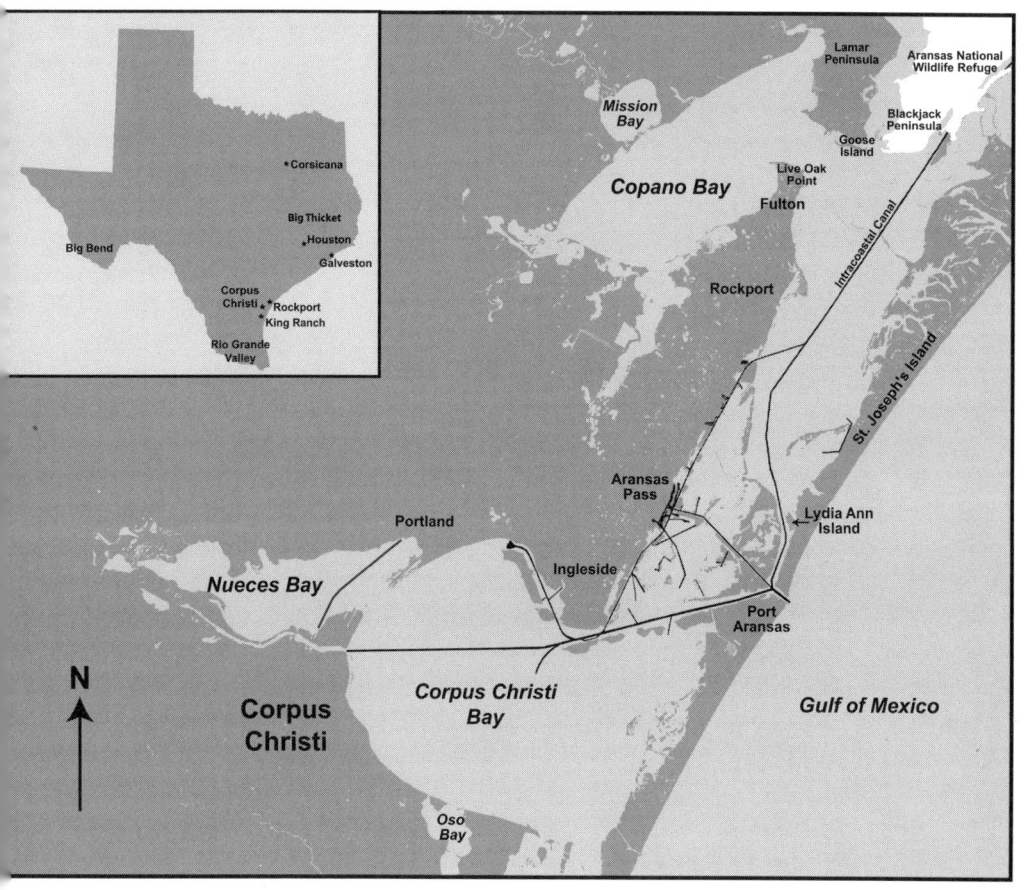

The Central Texas Coast

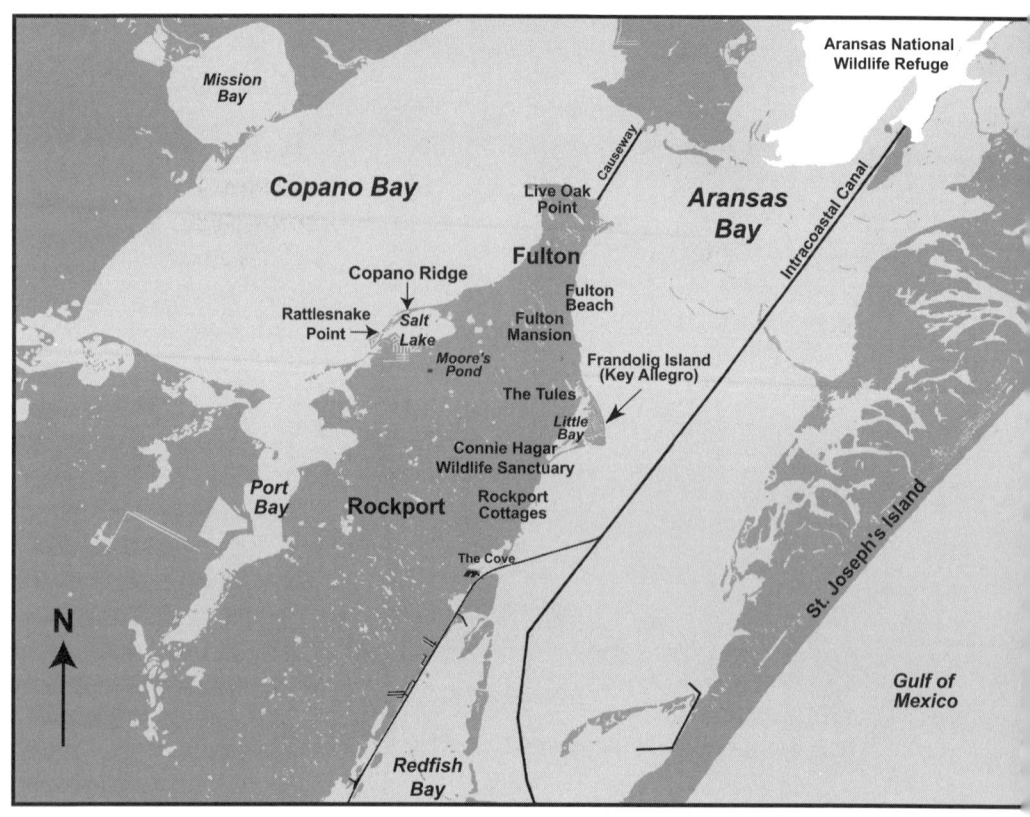

Rockport and Fulton

THE
LIFE HISTORY
OF A TEXAS
BIRDWATCHER

Chapter 1

Martha Conger Neblett was born June 14, 1886, in Corsicana, Texas, to Robert Scott and Mattie Yeater Neblett, their first of three children. Mattie named her daughter after her own mother, Martha Conger Yeater, the last of several generations of her family to grow up on the Conger plantation in Mississippi. Robert, an attorney and the mayor of Corsicana, was called "Judge" Neblett, a title bestowed gratuitously upon all lawyers in Texas in that era. His career did include a term on a district court bench.

Both parents were intellectuals who would teach their children to enjoy music, literature, art, nature, and history. Of Scottish and Irish ancestry, they came from aristocratic families of the Old South but were fiercely Texan and proud of the roles their forebears had played in pioneering and developing the state.

Robert and Mattie were married six years before Conger was born, having postponed the glad event until a suitable sum, five thousand dollars, was set aside for a college education and until a proper home could be built. Before the end of the baby's first summer, they moved into a house on Beaton Street, two blocks from the courthouse. The three-story, pillared white house containing fourteen rooms, six halls, and two verandas was built entirely of Texas timber. Walnut was carved for the front stairway; the several mantels were inlaid with walnut, ash, pine, oak, and mesquite. Here was room for all the hand-embroidered linens, the china and silver, and the heirloom furniture that had been Mattie's portion as a bride. More servants were hired, one to help with the baby and, especially, to launder her lavish layette, enough for three babies, with each garment hand-stitched and daintily embroidered. The cloud-thin christening robe, long as a lady's dress, was so transparent that Mattie had provided two petticoats, "for modesty."

Each parent had definite plans for the child. Mattie would teach her to be a lady—no other future was thinkable for a daughter. She would learn to exercise the social graces; to entertain; to be agreeable to gentlemen; to manage servants; to embroider, dance, and sing; to recite verses for company at an early age; and later, to read poetry for parlor gatherings. Bob Neblett proposed to develop her mind; above all she must be able to think.

But the infant was puny. Milk disagreed with her, but milk, being mandatory for babies, was forced down her. Allergies were unknown at the time, as were substitutes for milk. When the baby was a month old, her parents so despaired of her life that they had the minister come to the home and baptize her. Two years later they had a proper ceremony at St. John's Episcopal Church. By then, free of the milk diet, the fragile daughter was a tomboy. She climbed trees almost as soon as she walked. Lying flat on the ground, she teased ant lions: "Doodlebug, doodlebug, your house is on fire." Aboard her father's back she galloped miles through the house, whooping for more speed, until her mother called a halt.

"Get up off the floor, Mr. Neblett. You're spoiling the child."

Although the mother had become "Mama" to her husband, he was still and would always be "Mr. Neblett" to her. This formality she extended to Conger, refusing to allow a nickname for her older daughter. She did, however, allow a nickname for her second daughter, born when Conger was two. "Mr. Neblett," no longer hoping for a son because of his wife's failing health, gave this child his own name, Robert, with the last syllable accented for femininity. She became Bert.

While waiting for Bert to grow into a playmate, Conger acquired another. One summer morning she set out for the ice cream parlor, where she was a steady customer with a charge account. On the corner of the courthouse square she was transfixed by the sight of a man holding seven small donkeys by ropes. Ice cream was forgotten; before her was a far more pressing need, and she knew that the man would not deliver the merchandise if she offered only the words "Charge it." Approaching him, she asked timidly, "How much for a donkey?"

Fanning himself with a broad-brimmed hat, the owner answered teasingly, "Three dollars and five cents."

Without a word Conger sped across the street, raced up the stairs to her father's office, and faced him with shining eyes.

"There's a man with little donkeys! I want one to ride!"

Smiling, Bob Neblett drew two butterscotch wafers from his pocket, pushed one across the desk, and popped the other into his mouth.

"How much are they, honey?"

"Three dollars and five cents."

He pushed three silver dollars in the wake of the wafer, saying, "Take these to the man. I'm sure he will trade."

Conger disdained to dicker. "It takes a nickel, too," she said firmly. The lawyer tried to explain the art of barter, but his daughter was adamant, and finally the nickel crossed the desk.

She raced back to the square and thrust the coins into the man's hand. "Which one?" he asked. Heart pounding, Conger studied the motley remuda. A little gray with black ears and tail and huge, melting eyes nibbled at her, settling the matter. The man handed her its rope, and, walking on air, Conger led the animal home.

At her needlework beside a window, Mrs. Neblett heard the gate open, glanced out, and thought she might faint. Speechless, she watched the procession through the yard and could not even scream when the creature swiped a mouthful of her prize maidenhair fern. On past the servants' quarters, the washhouse, and the woodhouse they went, the donkey sniffing at the big iron washpot fragrant with fresh lye soap. In the stable Conger found a currycomb and set about grooming her steed. No Derby debutante ever had more loving treatment. The animal emerged

[5]

smelling like a rosebud, its handmaiden like the barnyard. Mrs. Neblett, holding her nose, shoved Conger into a bathtub and tossed a block of lye laundry soap in with her.

Judge Neblett was more appreciative. With due solemnity he walked around the donkey, nodding agreement to all the fine points cited by its proud owner. Next day they went to the saddle shop and chose a tan sidesaddle featuring an enormous red rose on the velour seat. Thereafter, until she outgrew her mount, Conger knew the ecstasy of roaming "burro-back" wherever and whenever she pleased.

The little sister took to more ladylike ways; she was no tomboy, but both girls were given the prescribed social training for that era. Together, they were initiated as "observers" on their mother's "day." The engraved calling card read:

At Home
Mrs. Robert Scott Neblett
Tuesday

Tuesday afternoons the girls, starched and beribboned, were ensconced on Grandmother Yeater's damask-covered Victorian love seat. Their short legs sticking straight before them, the girls viewed the procession of ladies in rustling silks; long, dark kid gloves; and high buttoned shoes that streamed through the parlor.

Conger escaped one Tuesday by going with her father to Austin to call on his good friend, Gov. James Stephen Hogg, of whom Neblett spoke proudly as "the first native Texan elected to that high office." Noted gourmand as well as statesman, Governor Hogg was further distinguished by an enormous abdomen.

"Come here, child," the governor invited cordially, pulling five-year-old Conger to his knee and holding her closely. The conversation was jolly; the governor laughed often and heartily, his ample abdomen and his guest jiggling in unison. The sensation made a lasting impression on her.

Hand in hand, Conger and her father strolled their big, shady yard in late afternoons of spring and summer. From sections of gutter pipe he had made birdbaths, and it pleased him to introduce his daughter to their patrons. "That is the Texas mockingbird, the greatest singer in the world," he declared. "And that is the bird of paradise. Some call it the scissortail, but it is the Texas bird of paradise." Conger believed it. The exquisite flush of coral under the wings, the pearly head, the magnificent tail— it would always be her favorite. "The mourning dove," he continued, as a pair approached timidly through the foliage, "gets its name from its sad call. It is a gentle bird." A noisy spurt of blue scattered the doves. "The blue jay, now, is a cocky fellow. Some people do not like his thieving, arrogant ways, but he wears a handsome coat."

Most of the summers were spent traveling. Mrs. Neblett, always hoping for relief from her chronic nervousness, took the girls to various Southern resorts, her husband joining them at times. On her seventh birthday, Conger had her photograph made at the Chicago World's Fair, where she was enthralled by the Swiss exhibit—a full-size horse of solid chocolate.

In New York the little girls made short excursions unescorted, but they were admonished to consult a policeman if trouble came their way. Conger fell head over heels in love with the uniformed policemen, and she was puzzled and distressed that her father, surely the smartest man in the world, was not a policeman. She brooded over this apparent shortcoming for months, and one winter evening, as she cuddled in his lap, listening to him sing, she decided to have it out with him. Why couldn't he have been a policeman? Offhandedly, he said he probably could have. His daughter waited anxiously for an explanation. Finally, she blurted accusingly, "But you weren't."

"No, I wasn't," he said, and he went into another song. Conger was hurt, but she loved him anyway. It was her first sad adjustment to a situation she could not change to her heart's desire. She stifled the hurt, as she would throughout life, making the best possible whole of the pieces at hand.

Sunday afternoons Judge Neblett hired a surrey from the livery stable and took his family on drives into the countryside, stopping to point out native trees, shrubs, and wild flowers. His respect for oaks bordered on worship. Stroking the bark of a fine specimen he would say, "Let my remains be buried at the roots of a great oak, to nourish its growth. That is immortality, the only resurrection I want." April outings were made specifically to view miles of Texas bluebonnets, set off by patches of Indian paintbrush, winecups, daisies, and prickly poppies.

Mrs. Neblett's flower garden was a showplace that drew a variety of butterflies, whose names she called to her children's attention. On starry nights she pointed out characters in the sky—the Bears, key to Polaris; and Cassiopeia; Orion; and others. The lessons were not intended to teach astronomy at all; they were to teach the girls to appreciate references to constellations in poetry and mythology. The day after the stargazing, Mrs. Neblett would read passages that made the lessons meaningful.

The family read together until the girls could choose books of their own. Conger shed tears over *Black Beauty*, and to console his daughter, Mr. Neblett gave her a bay pony named Ginger, and the saddle with the red rose seat came down from the hook (the donkey having been put out to pasture). Once again she enjoyed riding far and wide, and again Mattie Neblett was complaining that "Conger always smells like a horse." Titles on the bookshelves reflected the growth of the readers, from *Little Lord Fauntleroy* through *Little Women*, the interminable *Elsie Dinsmore* series, to Longfellow, the *Waverley* novels, and Dickens. Conger memorized vast stanzas of poetry, but Bert scorned such tedium.

Around the piano, with Mattie at the keyboard, the family sang together. By watching her mother's fingers, Conger learned to pick out tunes with her own; Mattie explained the staff, and soon the child could match notations on sheet music to the ivory keys. Piano lessons began when she was eight, and practice was never a chore. True tones came naturally from her throat, too; she began singing to her own accompaniment and at ten joined the St. John's Episcopal Church choir. Every Sunday, in white mortarboard and cassock, she marched behind the acolyte leading the procession of singers, which ended with the tallest adult. For the next seventy years, with few interruptions, Connie would sing or play in some church on Sunday. The denomination never mattered because none of the doctrines she heard so thoroughly expounded ever won her complete allegiance.

[8]

She began voice lessons when she was fourteen. By then Conger was an accomplished elocutionist, reciting poems and ballads on social occasions, as her mother had planned; dancing lessons, recommended by Neblett to make his "pony-built" daughter more graceful, were now paying off in beaux. But against one genteel art she firmly rebelled—she would not do needlework. Besides, she pointed out, all those acres of embroidery turned out by her mother should suffice for generations, most certainly for the hope chest she was expected to have when she became a bride.

In every other way Conger sought to please, for by now it was clear that her younger sister was far prettier than she. Conger's heart-shaped face; fair skin; gray blue eyes; and her hair, the color of ripe maize, were pleasing enough but stopped just short of beauty. She was never deceived by compliments, nor could she be, for Mattie Neblett openly gloried that at least one of her daughters had inherited her dainty loveliness. Both, however, inherited her small stature; at five feet, eleven inches, Bob Neblett was a giant among his womenfolk.

When Conger was fifteen, Neblett's once-abandoned hope of a son was realized. He too was named Robert, but since the father was called Bob, the daughter Bert, and the son Sonney, there was no confusion. The sisters adored the baby.

On June 4, 1903, Conger graduated from high school amid a mad round of dances and card parties and dinners. She had a leading role in the senior play, *Cricket on the Hearth*. At commencement the graduates sat in a half circle on the stage, the young men with high stiff collars and the young women in gauzy white frocks, their hair piled high on their heads, bouquets of roses in their laps. Judge Neblett, president of the school board, presented the diplomas. Mrs. Neblett's gift to her daughter was a Knabe piano, the first grand piano in Corsicana.

For most of the graduates marriage was the next objective. But not for Conger; she would go to college. Her parents chose Forest Park College, a "select" girls' school in Saint Louis where music and literature were emphasized. No one in the Neblett circle dared criticize openly, but there was whispering about "sending a sweet Southern girl up north to school." Indeed, why send a girl to college at all? Conger loved college. The years

[9]

were deliriously happy. She made friends with students from strange places. She learned about their lives over bubbling chafing dishes of fudge or welsh rarebit. She fattened to 105 pounds, the only time in her life her weight topped 97 pounds. English and "vocal" were her majors; she came to love Browning, making scrapbooks of his and others' poetry, which would be read and re-read through the years.

Another scrapbook she compiled in her head; for the sheer joy of knowing them, she memorized hundreds of poems. Unwittingly, she thus bought insurance against boredom; whenever subjected to a sermon that was less than inspirational, she could shut her ears and listen to the poets.

Summers at home and Christmas holidays were festive with parties and dances. At card parties they played euchre, cooncan, five hundred, and whist. Dances were in the homes of friends in their social circle; the Neblett girls did not attend public affairs. One summer Conger wore out twelve pairs of dancing slippers; she never tired of waltzes, one-steps, two-steps, polkas, schottisches, the Virginia reel. The sisters were expert buck-and-wing and possum-a-la performers, but their specialty was a strutting cakewalk in which one of them had to lead because no gentleman could match their steps. Sixty years later, nursing a damaged leg, Connie would assert firmly, "I could do it now if the doctor would let me use this knee."

The Nebletts held open house at both Christmas and the New Year. Preparations began two months ahead—raisins were brandied, nuts salted and stored, fruitcakes baked and periodically doused with rum. Near the holidays extra help came into the kitchen; country women called more often at the back door with freshly churned butter and eggs just laid—nobody bought those things from the store. More cakes were baked and put under glass until the punchbowl was filled with eggnog and the french doors were opened to make one big room of the first floor. Winters in Corsicana were often so mild that roses could be gathered from the garden to adorn the rooms.

One such Christmas had an unfortunate aftermath. Returning to college, Conger stepped out of an overheated train at midnight in Saint Louis and into a howling blizzard. She stood in the cold for an hour waiting for her streetcar and arrived at the school stiff from head to heels and barely able to speak. She lay in the infirmary for two months, consuming gallons of wintergreen, then a favored treatment for inflammatory rheumatism. The ailment would recur in later years as acute arthritis. In March, barely able to travel, she went home to spend three more months convalescing.

Her little brother was a beam of sunshine in the sickroom. They became great pals; Sonney called her Connie, and Mattie Neblett let him get by with it. A bright child, he had begun to read at two and was his mother's pride. She often remarked, so often that her elder daughter became inured to the slight, "Well, Bert got the beauty and Robert got the brains. Poor Conger. But you can be clean, and you can be pleasant—and you'd better!"

The convalescent spent painful but ultimately triumphant hours at her piano. She practiced relentlessly with her stiff fingers, determined not to be robbed of her music.

That summer, at nineteen, she found that she must wear spectacles. Friends thought it tragic for one so young, but Conger accepted them without resentment, indeed with gratitude—that she could see better. She returned to Forest Park in the fall and completed the requirements for a diploma in voice. She received offers to sing professionally, stemming from her roles in college productions and the Saint Louis Civic Opera, but she turned them down, her mother having ruled that "no lady would sing commercially." Her talents had been cultivated for her own pleasure and that of family and friends.

Judge Neblett offered her a year abroad but was pleased that she chose to postpone it and simply enjoy being at home. Bert was at home, too, and they still enjoyed one another as they did no one else. They were a mutually critical, mutually challenging, mutually inspirational pair. They went with their mother to Mineral Wells to take the waters and often accompanied their father, then in the state legislature, to Austin, where they acquired more beaux among the university students. Conger also went with "Papa" on business trips concerning title work for oil companies. Oil had been discovered in Navarro County in 1894—by accident. Drilling for a water supply, city fathers were annoyed that the well flowed a greasy iridescent substance instead of good clear water; they closed the well and sought another location.

Others, however, were excited by the discovery, and the following year the first oil well in Texas to produce a commercially important flow was drilled. The first fully equipped refinery in the state soon followed.

Judge Neblett wrote charters for two oil companies that would become majors in the industry, and thereafter his practice was largely related to the oil industry. Corsicana became a boomtown, growing in population from ten thousand to twenty-five thousand in a decade. The community welcomed oil prosperity, but old families of elite society turned their backs on newcomers associated with it—including some who would become the elite society in major Texas cities.

The Neblett girls were popular. Young men were constantly in attendance, but none could win Conger's heart. If she were in love, and she was not at all sure about that, it was with her childhood sweetheart, Lynn Brooks, whom she had not seen in five years. The families were longtime friends, living around the corner from one another. Lynn had carried Conger's books to and from school, escorted her to parties, and always talked about the wide world beyond "this hick town Corsicana." He had a wild streak in him, some said, and no one was surprised when, in the tenth grade, he quit school and joined the Navy. His letters to Connie (schoolmates had overruled Mrs. Neblett about the nickname) told of life aboard the USS *Oregon*, the ports he visited, and what he saw beneath the waves, for he had also become a deep-sea diver. Connie's letters followed him around the Pacific Ocean.

Then Lynn came home, loaded with gifts from foreign lands for the girl he meant to marry. He went to work for the Southern Pacific Railways and promised to settle down. Everyone thought it was "so romantic, so suitable." Everyone except Judge Neblett. He rather liked Lynn but was wary of that wild streak and could not give his approval. It was the first serious rift between father and daughter, and though Connie was twenty, her father was still her hero, and the conflict hurt her deeply.

She took her troubles to Grandmother Neblett in Anderson, a small town in Grimes County where Bob Neblett had grown up. His grandfather, Dr. R. C. Neblett, a physician from Virginia, had settled there in 1821 when Texas was still part of Mexico. Bob's father practiced law in nearby Navasota but lived on and managed the family plantation. Bob was ten when the slaves were freed, but little change occurred on the plantation; the slaves stayed on as field hands and "house darkies." Bob rode horseback to Tehuacana College, a Presbyterian school later to become Trinity University, and to read law in his father's office.

Independence characterized Lizzie Scott Neblett. An articulate Free Thinker, she strongly influenced her son and her granddaughters, especially Conger, with whom she had particular rapport. Character study and astrology were among her consuming interests, and she still believed in the horoscope she had cast for Conger when this first granddaughter was born. The horoscope promised a child of tremendous intellect, talented and loving, but alas, there was a flaw—intolerance; it would be her downfall unless controlled. Grandmother Neblett assumed the task of helping her defeat this tendency, and Conger dutifully tried. Lizzie Neblett could easily trace the source of the flaw—she believed it came from a grandfather on the other side of the house, the Reverend A. J. Yeater. "Outside the pulpit, where he was splendid, he was impossible to get along with," she affirmed, "violently impatient."

But the grandmother could not resolve Connie's problem, and Lynn was impatient, too. She wore his ring and soon was swept into wedding preparations. Much of her trousseau was bought at the Neiman-Marcus store in Dallas, where the elderly Mr. Neiman sat at the doorway inspecting customers. Women had to be hatted and gloved lest they be frowned upon.

The wedding was simple, in deference to Judge Neblett's feelings. The young couple moved to Ennis, only twenty-one miles away and with an hourly interurban train service that enabled Connie to maintain her Corsicana ties. Lynn did not want to be tied to a home, so they lived in a boardinghouse; his job kept him away from home much of the time. With time on her hands, Mrs. Brooks became choir director of the Baptist church

[13]

and gave voice lessons. She also learned to cook, and though she would never excel in the kitchen, the attempt disgusted her mother—cooking was a servant's job. In time Lynn agreed to a house, and Connie's piano was moved into its parlor.

Worried that his wife was so often alone at nights—Ennis was a railroad town and a magnet for drifters—Lynn bought her a small pistol, an Iver and Johnson hammer-and-hammer, and taught her to use it. Another day he came home leading Mark Antony, a trim pit bulldog, all white except for one tan ear. It was love at first lick. The dog slept on a small mattress at Connie's bedside, escorted her to choir practice, and trotted along on dusty walks when Mrs. Brooks chaperoned her favorite pupil, Blanche Morton, and the girl's beau, Bob Bush, who would marry and remain her "children" for life.

The choir director, the pistol, and the bulldog became a sometime auxiliary to the Ennis Volunteer Fire Department. Twice in the night Mark Antony sensed fire in the neighborhood and pawed his mistress until she woke and went into the street to fire the gun and rouse the town. Shots in the night were a customary fire alarm.

Lynn never came home without a gift for Connie, often an extravagant one. He handed over his paycheck and never asked where the money went; he had other resources—an uncanny talent for rolling sevens and elevens and a canny awareness of the odds against filling an inside straight. He was fond of liquor, but Connie never saw him drunk.

In letters to Grandmother Neblett she unburdened her secret worry, never even hinting to anyone else that Lynn was bored, that this life was too tame for him. It was sad, for they truly loved one another, but they had so little in common and were together so seldom.

Suddenly, all other worries faded when she faced another that could change her life—she was going blind. At first she refused to believe it, but a second doctor confirmed that she had glaucoma and must adjust herself to gradual loss of vision. In despair she went home to her parents to await the inevitable. Still hoping, they took her to a Dr. D. T. Atkinson in Dallas, who was said to have worked miracles for others. She was prepared for a hospital stay; instead, Dr. Atkinson had her stay at a hotel and saw her every day for ten days. On the eleventh day he had glorious news. "You do not have glaucoma," he said. "All symptoms indicate a nervous disorder and undernourishment. Proper glasses, which may need to be changed twice a year, with rest and a proper diet should help you."

What a relief! Just to be alive and aware with all one's senses was happiness enough. She detested the prescribed twice-a-day malted milk with egg, but she never cheated. She rested long hours when she preferred to be up and about, the spectacles were changed as needed, and after two years of her faithfully following his advice, Dr. Atkinson pronounced her a healthy woman, prescribed bifocals, and suspended the egg malt.

World War I provided a solution to Lynn's restlessness. He snatched at a proffered commission, requesting immediate sea duty, but he was assigned to a training station in New Orleans, where he took an apartment in the French Quarter for Connie.

She tried but could not fit herself into the rank-conscious Navy circle that Lynn cultivated. She resented the privileged wastefulness she saw and the jeering at "sacrificing for the war effort," which she knew to be very real to many people. She was polite at the rowdy parties but escaped as often as possible to the saner world of home in Corsicana.

She was there when Grandmother Neblett died in her eighty-fifth year. Conger had come to think of her as imperishable. Her spirit had not aged with her body, she wrote as one still in quest of truth, but she had known that this September, 1917, would be her last. On her bedside table was a letter of instructions for her funeral: It was to be simple and inexpensive, homegrown flowers were to be used, no one was to wear black, and she was to be buried in a white robe and a white casket.

Her son and granddaughter stood at the head of her grave in the family cemetery and fulfilled the remaining wishes of the deceased: Conger sang "Flow Gently Sweet Afton," and Judge Neblett delivered the eulogy, giving thanks for the life she had lived in the pioneer period of the county. He mentioned her studious habits and strong character, saying, "She read with an open mind, spoke with a polished tongue, and wrote with a gifted pen." In conclusion he recited "Crossing the Bar," and Conger sang another of her favorite hymns.

Bob Neblett survived his mother by only a few months. Demands had been heavy upon him that war winter—Red Cross and War Bond drives, Salvation Army appeals, United Charities. As he had so often said to his children, "The rent you pay for the space you occupy on this earth is to do what your community asks of you." He had paid his rent many times over.

A kidney infection forced him to bed shortly after Christmas, and pneumonia set in. They took him to Scott and White Clinic in Temple, Mattie sitting beside his stretcher in a baggage car of the Cotton Belt Railroad, the children in a coach behind. They knew what would happen, for pneumonia was a killer before the discovery of antibiotics.

Sadly, they returned over the same route a few days later. As he had directed, they proceeded to the cemetery at once and laid Bob Neblett beneath the post oak he had chosen years before. A slab of Texas granite would be placed later. There was a Masonic burial service. Nothing more.

The three small women and the sixteen-year-old son, grown as tall as his father, masked their emotions in the presence of others. Returning to the big white house, each sought comfort in their individual ways. The widow reached for a volume of poetry, Conger went to the piano, Bert to the dictionary, and Sonney to the attic he had preempted and filled with a maze of electrical equipment.

Connie came to regard the simplicity of her father's burial as a great blessing, for the next winter found her singing many times in the presence of death. Victory in Europe was followed by an influenza epidemic at home that devastated the country like a war. Few Corsicana families were spared; people were stricken and dead within hours. Schools and theaters were closed, and public gatherings, including church services for the dead, were forbidden. Rites were held at the graveside, and for weeks on end, at least once a day, Conger Brooks followed the hearse to the cemetery to sing such comfort as she could to the bereaved.

At first there was a quartet singing "In the Sweet Bye and

Bye" in the bitter cold and wind. When the tenor was stricken, the trio continued, singing "Shall We Meet beyond the River?" The soprano succumbed, and for her Connie and the bass sang a duet of "Rock of Ages." When the bass was taken, there was only the mezzo soprano soloist to sing "Whispering, Whispering Hope."

Lynn decided to stay with the sea. From the Navy he went to the United Fruit Company as skipper of a ship on Caribbean and Gulf routes, with New Orleans their home port again. Connie boarded a train, with Mark Antony relegated to the baggage car along with her piano. They took an apartment on Thalia Street in an old but still gracious house of the French colonial period. When Lynn was in port, they celebrated at French Quarter night spots; he was exceedingly proud of his doll-like wife and loved to squire her about. Though they rarely ate at home, she learned to cook things he liked. When he was at sea, she moved in an entirely different circle and became choir director and soloist for the St. Charles Avenue Christian Church. She also spent several summers in Chicago, taking college courses in English literature. At the American Conservatory she took voice lessons.

From tropical ports Lynn brought gifts; love birds from Panama in a big gilded cage, exquisite aigrettes from Guatemala for her hair, and from Jamaica a small, stuffed white bird poised in flight to adorn a hat. She did not know that the bird was a least tern, or that such a bird existed.

Cage birds were fashionable in New Orleans. The French Market offered exotic varieties and others trapped in the Mississippi delta by little boys who got a nickel from the dealer for each bird. Most popular were "little green pops" and "little red pops," also known as nonpareils. Connie's landlord gave her a little green pop to occupy the tasseled cage when the love birds unaccountably succumbed. It was a charming little green finch with a yellow green breast. The landlord tended it whenever she was away.

In the fall she noticed a few blue feathers on the little bird's head, and through the winter more and more blue appeared until it had a solid cobalt blue head. Connie was mystified. The

[17]

next winter brought another surprise, another transformation; from throat to tail the bird became bright red. Crimson rings encircled his eyes, and a patch of chartreuse appeared on his green back. The little green pop was really a painted bunting. This she learned from *Land Birds East of the Rockies*, a small handbook by Chester Reed, which she had found in Sonney's collection. He was now at Georgia Tech.

The bird was dear to her, but Mark Antony was her favorite. One day he disappeared. He simply was not in the patio when she called him to go to market; he always accompanied her. Since he had never left home, she concluded that he must have been stolen. She put ads in the newspapers, went to the police, and drove around the district calling his name. In desperation she hired a private detective. She worried more about how miserable the dog must be than about her own loss.

He had been gone two weeks when a delivery boy, fearful and begging not to be "told on," whispered that he had seen her dog tied up in a back room at a laundry several blocks away. She set out at once. Anger and hope swept through her, but not fear. It did not occur to her to be afraid or to ask for help. The proprietor, alone in the laundry, eyed her suspiciously, sensing trouble. Behind the counter Connie saw a long hall with closed doors on both sides, and she wondered how many she would have to force open if this heavy-set man proved difficult. She made herself be polite.

"I understand you found a white dog, which may be one I lost," she said. "May I see him?" The man played stupid, then cagey. She handed him a photograph of Mark Antony, insisting, "I don't want him if he is not mine. You will know if he is." The man was still evasive.

Her fury mounted, and the laundryman wavered. Then he reluctantly turned and went down the hall, opening doors as if debating whether to discover the animal. Then Connie heard feet racing in the passageway. Mark Antony leaped the counter and in his joy, knocked her sprawling on the floor. Her tears and the dog's happy licking washed her face clean of makeup.

The laundryman made a final attempt, declaring he had paid twenty-five dollars for the dog. With a barely civil "Thank you," she marched from the shop, Mark Antony prancing at her side.

Chapter 2

One dim light burned in the Corsicana railway station at five o'clock in the morning; up the street a brighter glow came from an all-night cafe. Everything else was dark; the town slept as the train ground to a stop. The conductor swung down the steps of an unlit coach, placed a square stool on the ground, and reached up to assist a diminutive woman carrying a tasseled bird cage. He set a large suitcase beside her and looked around for someone to claim his passenger, but no one was there. "I can handle it," a contralto voice assured him. "It's not so heavy." She set the bird cage beside the suitcase and walked forward to the baggage coach, where another trainman handed her a leash. A white dog jumped down. The engine puffed, wheels screeched, and the train rumbled away into the night.

Connie was coming home this time to stay. After fourteen years she was abandoning the effort to be Lynn's wife. She was thirty-five years old; the best years of her life were behind her, people would say, and she would probably agree.

She stood a moment to drink deeply of the fresh air, so welcome after the stuffy train. Stars gleamed overhead; she could name many of them, having been introduced years ago by her mother. Now her mother was ill and needed her; Lynn did not.

Squaring her shoulders, she retrieved the suitcase and bird cage and set out for home, twelve blocks away. Mark Antony trotted along. In front of the cafe a middle-aged man, hat tilted at a rakish angle, stood whistling softly. A quick glance told her he was no one she knew, and she was glad of that as she marched by, eyes straight ahead. Then the stranger was beside her. "You seem to be loaded down," he said. "Let me help you." She would have refused, but he had already taken the suitcase and was in step with her. Oddly, she noted, Mark Antony made no objection.

"I am Jack Hagar," he announced, as if the name were entrée anywhere. He reached for the bird cage, and she surrendered it, too, grateful now because the big bag had been heavier than she thought and hard for her to manage while walking in high heels.

"I am Mrs. Lynn Brooks of New Orleans," she responded. "I have come home to be with my invalid mother, Mrs. Neblett."

"Might have known you would be Mrs. Somebody," her escort grumbled in mock sadness. "All nice women seem to be married."

"Maybe so" was the not-so-encouraging reply. The stranger chatted on; he was an oil man and real estate broker, native of Boston, recently of Oklahoma, but now committed to Texas, especially to Corsicana. Connie barely listened; she was nearing home, honeysuckle and four-o'clocks perfumed the night, and big trees made deep shadows.

She thanked the gentleman—what was his name?—at the door, opened it, and called softly, "Mama."

The helpful stranger was forgotten the next day in the tide of things to do for her mother and the house to be explored. It had been remodeled after a fire the previous winter had damaged the upper floors, and now it was only two stories high. News of her return spread that day, and friends came to see her. But the helpful stranger would not let her forget him. That afternoon at four o'clock, the "proper" hour for social calls, he telephoned. Was she okay? Everything all right at home? Yes, and thank you again. He persisted. There was a circus in town, would she like to go? It would be nice, but unfortunately she had a headache.

"Now," he drawled, "you hadn't ought to do that, Mrs. Brooks." At that she perked up, giggling, unable to resist throwing a verbal dart.

"Are you sure you're from Boston, Mr. Hagar? How come you say 'hadn't ought to'?"

[20]

"Oh, I've been down here a long time," he explained airily. "I've picked up the language."

He telephoned the next afternoon; another invitation was declined. None of her friends knew him or any other oil man; they remained aloof from oil people. They were destined, however, to accept one oil man. Jack Hagar finally made an offer she could not resist. He had tickets for the Dallas Symphony's opening concert; would she care to go? They heard the full series that winter, on season tickets he had confidently bought at the beginning. Jack was different from the other men Connie knew, refreshingly different. Cocky, independent, he held his own among the roughest of the oil fraternity but knew his way around a drawing room. He teased and sometimes provoked women but was always gentle and thoughtful with Connie. He had ideas for fun and play; he made her laugh. His kindness embraced Mrs. Neblett, who failed to awe him despite her snobbish efforts; soon she was laughing with him, too. That he was a Republican was rather a jolt; Texans were either Democrats or untouchables; therefore, Connie had never examined the policies of either party. Jack was ardent in his convictions and eventually convinced her of the existence of some merits of his side.

Music was a bond between the new couple. Jack had studied piano and still played for personal satisfaction, but he preferred to listen to Connie sing and play, as she did many evenings.

The community was quick to reclaim Connie's talents. She took charge of another church choir, began teaching voice again, and rejoined the music and study clubs. Often she and Bert, now married to attorney Robert Malloy, gave whole programs together. With their mother they belonged to the Thankfull Hubble Chapter of the Daughters of the American Revolution (DAR) in Austin and helped organize a local chapter of United Daughters of the Confederacy (UDC). That called for digging into old trunks for letters and records and for reliving the hardships their families experienced during the Civil War, and their research spawned such a wave of Rebel loyalty in Mattie Neblett, now much improved in health, that she was inspired to attend the UDC general convention in Savannah, Georgia, taking Conger with her.

The lobby of the handsome, old-fashioned convention hotel was draped with flags, the Stars and Bars sharing equal honor with the Stars and Stripes. As Connie and her mother registered, a commanding figure leading a posse of ladies wearing sumptuous corsages and hats sailed into the lobby. They recognized the leader, the president general of the UDC. The president general came to a ramrod stance in the middle of the floor, staring unbelievingly at the decorations. "Remove those flags!" she ordered, gesturing toward the Stars and Stripes. Indignation spread among the delegates. None would register until the offending bunting was taken down, leaving the Stars and Bars of the Confederacy uncontaminated by association with the victorious banners. When the scene was repeated in the dining room at the convention dinner, the Corsicana delegates began to lose their enthusiasm for The Cause.

They were surprised and other delegates shocked to discover that the guest speaker was governor of a state north of the Ohio River—a Yankee. He was a popular speaker, and it was an accomplishment for the president general to have snared him, but he was still a Yankee. However, the governor of Georgia sat on the chair's left, so the Daughters felt safe.

In her lengthy introduction of the speaker, Madam President General stressed that having even so distinguished a Yankee as the visiting governor demonstrated to the world that the South was magnanimous. She went on to emphasize that the Confederacy had been "in the right," and when at last she yielded the floor, she closed with congratulations to the Yankee guest on having this opportunity "to get set straight about things." The guest speaker stood, surveying the audience with a still face until the polite applause faded. Then he spoke.

"Ladies and gentlemen, I have been brought here under a misapprehension. I am an American. My grandfather marched and fought with the GAR [Grand Army of the Republic, an organization of Union army veterans], and I am proud of that fact. So, with your kind permission, good evening." He bowed and left the hall.

Connie breathed an "Amen." Behind her a delegate snorted, "Serves her right for inviting a Yankee."

[22]

The governor of Georgia filled the void left by the Yankee keynote speaker—filled it to overflowing with glorifications of the men in gray and of Southern womanhood. Before he finished, two small women rose and quietly departed. "Out we two peanuts walked," Mrs. Brooks concluded in her convention report to the Corsicana chapter. "What we learned, mostly, was that nothing much has happened since 1861." She remained a dues-paying member but attended no more conventions.

From Savannah the "two peanuts" visited Sonney at Georgia Tech and went on to Washington and a reception at the White House, where they were charmed by the gracious Mrs. Coolidge. It was a much more pleasant experience than their first White House levee several years before when Mrs. Wilson and the ailing president received them. He had obviously been in pain, and they felt he should have been spared such public exposure.

The sisters were the core of their social circle, most of whom had grown up with the Neblett girls. Connie loved them all, but Bert was her comrade—and sharpest critic. With acid wit, Bert sometimes attacked almost viciously. It dismayed their friends on occasion, but Connie was never resentful, tossing it off with the comment, "If Bert takes me down a notch, it's because I need it." Both laced their private conversations with cuss words, but in public Connie was unfailingly circumspect. To outsiders Bert was Mrs. Malloy, but her sister was always referred to as "that sweet Miss Connie."

"Hell," raged Bert. "She is no sweeter than I am. That's just a front she puts on."

It was Bert who proposed the nature study. With Blake White, one of their closest friends in their circle, they were in the Neblett library working on papers for a club program. Connie's little green pop, animated by wild birds outside the window, twittered in his cage. Searching for a reference, Bert glanced along a shelf of books unread for years, and titles jumped at her: *Birds of the Austin Region* by George Finlay Simmons, *Wildflowers East of the Rockies*, and *North American Birds' Eggs*, the latter two in the Chester Reed series.

"It's a damn shame," she declared, "that we know so little

about Navarro County after Papa tried so hard to teach us. He was such an ardent Texan and loved wild things so. Why don't we learn, as an honor to him, all the birds in this county?"

Connie was seized by a sudden excitement, as if Bert had turned a key to a secret door. "The wild flowers, too! And the butterflies," she cried.

"And the constellations," said Mattie. "And the trees and shrubs."

Enthusiastic, they decided to keep lists, starting at once with familiar species. Pencils in hand, they compiled surprisingly long lists in all the categories, recalling more than they realized they knew. Perhaps, after all, there would not be so much to learn. But there was. The first excursion into the country was maddening: What is this? What on earth can that be? With blossoms, twigs, and bark they hurried home to consult the books. Some problems were solved, but more remained mysteries. This would take time.

Bluebirds and robins on the farms were unexpected. "Papa would have loved bluebirds and robins," Connie sighed, "but I don't think he knew them." In Oakwood Cemetery they found blue jays, scissor-tailed flycatchers, cardinals, and mockingbirds. An elusive voice whistled, "Come 'ere, come 'ere," from one tree, then another. They tripped over headstones trying to obey the command, finally locating the caller—dark reddish brown body, black head and tail, and wings with white wingbars. Connie flipped through Reed's book, Bert through Chapman's *What Bird Is That?* It turned out to be an orchard oriole.

"The pictures don't do it justice," they fumed, as they would hundreds of times upon other discoveries. Soon they would learn that the "come 'ere" call was the male's method of leading them away from a nearby nest on which his mate sat, wearing entirely different plumage, and that their fledgling would wear still another costume in his first year. Dimorphism was a word not yet in the vocabulary of the seekers; except for redbirds, sexes were alike in the species they knew, and the printed illustrations were of male birds in adult plumage. Beginners rarely went beyond illustrations.

On a sultry morning Connie took her book to the upstairs porch, shaded by a giant pecan tree. Glancing up, she saw a yellow-billed bird eyeing her through white spectacles. It was a robin at her very door, and again she wondered why robins had been overlooked in her childhood. When the bird dropped out of sight, she quietly moved her chair to the banister and leaned over. A small, damp platform of mud was welded to a horizontal joint of the tree. A robin alit, deposited a pellet of mud, and flew away as another came in with another pellet and with expert swipes of its bill, smoothed both blobs into the platform.

Thrilled to have a grandstand seat for a nest-building, Connie forgot her book and her lunch. The birds worked steadily, gathering mud from the fern bed where a dripping faucet overflowed a shallow bowl; they pecked out a dab of earth, twisted and shaped it into a ball, maneuvered the ball onto the upper mandible, and flew to the tree. The one with the paler breast did all the arranging and smoothing—must be the lady, Connie concluded. At intervals the robins ceased their labors to feed randomly about on the lawn.

Downstairs the grandfather clock sounded the hour—three o'clock already. "Damn," Connie exclaimed aloud. She must dress and pour tea in somebody's dining room darkened by heavy draperies and lighted with candles. Why were houses made dark for daytime parties? And what a waste of time, anyway.

Next morning she woke to bubbling song from the pecan tree, loud and clear in the hush of dawn. She lay and listened, trying to memorize the phrases. Watching daily, she saw the platform become a saucer an inch thick; grass and small stems were worked into the mud—like adobe, she thought. Adobe walls grew around the hollow center, and more grass was applied to the outside.

That done, the female set about molding the inside; on fresh mud pellets she twisted and turned, shaping and smoothing with her breast. The male delivered blades of grass for the lining, which his mate placed and re-placed until the result fit her specifications. Often, he perched on the rim, head cocked sideways, surveying the work, but most of his efforts now were directed at suspected intruders. A curious cardinal was scolded; another male robin set upon violently. In peaceful intervals he sang.

Finally the robins rested and foraged around the neighborhood as if on a well-earned vacation. Peering into the mud cup, Connie saw a turquoise-blue egg. The honeymoon lasted until four jewels were laid, and then the female began sitting on them. In the two weeks following, Connie could stand at the railing and exchange confidential looks with the sitter, sometimes seeing her turn the eggs with her bill. The sitter's mate sang and at intervals took her on foraging expeditions, always escorting her back to the nest.

The creatures that emerged from the pretty eggs were blind, squirming, nearly naked pink-and-gray blobs with wide, yellow-lined mouths that flew open whenever a parent alit on the nest. Song ceased; the father bird fetched food for the first several days that the mother brooded the infants. After each feeding she stood aside and waited until an ashy gray fecal sac was ejected from a chick; she snatched this in her bill and carried it far away, and the nest remained immaculate. But while still half-blind and downy, the little ones began to undertake nest sanitation on their own, backing themselves up to the rim, where they teetered a moment, and then dropping the waste overboard, and falling contentedly back into the nest to sleep.

The babies' eyes opened, quills sprouted and blossomed into feathers, and the parents hunted ceaselessly for grubs and bugs to stuff into their voracious offspring, which were fattening by the day. They crowded, then overflowed the nest but still were all appetite, gulping what seemed to be miles of earthworms.

"They should be earning their own living now," Connie reported to Jack one evening as they drove to Dallas for dinner. "They are so packed in there I don't see how they can stand it, but they won't budge. Those brats keep begging for more, and the poor mama and papa are worn out."

The weary parents had reached the same conclusion; next day Connie witnessed the unwilling debut of the otiose young. The adults made trip after trip with bills full of mulberries, which they poked as deep as they would go until the brats were stuffed to stupidity. Then, each parent pecked the behind of a startled child, prodding and pinching until the victims were inspired by pain and indignation to move out of reach—out on a limb. Then the elders went after the other two, nipping until they also climbed out. The four fledglings marched silently along the branch, stopped and sat morosely, then suddenly launched themselves into the air. The parents saw them off, shook their wings as if dusting off a problem, and flew in the opposite direction.

The nature study undertaken by the sisters interested others and resulted in the organizing of the Nature Club in January, 1923, with eighteen members. They affiliated the club with the National Audubon Society and the Texas Federation of Women's Clubs. Indoor meetings alternated with field trips.

They had Reed's little handbook, and old files of *Bird-Lore*, *National Geographic*, and *Nature* magazines contained a great deal of helpful information. *Nature* had a series of paintings with descriptive texts that included western birds, some of which occurred in Navarro County; most publications were devoted to species in the eastern half of America. Another issue depicted shorebirds—avocets, yellowlegs, willets, turnstones, and others. "Someday," Connie remarked to Bert as they turned the pages, "we must go down to the coast and see these birds." But the plan could wait; so much was yet to be learned at home.

Music was still her primary interest, although recurring arthritis robbed her fingers of the nimbleness and keyboard technique she once had; her voice was less true, now, also. No one else seemed to notice, but the musician knew. She did not hesitate, however, to undertake new studies, and she was soon learning the music of the Christian Science church as soloist and sometimes pianist. Most of their hymns were new to her. Jack could, and did, help. He came from a Baptist family but in his youth had often gone with friends to the Mother Church in Boston and was familiar with its practices and music.

Jack had been courting Connie for five years, making himself part of every aspect of her life, including driving slowly around the countryside so she could watch the birds. He had endeared himself to her mother, who asserted that he was the gentlest man she ever knew. Connie was reluctant to marry again. She was nearly forty, silver-haired now for years. Was she not too old for another romance? She did love Jack, that she admitted, but. . . . Mattie Neblett gave her middle-aged nestling the push she needed. "Oh, go ahead and marry him, for heaven's sake! He will never give up."

She capitulated and was radiantly happy. There would be a simple wedding in the spring, as soon as their brick bungalow was finished in Jester Place, a new subdivision Jack had developed. She selected draperies, rugs, and furniture to go with the pieces she would take from home, pieces that brides in her family had used for generations. Jack planted honeysuckle, clematis, verbenas, a hedge of crape myrtle, and a rose garden. For him, roses flourished.

Pewell Jones, the twin of Bert's maid Jewel, was hired for housework. Pete Raspberry, who worked a Neblett farm and tended Mattie Neblett's yard, would help in the garden.

The wedding date was set but kept secret. The ceremony would be performed by the Christian church minister, in whose home Jack roomed. On April 2, 1926, Connie and Jack drove to Athens, where the minister was preaching that weekend, and they were married with only the minister and his wife present. They drove back at once to the new home—Connie's first real home of her very own.

Almost immediately the home was blessed, in the bride's opinion, by blue-gray gnatcatchers nesting in one of the young trees. She kept an eye on the incubation and brooding, and one day saw thumb-size fledglings hopping along the limb. She had resolved to take the tiny nest as soon as it was vacated, but that afternoon she had to sing for a wedding and that evening go to a dinner. When she went to the tree next morning she found no trace of the nest.

The next nesting unraveled the mystery. This midget Old World warbler destroyed the nest within the hour of the nestlings' graduation, methodically taking it apart and scattering the pieces. So, at the next opportunity, Connie was ready to rush out and take the prize. She cut a section of the branch on which it grew "like a knot on a limb." The nest was lined with grass, the outer twigs bound with spiderwebs and covered with oak lichens. It was so well constructed that it remained intact for more than forty years, serving as an exhibit at hundreds of presentations Connie Hagar would give.

In a magazine article she read that the government needed volunteers to band birds. Pleased that the birdwatching hobby from which she derived so much pleasure could also be useful, she volunteered; Bert was enthusiastic because it would authenticate their county lists. They and others in the Nature Club qualified for bird-banding permits. With the packet of bands from the U.S. Biological Survey were instructions; banding must be done quickly and with utmost care to avoid harming the bird, especially a nestling. Practicing on sticks, they became expert at manipulating the small pliers and bands.

"I need four hands," wailed Connie, struggling for perfection. "Damn this arthritis!" She found that a struggling, fluttering bird became calm when held back-down in her palm with the head between her first and second fingers.

Blue jays, mockingbirds, cardinals, hermit thrushes, and Carolina and Bewick's wrens were trapped and banded. Bluebird nestlings were taken just before fledging from hollow iron fence posts at the cemetery. A straw cup full of Bell's vireo babies was found in a clump of gaillardia, not a foot off the ground, in Connie's own yard.

Cruising the county in the coupe Jack had given her, a twin to his own black Ford, she found red-winged blackbirds congregated in reeds beside the city waterworks. From a saucer-shaped nest of grasses and leaves fastened to reeds at the edge, redwings fledged four young and promptly laid another bed of grass upon the old one and hatched five young from it. Not yet finished, the parents brought forth from a third layer of grass and leaves still another brood. Connie thought this interesting enough to write for the *Wilson Bulletin* and was flattered when it was published. It was the first of several notes and photographs the *Bulletin* would accept from her.

During that first summer of banding, Sonney and his wife visited their families. Upon graduating from Georgia Tech, he had married his hometown sweetheart, Alice May Kerr, and had gone to General Electric in Schenectady, New York, where he would become an executive in the company.

When Sonney saw his sisters in boots and baggy denim jeans, he let out a derisive whoop and laughed until they left in a huff. Grabbing a camera, he trailed them to the farm where they were intent on banding nestling Carolina chickadees, removing the little ones with a teaspoon without touching the nest. He snapped a roll of film and was gone before they finished.

Neither Connie nor Bert really liked the jeans (denim then was a coarse material used mainly for workmen's clothes), and one look at Sonney's snapshots settled the matter forever—bird banding did not, after all, require such desperate measures. The boots they kept, but neither ever wore any type of trousers after that.

The honeymoon year in the house that Jack built was cut short when a stroke paralyzed Mattie Neblett. Sadly, they closed the bungalow and moved to the big house. It could not be for long, they thought. The stricken woman looked so hopeless, so frail and small. For a year she lay in bed, attended constantly by nurses and her daughters, crying most of the time. She managed to utter a single word, "Mercy"—her entire vocabulary for the rest of her life—but by various inflections of the word she made her wishes and opinions known and continued to dominate her household. She lived for three years after the stroke. They were dreadful years. Connie curtailed club activities, gave up card playing forever (without regret), and spent much of her time with books at her mother's bedside.

The urge to list daily observations moved her one winter day when she came across a blank ledger in the library. Across the first page she wrote "Nature Calendar," and below that the date, January 17, 1928, and "Saw waxwings, robins, white-throated sparrows, juncos, myrtle warblers, hermit thrush, flickers, sapsucker, cardinals, mockingbirds, blue jays. Standing honeysuckle and japonica budded, cut forsythia and narcissus. Elms swelling. Found crippled myrtle warbler."

She would have been stunned that day to know that her

Nature Calendar would go on for more than thirty-five years, with few lapses, and that her records would interest professional ornithologists. To her, ornithologists were shadowy people who wrote the books; she knew only amateurs.

The Calendar was the only diary she ever kept, and at times it contained other notes—"Jack's birthday. . . . Went to Dallas concert . . . Mama better today." The ledger was succeeded by a hodgepodge of notebooks, mostly pocket-size engagement books distributed free by insurance companies. Anything with blank pages served; she never purchased a notebook. And if the current calendar were mislaid, she would jot down the day's notes on any other with space available. Dates were always entered, but accounts were not always consecutive—to the future dismay of professional ornithologists.

A spring date in the Calendar contained a jubilant item: "Painted bunting nesting in Corsicana!" Pete Rasberry brought the news; his wife had found a nest over which a bird just like her little green pop was singing. Connie had never seen a painted bunting in the wild. At the little farmhouse Mrs. Rasberry led her to a hawthorn in full flower under a hackberry tree from which a sweet little song came; she looked up and saw the male—red, blue, and green, much brighter than her pop had been. The singer's mate, a pretty green, but without the trimmings, slipped quietly from the hawthorn to a cedar elm. Connie parted the bush and found low in its branches a well-woven cup containing three freckled eggs. She scrutinized them and withdrew quickly.

She returned often to see the brood through a successful fledging, and since she now knew the song, she discovered numerous painted buntings in the area.

She had learned much from her little pop, the last lesson being that wild birds reared in cages were happier to remain so. On a bright morning early in her nature study her pet had seemed unusually restless, as if, she thought, he longed to be free outdoors, and she let him go. It was mistaken kindness; a few days later her little pop was found clinging to the outside of a cageful of canaries, apparently trying to get inside. The owner of

[31]

the canaries telephoned Connie, saying she would like to keep the bird, and Connie consented gladly. She no longer liked to see birds in cages.

The Biological Survey wrote to advise against banding nestlings, lest the human odor attract predators to the nest, so the banders learned to be ready and on hand when they knew nestlings were to fledge.

Mattie Neblett always brightened when listening to reports of her daughters' outdoors activities. Connie told her about the hairy woodpecker at the birdbath and the hermit thrush that managed to filch boiled egg from the trap without being caught. The willows were red and the elms in bloom; crow poison, vetch, and wild geranium were up. Her mother would utter weakly, "Mercy," clearly meaning "Tell me more," and Connie went on, chuckling over the fledgling Bewick's wrens found yammering under the japonica.

"Cutest things you ever saw," she said. "No bigger than grasshoppers but, God, those feet! Big as they will ever be; those babies will have to grow a lot to match them."

Autumn wild flowers were exceptional that year; the Nature Club gathered bouquets to display in the public library, and Connie took some to her mother—bluebells, smartweed, asters, gayfeather, goldenrod, boneset, summer snow, and blue sage. Two sandhill cranes dropped out of the blue to forage a nearby field, and flights of hawks soared overhead—they were just hawks, never coming close enough to be identified; the observers possessed neither field glasses nor binoculars and were unaware of such aids to their hobby.

Swarms of butterflies danced through November—red-spotted purples, buckeyes, cabbages, and sulphurs. But December brought icy winds that attacked, retreated, and attacked again. For three days the world was frozen, and then came snow. Mrs. Neblett was wheeled to a window to see a white landscape, eighteen inches of snow, the deepest she had ever known in Corsicana. Birds flew from the feeders to huddle in shelter. They would survive the icy blast, but the patient at the window would not. Three days later Mattie Neblett slipped quietly away, and on Christmas Eve, under a warm sun that melted snowdrifts on the graves, she was laid beside her husband in Oakwood Cemetery. She left a void in her daughter's heart, but Connie would not pretend a grief she did not feel; the illness had been tragic, but not the death. "Of course I am not sorry," she said. "It's a blessing to all of us, most of all to her."

Pewell Jones moved the Hagars back into their bungalow, and the Malloys moved into the Neblett house. Gradually, the neglected threads of their lives were woven back together.

Severe cold returned in January. On the Nature Calendar's second anniversary the thermometer fell to two below zero, an unusual punishment for Corsicana; long-standing shrubs were killed, and birds thronged feeders and warm water. As the weather relented, unusual birds arrived; purple finches January 21 and redpolls February 5. Connie had come to associate unusual weather with unusual birds, but she did not realize just how unusual the redpolls were.

The Nature Club obtained permission to make Oakwood Cemetery a wild flower sanctuary, and in the spring they transplanted additional species to the already colorful site. From the rich Trinity River bottoms they brought puccoon, redbud, blue curls, dogtooth violets, and others. In April the members formed a caravan of five cars to tour East Texas and see acres of dogwood in bloom. With *Texas Wild Flowers* by Ellen D. Schulz in hand, they learned many new species, including the true buttercup, the name they had always mistakenly given the yellow evening primrose.

Later in the month Jack took Connie to Abilene for the annual meeting of the Texas Federation of Music Clubs, of which she was corresponding secretary. From there they drove westward, just roaming, suddenly intoxicated by freedom. It was their first real trip together. They explored the Big Bend, destined to become a national park but not easily traveled at that time. Prickly pear, sotol, yucca, and maguey were blooming, and low-growing varieties of cactus had silky petals of pinks, green, brown, and yellow among their sharp spines—delicate beauty in a forbidding setting.

Flocks of lark buntings in black-and-white mating plumage swirled through the Davis Mountains; a fiery-red bird with black upper parts was acting like a flycatcher beside Limpia Creek. It proved to be just that—a vermilion flycatcher. Connie gathered red penstemon to show the Nature Club.

In mid-May a painted redstart visited Corsicana briefly, and a Lucy's warbler worked the mulberry trees for three days. Neither of these species belonged there, Connie knew, but she could identify no weather condition to account for their presence.

With each season offering new wonders to explore, the years rolled by. The Nature Club found kindred groups in nearby cities; they heard astronomy lectures in Fort Worth, studied bird skins in the Dallas Museum of Natural History and in the Attwater Collection in San Antonio, the latter owned by Roy W. Quillin, who also had a comprehensive egg collection over which Connie pored for hours. His wife, Ellen Schulz, director of the Witte Museum in San Antonio and author of the flower book that had become Connie's botanical bible, joined them on field trips. With them on other occasions was Dr. Eula White-house of Southern Methodist University, a botanist with a flower book in the works, and sometimes Norma Stillwell, who wrote a nature column for the *Dallas Morning News*.

Banding was to Connie the most instructive phase of her study. The specimen in hand told her more than books, and often she studied them together, bird in one hand, book in the other, and thus was able to identify the western form of the rufous-sided towhee; it differed just enough from the familiar "chewink" to make her curious.

Most finches could be lured to traps with seeds, while mockingbirds, thrashers, and thrushes would risk anything for boiled egg. Connie did not depend entirely on traps; a small leather pouch containing bands, paper and pencil, and small long-nosed pliers was carried on every drive in the country, and in her head she carried a schedule of probable fledging dates. Fledgling mockingbirds were easy; they always sat around in the grass for three or four days, yammering incessantly for grub, but she had to approach cautiously because once the youngsters spied her, they ceased their cries and froze in a crouch, becoming nearly invisible and thus, likely to be stepped on.

Blue jays preferred bois d'arc trees for nests; bluebirds, tufted titmice, and Carolina chickadees used hollow iron fence posts; great-crested flycatchers preempted mailboxes; and the sora, saltwater marsh hen to hunters, was taken at the waterworks.

The mourning doves with their changing colors were puzzling. They came to the waterworks by the hundreds, but winter doves were different. Extensive reading convinced Connie that the ones she banded were the eastern race, the paler winter doves the western race. But mourning doves were said to be nonmigratory—or were they? The Biological Survey was asking for evidence of "possible" migratory routes, and Connie was pleased to learn later that one of her own had furnished evidence. A fledgling she had banded in July was taken six months later by a Mexican doctor forty miles south of Mexico City.

Common grackles brought news from the opposite direction; among the swarms trapped at a winter roost in Blake White's trees were many that had already been banded. They had come from Kansas, the Survey reported, and the next summer the Kansas birder reported grackles banded in Corsicana.

News from afar about her birds, however, was scant; most of her returns were repeaters in her own traps. White-throated sparrow no. 519,867 repeated so often one spring that it became a pet, waiting docilely for her grasp when the trap was opened.

All this was so absorbing that Connie neglected to see a doctor about a pain in her cheek until it became too severe to be ignored. What appeared to be a small abscess did not heal, and further examinations led to diagnosis of glaucoma—again. Jack was crushed. Glaucoma meant blindness, he feared, but Connie was determined to find Dr. Atkinson, wherever he was, and she did. Stationed at Fort Sam Houston during World War I, he had remained in San Antonio to practice.

"Come at once," he advised.

This time Dr. Atkinson was alarmed, too. He ruled out cancer, but the abscess was deep, and decayed bone was likely; surgery was indicated. Confident of another miracle, Connie was not disappointed. The operation was done through the nasal cavity, and two inches of bone was removed, but there was no scar, only a soft emptiness in her cheek that only the patient could detect.

Serious illness was rare for her. The "Neblett sick headache" she accepted as a matter of course, never associating it with diet until Dr. Homer Jester returned from New York with new knowledge of allergies, and he ascertained that the headaches were attributable to certain foods, mainly milk and fish. Connie thought of all those mounds of tuna salad she had consumed at parties and wondered how she had survived. It was simple enough to forgo such items—and another miracle was wrought. Without the least comprehension of what allergies were all about, Pewell was able to provide safe meals while still upholding the tradition of rich Southern food, long on carbohydrates but abysmally short on proteins.

The sixth year of the Nature Calendar, 1934, began with notes on fine weather, abundant wild flowers and birds, and the vast improvement in field study made possible by Jack's gift of Zeiss 8 × 40 binoculars. Often on warm spring nights Nature Club members lay on cots in the Hagar backyard and named constellations while Jack, in a rocker on the back porch, presided over a pitcher of lemonade.

Often, too, the club made excursions into other parts of the state, traveling back roads, the better to find birds and plants not found at home. Connie and Bert, alternating yearly as district conservation chair for federated clubs, were in great demand as speakers. Both also served as counselors for Camp Fire Girls.

On visits to distant clubs, Connie would leave early, wearing flat heels so she could stop en route to explore interesting habitats. One such place was a cemetery on the outskirts of the town where she was due. The cemetery was a garden of wild flowers; she gathered an armload of specimens to illustrate her talk that afternoon. At the clubhouse the speaker changed to high heels, drew on white gloves, and entered with her display. The audience was attentive as she exhibited bluets, pussytoes, a branch of red maple, anemones, saxifrage, spiderwort, and puccoon and talked of their uses and habits. Finally, she confessed that she had robbed their own cemetery, and she congratulated the community on its use of native plants. A ripple of embarrassed laughter from the listeners brought out the truth—the cemetery was merely neglected.

Amid the compliments with the tea that followed, one woman commented "You have opened my eyes! I go by that cemetery every day and have never seen those flowers."

To Connie this was a cue to continue her club activities. She would have preferred to resign from everything and devote her time to the studies she so enjoyed, but invariably, when the temptation to quit was strong, someone would come forward and declare, "You have shown me a new world," or "You have opened my eyes," and she felt obliged to go on.

Bird talks were more difficult to make interesting; she had some color pictures from calendars and similar sources—this was before projected color slides, of course—so she relied on her collection of bird nests, packed in tissue in a large basket. These she displayed as she described the builders, their habits, and some of her experiences in the field. The small wallet of grasses bound with spider silk and decorated with lichens was built by a Bell's vireo in a redbud; there were also nests of ruby-throated hummingbirds, cactus wren, verdin, and others. The eastern bluebird nest, still holding the shape of the box Jack had built and placed by a living room window, was one she had kept notes on from the first straw installed until the last youngster fledged. (The record would later be deposited in the files of the U.S. Biological Survey.)

Relating the experience to a club one day, Connie cited bluebirds as "immaculate housekeepers," and explained how, after each feeding of the young, the parent carried away the droppings in little fecal sacs. A puzzled listener raised her hand.

"What I want to know," she queried, "is where do bluebirds get these sacks?"

Chapter 3

The pictures of shorebirds in the books Connie leafed through so often had kept alive her dream of vacationing on the coast, where she would be able to see them. In late July, 1933, the dream was about to come true. Bert also had arthritis, which was affecting her legs as it did her sister's hands; her doctor recommended saltwater and sunshine—a month on the coast. Connie would go, too. It might help her fingers; the knuckles now were so swollen she had given up wearing her rings. Rejecting Galveston as too big and too popular, they chose Rockport, a resort village on the Coastal Bend.

The night before their departure the Nature Club had a "last fling" at the stars in the Hagar yard. Next morning's first light found Connie and Bert kissing husbands good-bye and heading south. Their spirits rose with each dusty mile; they sang, Connie recited poems, and they laughed at everything. At Port Lavaca they stopped to fill their lungs with the salt air. Then, hugging the coast, they crossed bayous clogged with lavender water hyacinths; strange, long-legged birds flew up from the marshes. At midafternoon they rattled across a two-mile wooden causeway spanning the mouth of Copano Bay, ten miles from their destination.

The road cut through dense live oaks, many huge and sprawling, others growing to the very edge of Aransas Bay and leaning away from it with long, leafy arms reaching inland; strange shrubby undergrowth promised interesting investigations. Houses scattered among the oaks became more numerous,

[38]

closer together, and surrounded by oleander fences in rose pink bloom. The road widened into Market Street, the main thoroughfare of four or five business blocks; the street's center strip of paving was flanked by crushed oystershell. A few cars were parked in front of the stores, mostly one-story wooden structures with two-story false fronts. A windowless corner grocery painted dark red had a real second story and bore signs of battering from many storms.

The first block had stores and the post office, on one side only; the other side was open to Aransas Bay shimmering in the July sun, its waters lapping gently at a wide, sandy beach. The beach curved into a stand of reeds fringing the small harbor behind stores in the next block. In the harbor, shrimp trawlers draped with drying nets rocked against narrow wooden piers. Gulls soared overhead, and a brown pelican sat on a piling, solemnly surveying the scene. No one seemed to be hurried.

Rockport's three tourist courts were south of the business district, two on the waterfront; the third, Rockport Cottages, was two blocks inland on the state highway but faced the bay over an uninterrupted expanse of sand blanketed by red-and-yellow gaillardia. Connie turned the car into the curving, shell-topped driveway of Rockport Cottages, a row of eight small, one-room white frame structures built on low pilings, just high enough to be cooled by the constant southeast breeze.

Assigned to no. 7, the sisters were unpacked and cozy by nightfall. They had a miniature front porch and a bedroom with a bare floor, double bed, dresser, and two chairs. Closet space was behind a curtain hanging on a broomstick across one corner of the room. A rear alcove contained a shower stall and tiny kitchen equipped with a two-burner oil stove, sink, icebox, table, chairs, and dishes. Only cold water ran in the shower and sink. The place was clean and deliciously cool. After a stroll to the beach the new guests turned off the single light bulb hanging unshaded from the middle of the ceiling and slept soundly.

They awoke ready for adventure. Slipping into bathing suits, they had a sketchy breakfast and tore out for the bay. They swam and splashed and sang and laughed in the briny water and marveled at a skein of large black-and-white birds skimming back and forth, carmine beaks cutting the water's surface. Ambling back to the cottage they gathered bouquets of wild flowers.

Pewell would have agonized over the meals Miss Connie and Miss Bert prepared. Both considered eating a damn nuisance, but the corner grocery, dark red on the outside, dark as a cave inside, tempted them with an aroma of onions, potatoes, fresh tomatoes, bell peppers, and fruits—all in open bins. The clerk, an elderly wisp of a woman, dispensed advice and news with cheese and crackers. Rockport, they learned, "the jewel of the Coastal Bend," had once been larger than Corpus Christi, a fashionable resort with big, four-story hotels. One had had a dance pavilion out on a long pier, where famous orchestras played for throngs of vacationers who arrived on excursion trains. Mule-drawn streetcars covered a five-mile circuit connecting the hotels with the railway station south of town. Everything had been wiped out, though, by the "Corpus storm," the clerk explained. The hurricane of 1919 had devastated both Corpus Christi and Rockport, but Rockport survivors always referred to it as the "Corpus storm," as if the neighboring city were to blame.

The courthouse testified to the town's former glory and commemorated an era in Texas history in which county governments had sprinkled the state with enduring and sometimes bizarre headquarters. Aransas County had achieved the ultimate of the latter type with a multistory Byzantine edifice of yellow brick and red stone topped by an onion-shaped dome with satellite "onions" on each corner. A wrought-iron fence enclosed the square. Radiating from the courthouse was a network of unpaved, weedy streets, here and there bending or splitting down the middle to bypass a giant oak that had sprung from its acorn centuries before the streets were laid out. Connie decided she liked Rockport people because "they had sense enough to save the trees."

The town was situated on Live Oak Peninsula, a finger of sand between Aransas and Copano bays. Roads topped with oystershell connected the county seat to scattered, smaller communities. Visitors were warned not to drive off the shell, lest they get stuck in the deep sand.

When the tide was low, Connie and Bert drove the beach

road the few miles north to Fulton, where they explored the Fulton Mansion, a neglected but still stately relic of the previous century's prosperity, and watched "sea gulls" trail the shrimp boats to Roquette and Wendell's Fish House. Up here the live oaks were bent nearly to their knees by centuries of prevailing winds; their trunks leaning landward were bare to the tops, where, on reaching sunlight, they burst into one-sided umbrellas of green. Beneath them it was dark and cool. South of Rockport, trees became scarce, giving way to brush and marsh grasses. In a field by Heldenfels Shipyard, now idle, lay a curious relic of World War I—a ship built of concrete.

Many names mentioned in the weekly *Rockport Pilot* were the same family names that had appeared prominently in the newspaper since its founding in 1867. The old families in Rockport set it apart from other coastal villages; only Rockport had an "aristocracy."

Originally a shipping point for tallow and hides produced on the ranches and subsequently a marketing center for truck gardening, Rockport had become largely dependent on fishing. Tourism was a small sideline, and though residents were pleasant enough to tourists, they did not mix with summer visitors or "snowbirds," who came to escape the cold of the Midwestern winters.

Residents were no help at all with the birds and wild flowers, Connie learned; all long-legged wading birds were "cranes," and those flying were "sea gulls." A high school boy, Pug Mullinax, who delivered the ice every morning, explained that coots were "pool dous," the Cajun version of *poule d'eau*, or "chicken of the water." The name applied to all species of the rail family. He lingered at ice deliveries to talk birds and urged the visitors to come back in winter for the ducks and geese—he could help with waterfowl. Pug meant to be a game warden when he grew up. "Those little bitty ladies from Corsicana," he told townspeople, "are the jolliest women I ever saw. They laugh all the time."

Poring over the books, Connie concluded that the "sea gulls" were laughing gulls, though not all of them matched the pictures exactly; the immaculate black-and-white "shearwaters" of fishermen were black skimmers; and the tiny swallowlike "gull" was the least tern, the very bird she'd worn on a hat in New Orleans. "At least I've learned the difference between gulls and terns," she told Bert. "Terns have pointed wings and bills and they dive."

Summarizing the month, she wrote in the Nature Calendar: "Learned 15 new birds, southern constellations beautiful, learned 45 new wild flowers." Among the latter were wild snapdragon, sida, inkberry, granjeno, sea purslane, sweetbay, dwarf passionflower, sea rosemary, water pimpernel, salt heliotrope, sandbells, and polypteris.

Reluctantly, the sisters went home for the Nature Club's skywatch of the Perseids, which proved spectacular, so said the *Corsicana Sun*: "Nature Club members met at midnight on the Hagar lawn to watch the Perseids until 4 a.m. They counted up to 179 distinct meteors. The brightest fireballs with the longest tails left an afterglow across the sky from east to west. Reports of them are to be sent to Fort Worth and Pennsylvania observatories."

"Nothing's holding us here, Connie," said Bert on the telephone next morning. "Let's go back." They did, for two more weeks of sun and sand and surf. They discovered swamp sparrows and golden-fronted woodpeckers, found sweetbay berries turned into a purple feast for winter birds, and one day they saw the weather flag above the bank flying an ominous message. The big red banner had a black square center—hurricane. In a dead, flat atmosphere Aransas Bay lay like a mirror, shrimp boats remained in port, and people waited anxiously, but the storm went in at the mouth of the Rio Grande, barely brushing Rockport, but creating stunning cloud patterns.

The summer's experiences were related in several of the many club programs Connie gave that winter, "in her pleasing and inspirational manner," according to the *Sun* description. But her subjects were varied and far-ranging—folk music, knighthood, birds of the Bible, and many others. Flipping through her engagement calendar one evening, Connie chuckled and remarked to Jack, "Just give Mrs. Hagar a subject and she will sound off."

[42]

The following spring Connie and Bert were introduced to the Big Thicket by Mrs. Bruce Reid of Silsbee and Mrs. J. L. Hooks of Beaumont, two of the few people who could get around safely in that wild, mysterious, and virtually impenetrable area of southeast Texas that covered much of ten counties. A past president of the Texas Federation of Women's Clubs, Mrs. Reid had become so deeply involved in studying the outdoors around her home, Pine Knot, that she eschewed all club work except conservation—and that she did mainly in the hope of preserving something of the wilds she so loved. Connie and Bert were awed by her knowledge; she was, indeed, an authority on the natural history of the region. Mrs. Hooks, learning birds around her summer home on High Island, within earshot of the Gulf surf, had sought Mrs. Reid's help and had become her constant companion. They were a congenial pair, unlike in most ways but drawn together by mutual interests and by convenience. Mrs. Reid had pursued her studies afoot, never having learned to drive a car, but Mrs. Hooks was an excellent driver and eager to exchange that ability for what she could learn from Mrs. Reid. Bessie Reid was small, feminine, soft-spoken; Mrs. Hooks was a large, tall woman with a deep, sometimes booming voice. They addressed one another formally, as Mrs. Reid and Mrs. Hooks, throughout the years. A day with them in the Big Thicket was exhausting and stimulating—they found frogs and flowers, moths and magnolias, snakes and sapsuckers. It was never dull.

Mrs. Reid was frequently to be found with sick or lame birds, which she nursed back to health and released. She endeavored to give each its natural diet, larvae for this one, spiders for that, seeds for another. For this purpose, paper bags were issued to each explorer as they left Pine Knot in early dawn, and all through the day at the sight of an abandoned farm Mrs. Reid would say to the driver, "Stop here, Mrs. Hooks, please," and to all she added, "Get to the outhouses, girls. Gather all the wasps, spiders, bugs, and worms you can find." Obediently, all hands piled out to harvest insects, dead or alive, from houses, barns, and privies.

At times they left the car to trudge deep into dense forest and undergrowth, where one could easily be lost without an ex-

[43]

pert guide. There were many bog plants familiar to the visitors but many, many endemics that only Bessie Reid could name. Mrs. Hooks led the way across a slough, following a trail made by a wandering cow and being careful to place her boots exactly in the tracks of the cow; just inches away one could sink to the knees in the boggy bottom. The others followed, also stepping in the tracks. In the dusk they drove back to Pine Knot, bone-weary but gloating over all they had seen. Stiff and aching, they crawled from the car and fell like sandbags into chairs. Bert was sure she would never walk again.

"It's the nearest pooped I've ever been," Mrs. Reid declared.

"No, Mrs. Reid," her driver countered. "Remember the time we tramped until we had to lift our legs with our hands?"

But when the night came alive with deep-woods sounds, Connie came alive enough to capture a luna moth, giant of night-flying insects, delicately green with spots and borders of violet.

At High Island Mrs. Hooks showed them a living picture of breathtaking color; atop a stand of gray-green scrub was a shimmering mass of bright pink against a cerulean sky—roseate spoonbills jostling on their crowded nests. Among them were black-crowned and yellow-crowned night-herons, also tending nests.

The scene intensified Connie's desire to return to Rockport, and she persuaded Bert to go earlier that summer and to stay longer. In mid-May they were on the road, slowing often to marvel at enormous flocks of swallows pushing northward—a true migration, like none they had ever seen. Under an overcast sky, they drove slowly into Market Street and saw in the marsh across from the post office a clapper rail stepping daintily through the goose grass, followed by two dusky chicks—a nice beginning. Their cottage was waiting, they dashed to the beach for a first swim, and next morning young Pug Mullinax came with ice and news of the village. Connie felt she had come home.

Though eager to get to the shorebirds, she was nevertheless diverted to the oaks behind the cottages; they were alive with orioles, warblers, buntings, vireos, flycatchers—far too many to count. Many that were new to her went past unnamed, but she did unravel an interesting oddity—a varied bunting. She did not realize that it was out of place here, or that she was seeing the final flourish of a spring migration; she did note in the Nature Calendar that by June 1 the colorful passerines were gone. Species remaining on Live Oak Peninsula were breeding birds.

Along the waterfront she learned to distinguish, even at a distance, the various herons, gulls, and terns. She had acquired the several then-available volumes of Bent's *Life Histories of North American Birds,* and when a hard-hitting tropical storm at the end of July left many dead birds, she collected wings, feathers, and bills of several species to compare with Bent's descriptions, and sometimes added in the margins notes on additional characteristics she observed. The specimens helped also with the later puzzling array of sandpipers and plovers.

Connie had not then learned of Roger Tory Peterson's *Field Guide to the Birds,* which had been published that year. When it did come to her attention, she said, "I felt as if an unknown friend had extended a hand to pull me out of a bog."

Early in their stay the sisters had been rediscovered by two sixth-graders they had met the previous summer. Annie Ruth Jackson and Clare Newsome were Girl Scouts working on nature projects, and upon hearing grapevine gossip about the doings of the Corsicana women, the girls realized that they were gold mines of information and promptly set about exploiting the mines. They often "just happened" to be on the beach when Mrs. Hagar and Mrs. Malloy were there. The girls had good minds and vast curiosity, and the women were pleased to help them and their Scout troop. In August they invited the girls to join them for a resplendent midnight Perseid display. Annie Ruth had already made up her mind that when she grew up she would be just like Mrs. Hagar—she knew so much.

Frostweed and sweet goldenrod bloomed in the damp places, and black terns in mottled plumage flocked south, followed by swallows. Suddenly there were orioles again in the oaks, and gnatcatchers and warblers. It was September already—fall—time to go back to Corsicana. Their husbands came for their last day on the coast and next morning the Malloys left for home, but the Hagars headed west for another tour of the

Big Bend; at this season it would offer scenes very different from those of April.

Connie's mind had been harboring an idea for many weeks. After they had returned home, she revealed it to Jack without dissembling, without preliminaries. "I would like to live in Rockport," she announced. "I want to study birds. Is there any reason why we should not move there?"

Startled, her husband saw that this was no idle suggestion. He meditated a minute or so, pulled her into his arms for an affectionate peck, and gave in. "Malloy could manage my affairs here—but what would I do while you are watching birds?"

That was a real problem. Jack was an active man; retirement at fifty-seven was unthinkable. There must be some solution, they agreed, but meanwhile—they would say nothing to anyone else. Life went on as usual, except that now and then the Hagars slipped off to the coast looking for a house to buy. Nothing suitable went up for sale. Jack proposed renting for a year, "Just to make sure, dahling," he said, "that you would like living in a small town." No, the move would be for good, his wife declared, adding that she would "learn those shorebirds if it takes the rest of my life."

A telegram from Mr. Bracht, who had been helping in the search for a house, advised that Rockport Cottages was up for sale, though he did not think they would be interested in that. On the contrary, Jack was intrigued; he could run the tourist court—a new experience, but interesting. He would hunt and fish in his spare time.

They hurried to Rockport. Eleven acres of land went with the court, six of those acres covered by oaks, sweetbay, yaupon, beauty bush, and wild flowers. The property was self-contained; a Delco plant furnished electricity (when it worked), butane gas in a large drum fed the heaters, a windmill supplied water, and its dripping storage tank created a pool in the sand that was patronized by wandering cattle. Jack, inspecting the eight cottages, mentally began making improvements. He would add a ninth, and larger cottage, put the others in pairs with covered carports between, and no. 1, at the head of the line, could be enlarged into an office and a home for themselves. "We'll take it," he told Mr. Bracht. Elated, they went home to break the news.

Their friends were aghast. Conger Neblett leave Corsicana? Unbelievable. And they would be losing their leader and inspiration. Connie laughed off their protests. She would miss "society," they insisted; she agreed aloud but silently hoped she would never again sit behind a silver tea service in a darkened drawing room. She would, of course, miss her friends, but the distance was not great; they could visit often.

December was a month of farewell parties. Columns in the *Sun* were filled with accounts of events honoring the departing Hagars; clubs outdid themselves with citations, scrolls, gifts. Connie was touched by it all and a little ashamed that she was so eager to get away. At middle age she was breaking out of the cocoon of love and friendships that had wrapped her so long; she would be fifty next June—starting a new life. She was exhilarated.

Quite out of character, Bert trod softly with her sister. She, most of all, would miss the one person whose ideas kept pace with her own. Sonney and Alice May were home for the holidays, and the atmosphere reverted to normal at the Christmas dinner in the big house, abloom with roses from Jack's garden. The three Nebletts engaged in raillery. Their spouses laughed and kept out of it; this was a family affair.

Bert predicted darkly that Con would get out of hand with no one to put her in her place. "Certainly Jack never will," she accused. Slipping an arm around his wife's small waist, Jack promised devoutly to whip her every morning before breakfast.

Remodeling of the home cottage was under way when the Hagars arrived at Rockport in early January, 1935. Leaving Connie to oversee the work, Jack went back for their furniture. The new bedroom opened off the old one, which would now be the office, and behind it was the living room. Connie saw at once that it would not accommodate her piano, so the rear wall was torn out and the room expanded six feet, with a bay window overlooking the oaks. Kitchen and bath were renovated. The living room was furnished with Victorian pieces she had grown up with: the love seat and matching chairs from her parents' parlor, the marble-top walnut table that had been Grandmother Yeater's (whose portrait was hung over a bookcase), and her rosewood fingerback rocker. A drop-leaf walnut table, to display Connie's antique glass twine holders, was placed in the window bay. On the walls they hung the painting of the sugar mill on the Conger plantation, prints from the *Botany Book* of 1790, and a set of Siron and Mager lithographs. Sheer pink crisscross curtains were hung in the bedroom, which contained her ivory-painted bedroom suite. Breakfast table and chairs were placed by the kitchen window, but there was no place for their heavy dining room furniture. It was sold, but Connie could not give up her grandmother's four-poster bed and gateleg table. These they put in Cottage no. 2, where the Hagars would house very special guests.

Once arranged to her satisfaction, the furniture was never rearranged but remained exactly where it was placed when they moved in. Connie did not care for possessions in themselves but only as they served a purpose or reflected facets of history—like the antique glass. Pretty things in shop windows attracted her only when she was shopping for a gift or, perhaps, to select ear clips and necklaces. She loved jewelry, real or fake, so long as it was colored, and since she had given up rings, she usually wore ear bobs and matching necklace.

There was so much to be done those first few weeks in Rockport that at times she almost regretted having denied Pewell's plea to make the move with them. She would gladly have brought the maid, but there was no school for Pewell's little son since only seven blacks lived in the area; the domestic servants there were of Mexican descent.

Tourists sought accommodations before the Hagars were settled. The Cedars, operated by the Daggetts, and Hunt's Cottages were full, and soon the Rockport Cottages were full, too. Fishing was the main tourist attraction. Jack fell into the role of boniface enthusiastically; he learned the lingo of the waterfront and the times and tides for best fishing from the post office fraternity that gathered every morning to exchange news and opinions. His own opinions were usually the opposite of the others', but the brotherhood recognized the basic goodwill of the new-

[48]

comer and welcomed him. Jack became a one-man chamber of commerce. Rockport had everything, he assured anyone who would listen. He was happy.

Owners of the wandering cattle, however, thought it unfriendly of Hagar to fence his property; they depended on the windmill overflow. Jack had other plans for his surplus water; he proposed to carpet the open space in front of the Cottages with St. Augustine grass. His plan was greeted with hoots and derisive howls at the post office. Only a Yankee would be so foolhardy. Everybody knew grass wouldn't grow on that sandy peninsula. The determined Yankee, tired of emptying sand from his shoes, had three hundred loads of loam spread and plowed into the sand. He set squares of sod in it and turned on sprinklers. Palms and oleanders were set out along the curving driveway, and native shrubs were planted by cottage steps. Weeks later, when a green carpet appeared between the driveway and the highway, there was a rush of orders for St. Augustine grass in Rockport.

Jack ordered small gas ranges and heaters for the cottages, replaced iceboxes with electric refrigerators, installed washbasins, and laid linoleum squares on the bedroom floors. The Rockport Cottages were then on a par with most coastal accommodations and as luxurious as they would ever be.

Connie declined to join the local bridge clubs but gladly agreed to sing or play or give nature talks. These occasions could be managed without neglecting her real life—with the birds.

Their daily routine began with breakfast at six o'clock. By seven, Jack had fetched the yardman and the maid, who tended the cottages and prepared their noon meal; then the car was at Connie's disposal. As she drove away, Jack was bustling about, cheerily giving orders, making gratuitous comments and jokes. She was back for dinner at noon and again in the afternoon to set her husband's supper on the table at six o'clock. Her mornings began with a slow drive along the shoreline, empty save for birds and intent anglers on the fishing piers. As the season advanced into the nesting period, the action moved inland. Horned larks covered eggs on a shell reef by the shipyard, where three young were banded one day and three more the next, just as

[49]

they departed the shallow scrapes where they had hatched. Three nests by the schoolhouse produced five baby Inca doves; two wide-mouthed fledgling nighthawks were found, examined wonderingly, and banded. A colony of red-winged blackbirds and great-tailed grackles held forth noisily in tules near Sparks Colony.

On Live Oak Point, the northernmost tip of the peninsula penetrated only by fishermen and the birdwatcher, she found pairs of Wilson's plovers with fuzzy, walnut-size chicks running after them on matchstick legs. Others were on nests. By easing the car onto a shell ridge she could watch the progress at several nests. The male guarding a mate on the nearest nest, a mere dent in the sand, always whistled a single alarm note at her approach, and the sitter slipped off the mottled eggs and into the brush, soon to pop up at some distant point. Following the apparently aimless wandering of the bird through her binoculars, Connie found that the bird invariably worked her way back secretly to those eggs. She watched the hatchings and the chicks' quick debuts into the world. A slight quivering of an egg signaled the start of hatching as an egg tooth slowly cut a jagged circle around the end of the eggshell; the cut piece fell away and a sopping wet form struggled out to lie trembling in the light, head bent helplessly over its back. Then the neck stiffened and with tremendous exertion was brought forward. The wet down dried to speckled tan above, white below, with a dark necklace. The chick staggered to its feet and was away in a flash. Chasing them Connie was deeply impressed by the sturdiness of these minutes-old wild things. Holding a captive, she studied its downy plumage, applied a band, and let it go to agitated parents hiding nearby.

Watching wading birds from a pier near The Cedars one morning, Connie was joined by a tail-wagging, bristle-haired terrier of mixed ancestry, and when she returned to the car, he was in it ahead of her. He wasn't a bit like Mark Antony except that he was a dog; his coat was a wiry golden brown with a blaze of white across his whiskered, smiling face. She hugged the animal. "If you want to go birding with me, little dog, you may." He sat on the front seat, jumping out when she did but never rushing the birds. At noon she took him home and told Mr. Daggett, "Your little dog went birding with me. He's a nice dog."

"Fuzzy just likes to ride," his owner said. "Don't let him be a nuisance to you."

Fuzzy found her on the beach next morning, and again the next and day after day. She always took him back to the Daggett home, but soon the dog was trailing her car to Rockport Cottages. Jack took him back. At the post office Fuzzy left the Daggett car to get in with Jack. It was a delicate situation; the Hagars definitely did not wish to offend a rival court owner, but Fuzzy was so persistent that Connie gave up. "To hell with it," she announced. "The Daggetts know I am not stealing their dog. He isn't tied here; they can come get him, but if he wants to be my dog, I'm willing." Fuzzy had known all along he was her dog.

Together they explored the Cove, a small bay and wide marsh south of the shipyard separated from Aransas Bay by an ancient oyster reef on which grew a botanical tangle of chittimwood, dewberry, coral bean, Mexican apple, slender-stemmed sunflower, lantana, and vines. Cow-itch vine with fleshy leaves bore purple berries favored by many birds; matrimony vine, bearing today's lavender flowers and yesterday's paper-colored flowers, would later produce red berries; dainty climbing snapdragon had tiny deltoid leaves and purple blossoms. In early morning the bordering mat of gaillardia, or Indian blanket, was mixed with the azure of Virginia dayflower, or widow's tears. The marsh nourished ironweed daisies, sea ox-eye, sea rosemary, purslane, and beach heliotrope, as well as herons and ibis, skimmers, sandpipers, and plovers.

North of the business district, where the road forked from the highway to the beach, was Little Bay, a haven for ducks, and Frandolig Island, a brushy area to which Connie had not yet gained access. Near Fulton the beach road wound around the mouth of a sluggish stream that passed under the highway and was lined all the way with cattails, or tules. Gallinules clambered up the stems.

Two miles inland from downtown a road branched off by Moore's Pool, a small lake surrounded by oaks, brush, and rattlepod, and half-covered with lotus. This road wound on past

Redbug Corner to Sparks Colony where one could turn off to Rattlesnake Point or go on to Salt Lake, a larger body of water separated from Copano Bay by a ridge of sand and shell. From Sparks Colony, Connie often drove the loop back to town by Lenoir's Landing and along the Copano shore to the highway. The few people who lived along these roads came to know Mrs. Hagar and Fuzzy early; she introduced herself, seeking permission to wander over their property. Though her mission puzzled them, she was never denied. In her high-centered Ford it was possible to get deep into the unfenced pastures, but many had to be negotiated on foot.

At least once a day Connie stopped at the Tules, a reed-grown swale near Fulton where the sluggish stream spread out before being channeled under the highway. Above the reeds on the south side of the swale loomed a dark mass of tall, dense oaks. And here, the rising sun illuminated a breathtaking scene of dark trees adorned with roosting blue herons, pink spoonbills, white egrets, and ibis. In the still water reflecting the pink dawn sky, black-necked stilts and avocets probed the shallows.

Annie Ruth Jackson telephoned about the owl in their trees. Connie, equipped with bird bands and pliers, went for her after school. The bird was high up in an oak, but the young girl, wearing gloves, as Mrs. Hagar insisted, shinnied up the tree and took it. A screech-owl, Connie's first. It played dead in her hands but came alive angrily when released.

Annie Ruth's long legs were a match for the young plovers, too; she captured many that would have gotten away from Mrs. Hagar. A good student, she worked on identifications as her mentor directed. "Start with the stems of plants, as you do with the legs of a bird—you know me and legs, Annie Ruth. Legs and bills first.

"I'll tell you something," she confided one day. "People are always saying how smart I am. Well, the truth is, I'm not really smart, I'm just a sticker. I stick on a problem until things unfold."

In a letter to Bert she wrote that clapper rails were nesting again in the ditch between the harbor and the post office. She had reached into the cattails and lifted the incubating hen from the plate-size platform she had built of reed stems. "She will sit

[52]

those eggs until death," she wrote. One day the parent rail even followed Connie across the street and into the post office.

She wrote on the stationery Jack designed, showing his pride in his new enterprise. At the top was a sketch of leaning oaks, beneath them in big black type "Rockport Cottages," with "Jack Hagar" in small type below. The upper right corner listed Rockport's advantages: Winter and Summer Resort—Bathing—Coolest Spot on Texas Coast—Hunting and Fishing—Home of Rockport Oysters. The left-hand corner extolled his court: Water Certified by State Dept. of Health—Gas and Lights—Clean Modern Cottages—Completely Furnished—Located on Hug-the-Coast Highway. The address, Box 339, was opposite "Phone-9." Their number was one of ninety in the telephone directory.

Jack blithely ignored certain drawbacks in his Eden, snakes among them. Snakes abounded here, Connie was warned, so she added a heavy stick to her field equipment. In addition to rattlesnakes, cottonmouths, and the beautiful but deadly coral snake, there were harmless, even beneficial snakes, but to native folk all snakes were vile. She knew better and sent for books that would help her tell friend from foe. Some friends were fascinating—blue racers, ribbon snakes, garter snakes, green garden snakes, and the "very dangerous" spread adder she was warned of proved to be the comic hognose that played possum in the face of danger. She learned to distinguish between the useful scarlet king snake and its look-alike, the coral snake. The latter, she found, was actually quite rare—and timid. It "ran" if given the chance and did not strike; coral snakes had small teeth and chewed. Anyone bitten by a coral snake had to be a fool, Connie concluded. A cottonmouth, though, would fight back, head reared and swaying, fangs bared, and strike as long as life was in it. "Makes a rattler look like a coward," she told Jack. Cottonmouths were fat and ugly and smelly. She despised them.

Mr. Glass, an elderly neighbor, was horrified by little Mrs. Hagar's snake encounters and that her defense was an ordinary stick. From a sweetbay root he fashioned a smooth four-foot club with a handle providing "a good heft" for her. Its first victim was a rattlesnake on Rattlesnake Point. Connie's binoculars were

[53]

focused on shorebirds when Fuzzy yipped his "snake bark," unlike any other bark. Then she saw the lark sparrow in the road, seemingly frozen to the ground, its wings limp and eyes paralyzed in a stare. A rattler, "big as an inner tube" slithered toward it. With the new club, she jumped from the car, and the coiled snake turned to her, its head high, tail buzzing. Like a golfer poised for a long drive, she took a stance, "got a heft" on the club, and swung hard. The snake's head snapped off with a loud crack; the lark sparrow relaxed and weakly fluttered away. Mr. Glass shuddered when he heard of it, but Jack shrugged and said, "When my little wife gets mad enough, everybody better look out."

Their first year in Rockport was passing so quickly, the dazzling spring migration had merged into the breeding season, which was still in full swing when, to Connie's amazement, birds were coming south again. It was July 15. In starched cotton frock and rubber boots, she, along with Fuzzy, followed the trail they had beaten out on the north side of the Tules. Far back from the highway was a small lake frequented by black-necked stilts, whose young now stood as tall as their parents on ridiculously long legs. Overnight they had been joined by a flock of least sandpipers. So soon? It was barely six weeks since the last of the northbound sandpipers had left Rockport. Did fall migration begin so early? It was indeed the overture of the autumn symphony of flight that would span the next five months. The date would become significant in future years; least sandpipers arrived in mid-July, leading the fall migration.

In September thousands of ducks began to pour from the sky to settle on Little Bay, so many drakes in such puzzling eclipse plumage that Connie despaired of learning them until the fall molt was over. With winter came sparrows, their young also puzzling; the song sparrow so familiar in Corsicana was scarce here, but flocks of chipping, savannah, field, and vesper sparrows were seen on the daily tours.

It had been a good year. Connie at fifty was young again, and Jack was having the time of his life.

Winter barely brushed the peninsula until well into the new year of 1936, arriving in February when ice formed on the birdbath and the first robins arrived with bluebirds, kinglets, yellow-rumped warblers, and many, many more sparrows. Rain followed the cold, and quickly the fields burst into bloom: golden corydalis, phlox, gaillardia, sleepy daisies, coneflowers. A veery lurked in a brasil thicket inhabited by a hermit thrush, orange-crowned warblers and cedar waxwings possessed the oaks, and a harrier quartered the prairies while kestrels scanned them from atop utility poles.

Scents of spring were in the air; cardinals, mockingbirds, and Inca doves went about in twos. The appearance of a yellow-throated vireo meant another spring migration was in the offing.

In the following weeks, the daily entries in the Nature Calendar began with "perfect day," followed by long lists. There were hordes of blue-gray gnatcatchers dining sumptuously on insects drawn to the nectar in creamy white heads of Spanish dagger, and goldfinches in winter plumage. But a prothonotary warbler was like a little torch illuminating the oaks for four days; a Carolina wren claimed territory with ringing songs. April brought wave after wave of warblers. Connie spent much of each day stretched out in a reclining lawn chair in her yard, with her eyes and binoculars directed at the treetops. The parade of warblers changed with the weeks. Black-and-whites, parulas, yellow-throateds, and ceruleans came first; then black-throated greens, Blackburnians, yellowthroats, hooded, Canada, magnolias, yellows, Kentucky, Tennessee, and worm-eating. Ovenbirds and waterthrushes came, and finally the redstarts and the chestnut-sided and bay-breasted warblers. Meanwhile, an American goldeneye, allegedly a deep-water denizen, spent a week in a shallow rain pool near the back door. And, as migrants poured through, nestlings of resident birds became eligible for banding.

On Easter, from a rear pew in the church, Jack beamed as his wife, in pink linen frock and flowered hat, rose to sing the solo passages of the anthem. No one in the congregation suspected that the Easter sunrise had found the soloist tramping a pasture inspecting nests of meadowlarks and Bewick's wrens. Most of the congregation, however, had become aware that Rockport's birdlife was somehow significant. Overwhelmed by all she was seeing and eager to share, Connie had volunteered several articles to the *Rockport Pilot*, and these had interested a San Antonio editor, who asked her to write for the *Express*. She was pleased. Though she had no literary ambitions, she was happy to tell the world about birds at Rockport. Her story was published the first Sunday in May, 1936, under a five-column headline, "Texas Gulf Coast Is Haven for Bird Life," by Conger Neblett Hagar.

Chapter 4

Having heard her bird talks to the schoolchildren, the school superintendent naturally sought Mrs. Hagar when he received a letter from George Williams, author and professor of English at Rice Institute in Houston. The writer was interested in bird migration and proposed to publish a bulletin, the *Gulf Coast Migrant*, summarizing spring and fall passages along the coast. Could the superintendent recommend someone in his area who might contribute reliable observations? Joyfully, Connie accepted. Professor Williams named three others who would help: Joe M. Heiser, Jr., of Houston; Arly McKay of Cove; and Irby Davis of Harlingen. Though they were new names to her, they were doing what she was doing; she would be a link in a chain of birdwatchers around the coast, and she would learn what others were seeing—a delightful prospect.

Her first report, covering many pages, inspired the *Migrant* editor to promise a visit at the end of the summer term. Jack was no less pleased than she; he understood how she longed to talk birds with someone who cared. "Someone who can help me," Connie said. And though Jack was convinced that his wife knew more than any college professor, he would reserve no. 2, the equivalent of a VIP suite at Rockport Cottages, for this one.

Connie was in awe of her visitor but thought the dark, square-faced man "quite good-looking" as she greeted him on her steps at the end of his leisurely drive, "looking at birds all the way." They sat late in her parlor making plans, talking birds and the *Gulf Coast Migrant*, and about one another. Williams had lived in Aransas Pass as a boy and knew the area well. (It was the setting for a novel he later wrote.) Birds were his avocation, the Rice campus his laboratory, where he had studied nesting robins for years. He published the mimeographed *Migrant* at his own expense and sent it to interested correspondents, including Dr. Harry C. Oberholser, senior wildlife research biologist in the U.S. Department of the Interior. Connie was elated to learn that Dr. Oberholser was working on a definitive book on Texas birds; it was to be his life work and already he had mountains of data.

Next morning they roamed the back roads, seeing many fall migrants; the afternoon was spent along the shoreline. Black terns in motley plumage dipped at the edges of Copano Bay, and Williams remarked that he had a skin of one in peak breeding plumage. Connie wanted to know how to save skins and if it was difficult. "Not at all. I'll show you," he promised. At Johnson's Drug Store they bought small scissors, tweezers, a sharp knife, sterile cotton, and borax. Needle and thread she had. After supper and comfortably established on a first-name basis, George coached her through the removal of a skin, curing it and reconstructing the bird on a cotton body, sewing it together, and finally mounting it on a small stick. The stick, he explained, was there so she would not have to "manhandle" the specimen. A longer stick, Connie realized, would give her that extra height she needed when showing birds to an audience.

Williams was accumulating data to verify, if possible, his widely contested theory that migrant passerines travel by land around the Gulf in their northward journeys, not across the Gulf, as others believed. He was to return for many more mutually rewarding visits, and soon there were others to share Rockport's birds. A couple from Dallas came on Labor Day at the recommendation of Norma and Jerry Stillwell.

"We are Terry and Maurine Gill," they explained, "hoping to learn shorebirds." The rapport they all sensed instantly deepened as they sat outdoors in the lengthening shadows of the oaks while the drone of cicadas crescendoed and waned and bobwhites came to feast on the ripe partridge peas that Jack zealously guarded from the mowers. Terry, an engineer with Lone

Star Gas Company, had begun casually noticing birds as he traveled his territory, often accompanied by his wife. Both had become more than casually interested, but Terry, Maurine insisted, was far ahead of her and knew the upstate land birds well. "But those pesky little water birds," her husband wailed. "How do you separate sandpipers in winter?"

"You will see" their hostess promised. And they did, working doggedly every day as Connie patiently detailed field marks. "When in doubt, make them fly. You cannot miss the flashy wing patterns of willets and sanderlings—but oh, look above us!" Drifting high against a wisp of white cloud was a great black bird, its long wings motionless, its long tail opening like scissors. "A magnificent frigatebird! The man-o-war bird," she breathed, gazing wonderingly. "You have given me a new species. What can I do for you?"

"Tell more about sandpipers," Terry answered promptly.

To avoid Labor Day crowds on the beaches, they crossed Copano Bay on the rattling causeway to Lamar Peninsula. Brown pelicans maneuvered and plunged for fish, while overhead, white pelicans were gliding on set wings. In a grassy shallow inlet beside Mills Wharf, fifteen wood storks sampled the menu in the mud with huge curved beaks swinging back and forth. "Watch the storks," Connie advised. "Look at the feet." One of the flock, deciding the bill of fare might be richer elsewhere, flapped slowly into the air, dangling big feet.

"They are pink!" Maurine shrieked. "Baby pink!"

"I wanted you to see that," Connie said. "None of my books mentions pink feet, and I wondered if I were seeing things. I am not sure, but I think maybe the color fades on dead birds, and since many writers work from museum specimens, they might not know about the color."

On the Gills' last day they stayed afield until dark drove them in. Terry sank to the steps of the Hagar cottage and said to Jack, "What a place! What a weekend! What a teacher! Your wife is quite a person, you know?"

"You mean Pure Nuts?" Jack asked airily, using a favorite nickname for her. "Why, I taught her everything she knows."

The Gills, too, would return often, and Maurine, a trained

secretary, always sent Connie typed lists of their findings. "So much more presentable than my records," Connie said, delighted to file them.

She watched the fall migration alone. Thousands of redheads rafted on Little Bay, soon joined by pintails, wigeons, and others. Fulvous whistling-ducks occupied Moore's Pool, and an osprey consumed its fish on a telephone pole near the Cottages. Swallows swarmed through, and scissor-tailed flycatchers, absent since August, reappeared in October in romping, chattering companies, playing their way southward. They were more brilliantly suffused with coral, even into the tail feathers, Connie noted, than they had been in spring. Oddly, most birds were more colorful in springtime.

The honking of geese aroused everyone in Rockport. The Canadas were in! Jack oiled his guns. But more exciting to Connie had been the river of hawks that streamed along the shore in front of the Cottages in late September. Jack, too, was impressed by the sight. From early morning and through the day hawks appeared from the north and disappeared on the southern horizon. She could not name them, but two weeks later when another migration occurred, she was better prepared, having studied industriously. This flight contained falcons—peregrines, merlins, and kestrels, but it was over the prairies and not the same species she had seen on the bayfront.

Flickers dominated the woodpecker scene, and a small band of red-headed woodpeckers came to spend the winter in a marsh near Copano Bay. Most of them were subadults, but before they departed, they had donned the elegant adult feathering. These woodpeckers, she would learn, did not come every winter.

"Saw my first great white heron," she wrote in the Nature Calendar October 25. It was no egret, she was sure, with those yellowish legs and huge yellow bill; besides, she did not question the wonders of Rockport. Anything seemed possible. "Warm and fair," was a November notation made after driving up Highway 35 to Green Lake. "Hundreds of spoonbills like big pink roses in the salt flats."

Between Thanksgiving and Christmas, species and numbers

built up overwhelmingly. Eastern bluebirds and American gold-finches flocked together near the Big Tree on Lamar Peninsula, then eastern phoebes, and an olive-sided flycatcher "whistled his order" from a high bare perch. "Quick! Three beers!" A brown creeper mined the oaks, and water pipits mingled with horned larks on sandy flats. Swarms of yellow-rumped warblers, hundreds of them together, were usual, but not usual was the mixed party that spent December 10 in her oaks—black-and-white, Blackburnian, and Kentucky warblers.

Fuzzy located Connie's first American bittern. As she studied two king rails in the brown grass of a roadside ditch, the dog kept muttering, impatiently twisting and wagging his tail at something on his side of the car. She turned, and there it was, camouflaged in the tall grass, slender and streaked, the bittern frozen in place, its yellow eyes aimed at her from both sides of its turned-up bill.

That two totally unexpected species of grebes should stray to Rockport, Texas, on the same day in December, the twelfth, was incredible even to Connie. She saw the large "grebe-like" birds cavorting on Copano Bay as she crossed the causeway and turned back to park on a jutting shellbank. She held her binoculars steady on the birds, diving and bobbing in the choppy water, until she made out the field marks—Holboell's red-necked grebes, though the necks were not red at this season. Going home along the Fulton Beach road, she passed the shrimp trawlers moored at the fish house and suddenly slammed on the brakes so hard that Fuzzy hit the floor. Another grebe was riding the surf like a swan, regally black-and-white, impossible to mistake—a western grebe. "Most beautiful grebe in the world," she told Jack. "I nearly fainted." Next day they were gone. Both would return in future years but at widely spaced intervals.

On New Year's Day, 1937, launching the tenth year of the Nature Calendar, Annie Ruth joined her mentor for a 7 A.M. to 7 P.M. Christmas Bird Count. They covered forty miles and listed eighty-six species—forty-two land birds, and forty-four water birds.

Connie had extended her observations beyond her home county. One day a week, taking a candy bar for lunch, she and

Fuzzy would drive up the coast, stopping often at the Tattons' Salt Creek Ranch for the small colony of Attwater's prairie-chickens there, or at the Hartman Ranch for ducks and geese, and on to Victoria. They would then return by way of Beeville, Refugio, and perhaps Corpus Christi. Another week she went west and south to Live Oak and McMullen counties, the King Ranch, and down into Kenedy County. She was always home by nightfall, lest Jack worry.

A March notation in the Calendar, "Laughing gulls are back," was to become an amusing reminder of her long struggle with that ever-present species. When the black heads of the breeding season disappeared, she had presumed the gulls were gone and had not known how to identify those gulls with the pale winter heads, nor had she identified the brownish young of late summer. But this summer she saw a proper laughing gull deliver a shrimp to a quivering, begging brown sea gull of equal size, and, she would tell laughingly, "lightning struck me." Of course the brown chick was her baby. How dumb can I be, she wondered. Soon she noted the gradual disappearance of adult gulls' black snoods and realized that laughing gulls were always there. How stupid she had been—would she ever learn all those changing plumages?

A varied bunting, her second, appeared with a wave of indigo buntings and was included in her list for the *Gulf Coast Migrant*. The same lists were now going also to Dr. George Lowery at Louisiana State University, at his request. He was a leading proponent of the trans-Gulf migration theory, and it intrigued Connie that although she sent identical data to Williams and Lowery, the recipients drew opposite conclusions from them.

She banded nearly one hundred birds that year. She always knew when a tufted titmouse (hers were always the black-crested race) was in a trap—its mate invariably fluttered and cried and "took on" until the prisoner was free. One cardinal repeated five times, twice in one day. (Several cardinals would reappear in the same traps a year later, including a mated pair caught the second time together, and a lark sparrow repeated after four years, missing the exact date by only two weeks.)

Shorebird nests were located by watching the comings and

[62]

goings of the owners. Black-necked stilts, Connie decided, loved nothing better for nests than old cow tracks. Least terns and black skimmers put their eggs in scrapes on sand flats, often in close community with one another.

Still another request for her observations was made; Dr. Oberholser had read her accounts in the *Migrant* and wanted details. Connie was flattered; this would be for his Texas bird book. Without delay she summarized the spring migration and the nesting species, including the warbling vireos that had nested in a fork of the oak outside her bedroom window—the same place they had nested the previous year. The senior biologist replied with formal thanks but asked, "Are you sure of your warbling vireo? You are too far south for this bird. Probably you have the Bell's vireo nesting in your oak, as you are within its breeding range."

She was taken aback, and a little indignant; she knew Bell's vireo so well in Corsicana. But her resentment cooled and she wrote again, giving details of the plumage, behavior, nest construction, and song. Noncommittally, Dr. Oberholser replied, "This is most interesting, the southmost nesting of the warbling vireo, it may mean an extension of the bird's range, for it is four hundred miles south of where it would remotely be expected to nest." He reiterated his wish for continued accounts of her birds.

The Gills came for a June vacation and to learn more about shorebirds, now on eggs or tending young. Fledgling willets raced over the flats. "Look like baby turkeys," Connie commented. Oystercatchers had eggs on Oystercatcher Point, and there, hiding in water pimpernel, were seaside sparrows. At one maternity ward they counted thirty-nine least tern nests and watched adults fly in with laden bills; they marveled that in such a crowded colony parents could unerringly find their own young to feed.

On the road to Rattlesnake Point a verdin hopped about in a huisache tree containing a northern oriole (Bullock race) nest, and nearby were young cardinals ready for banding. Terry and Maurine stood by as Connie parted the thorny granjeno branches to reach the nest of grasses with a bit of shed snakeskin woven into it. It contained two sleepy young redbirds and a

[63]

larger, blackish nestling with a long, pointed bill. This was their introduction to the wanton ways of cowbirds.

On the way home they paused at the little harbor to watch a brown pelican—uncommon in June when most of its kind were away on breeding islands. Another bird floated on the still water. Not a duck, not a gull, not a grebe—it had a funny bill. Connie called off her impressions of the bird with growing excitement. "I cannot say what it is," she exclaimed over and over. "It's different." The bird would not fly; it merely floated, occasionally snapping at bait shrimp a boy threw to the pelican.

"Well," Terry offered, "if you care so much about this bird I'll take a picture of it." He unhooked a small camera from his belt, and the three walked out on the old railroad trestle so they would be closer to the bird. Terry snapped the shutter several times. Connie clearly saw a tubular bill and knew she must read about shearwaters, a subject she had skimmed over, never expecting to see one.

Poring over the books, she decided it must be a sooty shearwater, and was more convinced the next day, when looking at the stranger with its characteristics fresh in her mind. It was there a third day, still floating, never flying, but was gone the fourth day. Dr. Oberholser accepted her report with polite reservations.

United States Department of Agriculture
Bureau of Biological Survey
Washington, D.C.

July 7, 1937

Mrs. Jack Hagar,
Rockport Cottages
Rockport, Texas

Dear Mrs. Hagar:

Your letter of June 14 has been received, and I am very much pleased to hear from you again.

From what you say it seems practically certain that you did have the remarkable good luck to watch a nest of the warbling vireo, so far south as Rockport, Texas. If, however, you can get any further light on the subject through your observations this year or next, I should be only too glad to hear from you regarding this.

The list of birds that you and Mr. and Mrs. Terry Gill observed in the vicinity of Rockport has been received and I am very glad to have this. There are several interesting records among them but you do not give any dates nearer than from June 15–18. I am wondering if it would be too much trouble for you to give an exact date for each of the species?

I note that you mention a sooty shearwater, which is a new bird for Texas. I should like to have all the information that you can furnish regarding this particular species, and to ask if you are absolutely positive of its identification. Also, how many of you saw the bird and at how close range. It is a species that, of course, should occasionally occur along the coast, but so far has never been reliably reported.

Any further notes regarding other birds that you can furnish at the present time or in the future I should greatly appreciate, bearing in mind that what I most desire are definite dates of occurrence.

With best wishes,
I am sincerely yours,
Harry C. Oberholser
Senior biologist, Section of Wildlife Surveys

P.S. The enclosed envelope does not require postage.

"He seems to doubt that I saw a sooty shearwater," Connie remarked to Jack, reading that passage to him. Jack was enraged.

"Nobody can question my wife's word," he stormed. "Throw that letter in the wastebasket and never write to him again."

"No, I will answer. I have told the truth, I think I know what I saw, but if I do not know I want him to tell me what the · bird was. I want the truth."

She sent Terry's best snapshots. "Not big pictures," she said. "But with a magnifying glass you can see details on the bird. If I did not see a sooty shearwater, tell me what it was." Annie Ruth and Albert Collier, marine biologist at the state game and fish laboratory, also saw it, she added.

[65]

Dr. Oberholser replied promptly:

Dear Mrs. Hagar:

I am exceedingly glad to have a chance to see the picture of the sooty shearwater, which fully identifies the bird and finally authenticates the record. This bird is very erratic in appearance and there is no inherent reason to doubt the occurrence in summer off the coast of Texas, but since there was never a record of the species before, it is desirable to make use of all possible means to authenticate the record before it is published. Of course, as a matter of fact, it has already been published in the *Gulf Coast Migrant*, and my own use of the record will, of course, give full credit to you and other observers. It was fortunate that Mr. Gill was able to get such good pictures of this bird. In accordance with your request I am returning the photographs herewith, and I trust they will reach you without incident.

Connie was content, but Jack was far from appeased. However, he was diverted by a confrontation with Bewick's wrens. During a draining and filling project, Cottage no. 8 had been jacked up, and over the weekend two pairs of wrens had chosen no. 8 for nest sites. One pair built in a paper sack full of nails in the carport. Another selected the slit between the floor and supporting crossbeams. Connie had seen the wrens inspecting the sites; a male liked a corner of the eave of the porch and there deposited a pile of wood shavings. His mate would have none of it; she kicked the shavings to the floor. The male then chose a flowerpot and amassed more shavings, also rejected. The fussy female scattered shreds in all directions. She was determined to have the slit beneath the floor. The cottage remained jacked up until Connie banded five young the day they fledged.

August was hot and dry; the peninsula sizzled in the heat. Cicadas began their chorus the moment the sun stippled Aransas Bay with yellows and pinks; it swelled to a deafening hiss like steam escaping from a giant valve, then waned and rose again all through the day. Inside the cottages, set to capture prevailing breezes, it was cool. In her grandmother's rocker by the window

Connie was reading about butterflies; so many danced through Rockport that month—monarchs, black and giant swallowtails, sulphurs, azures. She had collected a dogface with perfect profiles on the yellow-and-black wings.

A small green lizard slid along the windowsill searching for spiders and paused to "do push-ups" and expand a bright pink bubble beneath its throat. Because it turned brown against a tree trunk, locals called it a chameleon, but having looked it up, she knew the anole was no true chameleon. A cardinal family was at the sunflower seed feeder. The adults looked shabby—they were molting—but there was no sign of mockingbirds. There never was in August; they too were molting and much too proud to be seen in less than perfect plumage. They lurked under cover until new feathers restored them to their usual proud appearance.

She heard the car cross the cattleguard and looked up as Jack stood in the doorway. "Letters for you, dahling," he said, handing her a packet of mail as he sat down to peruse his own—more requests for accommodations than he could handle. Upon reading a letter at the bottom of her stack, Connie sat rigid a minute with mixed emotions. Was she glad? fearful? She was not sure, but she made her voice sound casual. "Jack, save a cottage for Dr. Oberholser on the twenty-third, please."

"Can't do it," he said flatly, scowling, "We are all booked up with nice people." Then he smiled, "I'll put him in no. 2," he said.

She learned more about Oberholser from the *San Antonio Express*, which covered his stopover there in detail. The face in the photograph was long, narrow, and rather forbidding, despite a hint of warmth in the eyes, deep-set and keen. The high forehead tapered to a point on one side where baldness widened the part in thin, closely combed hair. He wore a wide, starched collar. Connie admitted some trepidation; she had never met a professional ornithologist, and here she was starting with the best. What would he think of her activities? At any rate, she would look her best when he came. On the twenty-third she returned early from the bayfront, bathed, combed her hair, laid out the dress she would wear, and pulled on a loose robe. Jack left for the post office. The No Vacancy sign was out, and she felt secure from interruption. Barefooted, she propped against a pillow at the foot of her bed, her back to the door, and began listing species seen that morning. The doorbell tinkled. She was tempted to ignore it, but she could not be rude to Jack's guests. At the door she confronted a tall man whose face was vaguely familiar.

"Are you Mrs. Jack Hagar?" the man inquired in an unmistakably "Eastern city" voice. "I am Harry Oberholser."

Connie's hands closed convulsively over the front of her robe—and she had meant to look like a lady! "Oh, my goodness," was her dismayed greeting. "Here I am barefoot and in a kimono! Do come in, Dr. Oberholser."

In the living room he was barely seated before launching into the subject of birds. Unsmiling, very formal, very polite, the visitor appeared oblivious to his hostess's informal attire, but she could hardly follow the conversation—thinking of what her mother would have said of such a situation. Finally, she interrupted to suggest that Dr. Oberholser sit in the shade of the oaks while she made herself presentable. Minutes later, in a lilac voile dress and quite herself again, she joined him. "This sooty shearwater," the biologist pursued, "how near land was it? What was the weather? Did the bird land or take off while you watched?"

Jack came through the kitchen door. His frosty greeting and Dr. Oberholser's overwhelming formality rendered the occasion less than cordial. The inquisition was resumed, with Jack included.

"Looked like a mud hen to me," Jack opined. His levity fell flat. Connie proposed an immediate visit to the site where she had seen the bird. At the harbor they stood in the sun by Jackson's Fish House as Connie told of the discovery and subsequent studies of the pelagic species whose stopover had so agitated the Washington authority. They went to the marine laboratory where Albert Collier was questioned and to the Jackson's home to interview Annie Ruth.

Back in the Hagar living room Oberholser probed Connie's background on birds—her father's teaching, the Nature Club, and the trips to Big Bend with Jack were described, and she spoke of the startling beauty of the vermilion flycatcher they

[68]

saw. At that the man pounced. "In April, Mrs. Hagar? A vermilion flycatcher at Van Horn in April?" Yes, and in the fall, too. He could accept the fall sighting, but. . . . "Very odd," he remarked starchily. "That locality is entirely off course for that bird at that season. April!"

He cross-examined her on the warbling vireo; no aspect of plumage or behavior was omitted. Connie was glad Jack was not hearing this; he would have been furious. Near noon, she asked if Dr. Oberholser would like to drive out after lunch to look at birds.

"More than anything, Mrs. Hagar," he responded promptly. She thought there was an edge of grimness in his voice. Quite possibly a field test of her ability was the primary objective of his visit. Cruising the shoreline and the back roads, the visitor led the conversation away from birds but interrupted often to demand identification. "You say you observe every day, Mrs. Hagar?" Yes, morning and afternoon if not all day. "What's that?" You mean the willet, or those dowitchers?

"You don't mean every day, Mrs. Hagar. How often, exactly?" But she did mean every day. "Identify!" Yellowlegs. Mostly greater. Shorebirds had been coming in since July; purple martins were overhead and some barn swallows. They had been coming through for ten days.

"You play the piano?" Yes. "Identify!" Black-necked stilts, Wilson's plovers—they nest here, you know. Black terns, loggerhead shrike, white-rumped sandpipers. "Where did you study music?" Forest Park Conser—"Name that bird!" Sennett's titmouse.

"When does Mr. Hagar observe birds?" He doesn't. "Name them!" White-faced glossy ibis among roseate spoonbills, Hudsonian curlews. Black-and-white warbler on the tree, empidonax flycatcher above.

The trial went on relentlessly, giving the pupil no time to think. It was worse than any examination she had ever had in school—but she enjoyed it. This experience was confirming species for the Coastal Bend that were not entirely credited in the literature. Privately, Connie thought that Texas had been slighted by professional ornithologists, most certainly in recent years, and if this man was going to publish a book about Texas birds, she wanted the state to get full credit. Furthermore, and most importantly, she was learning from him; he had already illuminated numerous obscure field marks for her.

The quiz went on that evening over a sweet, red watermelon that Jack brought to the backyard, while nighthawks cut zigzag paths across a moonlit sky. Questions directed at Jack got unsatisfactory answers, but Dr. Oberholser could not and never would accept that Jack was not interested in birds. Sensing that his interrogation might sound hostile, the biologist finally offered an appeasing excuse. "I hope you will not think I am disbelieving by asking all these questions," he said, but rather gruffly. "It is necessary to be sure. The government cannot afford to report things not fully verified. This is for your protection, and for the protection of all people, that our records be absolutely reliable."

Connie nodded; veracity, reliability—these she lived by. Myth taken for fact did not amuse her. Jack was beginning to be mollified.

"A person like you," the guest went on with a trace of warmth, "can contribute very much. I do trust you will keep me informed of your experiences." She would, of course. She emptied the watermelon seeds at the base of a tree, explaining, "Redbirds adore them but won't get a chance; fox squirrels gobble them up."

The second day was more congenial; the guest seemed more relaxed, content, his questions were far less belligerent. A flight of scissortails going over prompted Connie to remark on the absence of this species between the time her nesters left and others came through, adding, "They are so much brighter and prettier now than in spring." His eyebrow went up, without comment, and again when she referred to a "migration of cardinals."

He examined her banding records and was impressed by her Corsicana notes on bluebird nesting and feeding. He recommended more titles for her library and added a word to her vocabulary—flyway. Birds followed definite routes year after year in their north-south movements, and he drew an exciting dia-

[70]

gram of known flyways. Many converged in South Texas and she would add to this list. After two exhausting, dazzling days Dr. Oberholser said good-bye with profuse, if formal, thanks.

"He nearly killed me," Connie sighed to Jack, "but I have learned more in these two days than I could have in two years without him." She sighed again, "You would think that after I had met him barefoot and in a kimono he would not have been so stiff and gruff. Maybe he can't help being so formal. Some people just don't know how to relax and be natural." Oberholser would never be natural in the easy way of Texans. He was to visit again five times, and for years thereafter they kept a steady correspondence, but he never addressed either of the Hagars by their first names. He recommended them for the American Ornithologists' Union (AOU) and urged their attendance at the forthcoming meeting in Charleston. Connie accepted the membership but shuddered at the thought of Jack at an AOU meeting.

One week after Dr. Oberholser's departure she had another guest who proved to be as strenuous. Young Edgar Kincaid, Jr., came with his father and a fishing friend for Labor Day and shorebirds. The lanky, long-legged lad well knew the birds of the Edwards Plateau, having grown up in Uvalde and visited often with his aunt, Mrs. J. Frank Dobie, in Austin. He had birded with a Dallas group and was an avid student, curious about everything in nature, but this trip was for a single purpose— shorebirds, which he pursued with killing concentration. His appetite for details was insatiable; it was not enough to point out great blue and Louisiana herons. He had to know why not all individuals of these species looked alike. He devoured Connie's explanations of immature and adult plumages. And how did she separate royal and Caspian terns, common and Forster's terns, dowitchers and willets? He all but dissected the birds through his binoculars as she talked, and he subjected her to extensive queries on more than half the species they saw that day, for many were new to him.

Connie found him a joy to work with. He learned quickly; she never had to repeat a lesson. She could see him growing up to be another, but less formal, Dr. Oberholser. He, too, would return many times, becoming one of her most satisfactory bird-

[71]

ing companions, one she would telephone immediately whenever anything special showed up at Rockport. Edgar was the youngest person at the meeting of the Texas Academy of Science in Dallas that November, where Connie heard Bessie Reid plead for preservation of the Big Thicket.

At Oberholser's request, Connie now recorded numbers as well as species, though it was a chore she did not relish—five thousand pintails, five hundred redheads, fifty gadwalls, four canvasbacks, fifteen red-breasted mergansers, two mallards, one hundred lesser scaup. The figures would change within days, American wigeons becoming the most numerous duck.

On Saturdays Annie Ruth helped tabulate. "September 12, big migration on, first norther. 14 Baltimore orioles, all males, 25 Wilson's warblers, 11 black-and-whites, 15 chats, 5 Maryland yellowthroats, 50 blue-gray gnatcatchers, estimated 1,000 eastern kingbirds, 20 great crested and 3 least flycatchers, 2 eastern pewees, 2 eastern phoebes, 5 kingfishers, 14 young black-crowned night-herons, 3 nighthawks, 1 scissortail, 1 green heron, 5 meadowlarks." They were all fun, but Annie Ruth wearied of counting commoner birds after the first hundred or so.

"Mrs. Hagar," she begged, "do we have to put down every herring gull, every single one?"

"Yes, honey. That's part of the program."

The lists intrigued Dr. Oberholser. Fifty gnatcatchers—they were not even supposed to flock in the fall. (Flocks were common to Connie.) The Swainson's warbler that spent the day, October 20, in her yard surprised him but had delighted her. Also surprising to him were so many Franklin's gulls still moving through at Thanksgiving when Bert, Blanche Bush, and Dallas birder Edith Winford were there. That holiday was memorable for the thirteen wood ducks found in a shady marsh pool surrounded by cattails off Fulton Beach. Connie visited the eight drakes and five demure ducks each of the four days they remained. She would never see so many wood ducks again.

Estelle Fiser of Chicago took no. 5 for the winter while her husband Al, a labor organizer, traveled the state. An excellent observer, she was especially good on sparrows, Connie learned. But Estelle refused to get excited over a discovery on their first day out, December 8. "Just an oldsquaw," she said. "But it doesn't belong on that pond. It should be out in deep water." Nor was she surprised by common loons that moved inshore on the blustery day; loons were common to her. This gratified Connie; she had seen a loon she thought was this species in late October and had reported it, but Oberholser's reply was that it could not be a common loon, that it was probably a Pacific, which in itself would be very unusual. Two weeks later, when a fisherman brought Mrs. Hagar a dead loon snagged on his line, because he'd heard she "liked birds," she prepared and saved the skin. It was indeed a common loon.

The Hagars went to Corsicana for Christmas but returned for Connie to make her count on New Year's Day, 1938. Of the 76 species seen, the three most numerous were brown pelicans (70), yellow-rumped warblers (270), and American coots (274). The four verdins for the day were all on Frandolig Island, where earlier in the winter she had found for the first time the sleeping nests built by this species for shelter in cold weather.

Sparrows increased in January, and Mrs. Fiser introduced Connie to a new species on the marshy stretch between the Cottages and the beach—six Henslow's sparrows. Together they learned the sharp-tailed sparrow and found twelve scattered over the area that day. There were also a few Le Conte's and song sparrows, never numerous here, and many of the familiar winter species—vesper, savannah, Lincoln's, field, lark, and chipping. Another lifer for both wound up their day at Sparks Colony— a green-tailed towhee. This wanderer from the West, Connie would realize in later years, would always be associated with dry years, as would white-winged doves, verdins, short-eared owls, pyrrhuloxias, and cactus wrens.

Dr. Oberholser wrote asking for "the very great privilege" of copying her Nature Calendar notes of previous years, if she felt she could "trust him with such valuable material." She bundled several volumes at a time to send. His having access to her notes solved one big problem over which her correspondents wrestled then and for years—her way of reporting birds as seen on "Tuesday," or "Sunday," though Oberholser insisted that what he most wanted was exact dates and localities. The Nature

Calendars, however, had exact dates. He no longer questioned her identifications, but he still asked for additional evidence on unexpected species, tactfully taking the position of instructor correcting what he believed to be honest mistakes. "Could I have misread your notation on yellow-headed blackbirds?" he wrote. "You are too far east for this bird." And "Is this correct about the black-throated blue warbler? You are too far west for this species." Grudgingly, he admitted that she might have small flights of yellow-throated warblers in the fall, though they were not known to flock at this season. And he allowed her a "few" Wilson's phalaropes. She and Annie Ruth had counted hundreds spinning on Port Bay.

He always thanked her warmly for her help, often mentioning her wonderful location for observations, which he frankly envied, and always urged her to keep sending notes, "since some of the species you mention are rare anywhere in Texas."

The geese that Jack bagged and Connie baked, after carefully measuring each, as requested, led to lengthy correspondence on that subject alone. Oberholser wanted exact dates on the Hutchins and the one she called "cackling goose,' and the exact measurements of future kills since identification of these races of the Canada goose depended entirely on lengths of exposed culmen, wing, and other features. It did not help that the names of the races had been switched, but the following season Connie faithfully measured seven birds, then laid them on the grass beside a yardstick and took photographs.

In April Connie shared the peninsula's riot of wild flowers with longtime friends Dr. Eula Whitehouse and Mrs. J. Frank Dobie, and as they departed, she welcomed the Gills for a week of dawn-to-dark birds. Discoveries awaited them: Sprague's pipits in the grass and a least bittern climbing reeds at the Tules, which was pointed out by Fuzzy, the bittern specialist. They found eastern bluebirds feeding their young on Lamar Peninsula. Connie had not known they nested there. Hummingbirds streaked from blossom to blossom in the tangle at the Cove. Most were ruby-throats, "and a black-chinned," Terry remarked casually. Connie perked up. She had suspected black-chins, but "they are not allowed here," she said.

"They weren't allowed in Dallas either, at first. But we have them," he said. Some of the laughing gulls had reached that fleeting stage of nuptial excitement during which their white breasts were suffused with exquisite pink.

A sharp norther, one of those vagaries of Texas weather that may cause temperatures to plummet as much as twenty-five degrees in an hour, blew in early one morning. "Loon weather," Connie announced. Donning wraps, they made for the Cove. Not far from the shore five loons bobbed on the crests of whitecaps and two were in breeding plumage. "Never did I expect this in Rockport," she cried joyfully, devouring them through binoculars.

Facing the blustery wind, they drove up Highway 35 to the new federal preserve, Aransas National Wildlife Refuge. It was too late for the fabled whooping cranes, but anhingas at Hog Bayou and a splendid bald eagle at Tivoli were reward enough. Homeward bound they saw a thin, dark line wavering across the sky ahead, big birds moving lazily toward them. Terry stepped on the accelerator, and the line grew denser, stretching from south to north as far as they could see. Hawks, thousands of hawks. Stopping beside the road, they marveled for half an hour at the spectacle before trying to name species. The great majority proved to be broad-winged, but among them were numerous red-tails, harriers, kestrels, two white-tailed, a caracara or two, several ferruginous, and a lone merlin.

Canada geese bound for the refuge crossed above the raptors at right angles, and flights of swallows darted beneath them. Finally, their necks too stiff to look up any longer, the party got back in the car and drove on. Hawks still flew above them, and when at last the numbers dwindled, Terry looked at his watch— they had been seeing hawks for two hours.

Very pleased with this report, Dr. Oberholser wrote back that only one other contributor, Mrs. Gray at Victoria, had mentioned this migration.

Most songbirds were late that spring. Relatively few appeared in April, when expected, but in early May small birds rained on the peninsula. People from all over town telephoned her: "My yard is full of little yellow birds," or "There are hun-

[75]

dreds of little blue birds on my lawn," or "There are dozens of little wild parrots in the trees," and so on. Connie could not budge from watching her own trees, also full of little blue birds (indigo buntings) and "little wild parrots" (painted buntings) and the quicksilver movements of hundreds of warblers. The first and biggest wave came May 4 with a cold northwest wind, but it continued in diminishing waves into May 16. On the first day she counted eleven species of warblers, but it became impossible to count individuals, except the bay-breasted warblers because they tended to keep together and sometimes fed on the ground.

Her account was almost too much for Dr. Oberholser. Thanking her for her "most interesting letter," he went on:

> In view of the importance of the records that you have been successful in obtaining, I should like, if at all possible, to have a complete record of all the species that you saw on each of the dates on which you did field work, including as far as possible the actual or relative numbers.
>
> One statement, concerning the bay-breasted warblers, is most unusual, since this is one of the rarest of all the warblers in Texas, and your record is all the more surprising in view of the fact that Rockport is so far west in the state. For this reason, particularly, I should like to have more definite information regarding the actual numbers, and all the dates on which you saw any individuals of this species.
>
> Still another statement in your letter is even more interesting. You mention that there were a number of Connecticut warblers in with the species seen on several dates. Since there is no authentic record of this bird for the state of Texas I am again troubling you to make sure that you have not confused this bird with the mourning warbler, which it closely resembles, and which is not so uncommon in your vicinity.
>
> I hope you do not consider me too critical of your identifications, since I have clearly in mind the correspondence we have regarding the warbling vireo, the final result of which was your convincing me that you knew perfectly well what you were talking about in recording the breeding of that bird at Rockport. I trust we shall have the same result

regarding the Connecticut warbler, but you can appreciate my desire to obtain all the information I can regarding a bird so rare and so unusual, as one will form a state record on the basis of your observations.

Obligingly, but wondering if the man would never believe that she did field work every day, Connie made a chart of fifteen-day periods showing counts of seventeen kinds of warblers and seventeen other kinds of migrants. The fifty-two bay-breasts seen on the fourth were gone next day, but on the eighth and ninth, there were twenty-five and on the tenth there were twenty-four. Perhaps these were all the same birds. As for the Connecticuts, there were four on the fourth, and eight on the eighth and ninth. She had not seen a mourning warbler that spring.

With mixed feelings Connie greeted Walter Miller, director of the Dallas Museum of Natural History, and Willie Mayer, taxidermist, late in May. They had a permit to collect water birds to be made into study skins and exhibits. To her, killing birds even for science was distasteful, but she could not forget how much she had learned from skins at that museum. She agreed to go with them to the breeding islands.

Their boat cut a wide wake on a mirror-still Aransas Bay as the sun rose. They made for Lydia Ann Island nestling in the lee of St. Joseph's Island and beached the craft on the muddy edge of a shellbank. Clouds of screaming gulls, terns, and skimmers flew up in protest. Connie pulled on boots and waded ashore with the men. Eggs were everywhere in little hollows scraped from sand and shell, so close together there was hardly space to put one's foot. Many scrapes held chicks of various ages. Connie paused for quick scrutiny of egg markings and downy plumages, but the party moved swiftly from one area to another so that no nest should be too long untended. Agitated parent birds dived constantly at the intruders. She turned her back on the collecting process, intent on determining owners of eggs and young. One large splotched egg was guarded by an American oyster-catcher; on a low stand of brush, reddish egrets poised uncertainly over platforms of sticks and trash, from which a few shaggy-necked young peered. Well before noon the collectors returned to the mainland; the sun was now too hot to risk further disturbance.

Magnificent frigatebirds showed a peculiar attachment to Rockport that summer. Local folk called them stormbirds because their appearance was usually associated with turbulent weather somewhere in the Gulf. Four to seven were seen almost daily for long periods, suspended in the air, hanging motionlessly, most often directly above the spire of the Presbyterian church. No storm, however, affected the town that summer.

Four stormbirds were hanging over the Cottages when Sonney and Alice May visited in June. So many birds were nesting on the grounds that her brother accused Connie of operating a hatchery. For nest construction, scissortails and blue grosbeaks used the colored yarn scraps she had supplied after they had all but demolished her butterfly net. Titmice, however, did their shopping in the wiry coat of Fuzzy, dozing under the turk's cap. One titmouse gathered so many hairs on one trip that it seemed to have a long beard. The hatchery was producing when Bessie Reid visited at the end of the month and helped band the crop. A baby roadrunner, all beak and virtually no tail, lurching awkwardly after a lizard, was caught and banded.

Business brought Dr. Oberholser to Texas in July, and he extended his trip to include five days at Rockport, bringing Larry Whitehead, Texas agent for the service, with him. His arrival coincided with that of the first returning sandpipers, and he was impressed by her ready identification of the "peeps." "Many experienced fielders in the East still fumble over sandpipers," he said. "But, of course, up there they cannot sit in a car and have a parade of peeps within a few feet. Here you scarcely need binoculars." He counted eight adult Wilson's plovers tending ten young.

They spent a day on Aransas National Wildlife Refuge, and again Connie felt that she had received more than she had given; the seventy-five glossy ibis feeding in a swale were the white-faced glossy, not the glossy, he explained. The white face was evidently only in breeding plumage, when the birds wore their gorgeous iridescence of mauve, rose, and green. Other times they looked like true glossy ibis, which did not occur so far west. He also detailed differences between double-crested and olivaceous cormorants and between the two races of loggerhead shrike, white-rumped and migrant, requesting her to separate these in her reports because they might be separate species. Also, he would like notes on weather in connection with occurrences of birds; weather could explain much.

Oberholser was pleased to tell her that his book on Louisiana birds was finally in press and that she would receive a copy soon. Now he could devote full attention to his Texas work, and she must continue to supply him with her most interesting observations. This she did, as always, including along with her own notes the carefully dated list, with numbers of individuals, of 111 species that Maurine Gill prepared from the visit she and Terry made October 4–8. To Connie the most interesting items were the 179 hummingbirds counted their first day, 169 of them feeding on the late-blooming silverleaf sunflowers at the Cove. All were probably ruby-throated, though they suspected some were rufous hummingbirds.

They had estimated as many hummingbirds the second day, but numbers decreased thereafter. They had been numerous since mid-September, Connie wrote. Dr. Oberholser questioned nothing in the report except five brants seen feeding with white-fronted geese near Tivoli. He asked for details. Connie reminded him that brants had been taken by hunters the previous year and that she had sent him their measurements. His apology was prompt:

My dear Mrs. Hagar:

I am sorry I troubled you regarding the data for the brant. In some way I overlooked the fact that this was the real American brant, and I was so surprised to read in your letter that you had observed this bird. Since there are so very few records for Texas or, as a matter of fact, anywhere in the interior of North America, I was particularly interested in making sure of the exact date and locality. Your list was being copied and was mixed in with a large number of other records of similar kind and, therefore, was not of easy

[79]

access at the time I wrote you and, anyway, I did not know it was on that particular list.

As you know, this is one of the very rarest of all Texas birds and you are fortunate to have been able to observe these at Rockport. However, apparently all the birds of Texas come to Rockport to call on you sooner or later! I am not at all surprised that someone from the Valley was surprised at the large number of birds at Rockport, since it is my opinion that for migratory observations there is no place on the Texas coast that is equal to yours. Probably the lower Rio Grande Valley harbors a larger number of birds in the winter and during the breeding season but certainly the migration and early winter at Rockport are a revelation to anyone who has not been there before.

Sincerely yours,
Harry C. Oberholser

Happily for both of them, two of the brants remained for Oberholser's third visit November 6–10, 1938. They went again to Aransas Refuge and saw three whooping cranes that had recently reached the end of their long journey from the Northwest Territories. They spent another day at the Hartman Ranch, where the brants were found among thousands of Canada, white-fronted, snow, and blue geese. When the flocks rose, "they covered the skies," Connie wrote in her Nature Calendar. On South Beach he marveled at the marbled godwits. "They are so rare," he said. It pleased him that she always referred to great blue herons as Ward's herons; he had insisted on the subspecific name.

Although still very formal, Dr. Oberholser was more at ease each time he came, and this time, Connie realized, he had something on his mind that he meant to clarify. It came out as they watched a seaside sparrow slipping through the grass.

"I can understand," he said, "How you, with your interest in birds, are content in Rockport, but I do not see what Mr. Hagar gets out of it. How can he be satisfied? What is his hobby?"

Her laugh rang out merrily as she said, "When we get home you can ask him."

[80]

Their guest asked the question again that evening in the living room, where Fuzzy snuggled against Connie on the antique love seat. To answer, Jack rose and wedged himself between the two, one arm resting lightly on his wife's shoulder, the other around the wire-haired dog.

"My hobby," he sang out with a devilish gleam in his eyes, "is to see that my wife and our little dog get everything they want."

Dr. Oberholser smiled stiffly. He had expected a sensible answer, but this one made no sense at all. He remained mystified, ever unable to accept Jack's indifference to birds, but he ceased urging him to attend AOU meetings, and the books he sent thereafter were inscribed as gifts to "Mrs. Jack Hagar."

He returned again a year later and saw a rewarding November parade of herons, shorebirds, ducks, terns, and pelicans of both species as well as waves of arriving songbirds and numerous raptors. He thanked her again for the sooty tern she had sent in September, "the only specimen of this bird we have from Texas." The Gills had found the bird dead near a dredging site and brought it to Connie for identification. An immature bird, Connie could not name it until she searched the books. Then she had prepared the skin and sent it to the biologist for verification. At his request, she had let him keep it.

The Texas book was progressing, he said; it was to be his monument, "the only monument I want." But Connie, without revealing them, now had misgivings, having heard from other sources that the manuscript was too long, so full of detail that publishers were shy of it. Taxonomy was Oberholser's forte; he was a "splitter" among ornithologists at a time when most of his colleagues were "lumpers." It made for some unpleasantness in professional circles, but he would not compromise; he kept dividing species into as many races as could possibly be justified by the most minor deviations, and he insisted on giving each race the full treatment.

His last visit to Rockport was the first weekend in January, 1941, realizing for him an often expressed desire to "bird with Mrs. Hagar in winter." Winter was hard to believe that year, with roses, poinsettias, hibiscus, and bougainvillea blooming in

Rockport dooryards and fields bright with gaillardia, "Texas fire-wheel," Connie called it, saying she had seen it in bloom in every month of the year.

She had saved for him to see the strange duck two young hunters had taken New Year's Day and brought to her—her first white-winged scoter, a female. Around the Cottages were both red-shafted and yellow-shafted flickers; Bewick's wrens; and white-throated, lark, and field sparrows. Mourning and Inca doves came to the birdbath, and ground doves foraged under the oleanders. "Country birds," the biologist proclaimed. "One would not expect ground doves in a dooryard." He savored the multitudes of ducks rafting in the bays, the shorebirds along the waterfront and ponds, and hawks on country lanes—harriers, kestrels and, for Connie, a new one—Krider's red-tailed hawk.

"What a place! What a place to bird in winter!" he remarked over and over, shivering to think of the cold in Washington.

Dr. Oberholser retired from government service at the end of 1941, but his correspondence was continued from Cleveland, Ohio, where he had gone to serve as curator of birds for the Museum of Natural History, to which he had long been a consultant. He expected to have more time for the book and hoped she would continue her reports. From time to time he sought reconfirmation of early records, the vermilion flycatcher in the Big Bend in 1930—precisely where? The "large migration" of varied buntings at Rockport, April 25, 1937—had they miscopied her account? They had, indeed, Connie hastened to reply; it was a huge migration of indigos. The lawn had been blue with them. A few painted buntings, but varied buntings were something else; she recorded only three over the years.

In 1942 he wrote, "Unfortunately, there is yet no assurance of immediate publication of my book, which is practically ready for the printer. However, I have not given up hope." Again he wrote of having too little assistance and admitted, at last that the manuscript was getting out of hand. "You can have some idea of the size of the text when I tell you that I have between 300,000 and 400,000 records that have to be consulted in updating the work." Hereafter, he added, she need send only unusual records. But unusual records kept occurring; hardly a year went by without one. The black scoter, new for the state, and a surf scoter prompted Oberholser, in a rare lapse into levity, to respond, "I presume some day you will see a great auk or a Labrador duck in Rockport."

Connie wrote to both him and George Williams before she went to bed the night of July 27, 1943—to tell about the flamingo. She had gone with Fred Stark of San Antonio's Brackenridge Park and his party to collect young birds for his zoo. Pug Mullinax, her one-time ice boy and now a captain with Texas Game, Fish, and Oyster Commission, piloted the boat. The enterprise was unpalatable to her, but Pug, with whom she often made patrols on the bay, insisted that only she knew where to find nestlings of the right age to adapt to zoo life. Also, she told herself, it was for education; many people never saw such birds except in zoos, and they should have the privilege.

They left the yacht basin at 6:00 A.M., cages and gear stacked on the deck, and already the morning was hot. There was a tropical storm in the Gulf, apparently headed for Galveston, but Aransas Bay was as still as glass as they headed north to Second Chain of Islands. Connie sat beside Pug in the high pilot's seat. Carroll Island, an Audubon sanctuary, came into view like an enormous bed of pink roses bordered by green foliage; at least five hundred roseate spoonbills were crowded upon it, she estimated with binoculars aimed at the picture.

"Stop, Pug. Please stop." she cried, her voice trembling with excitement. "I think I see something." She did. Among those pink birds was one taller, deeper hued, longer-necked—a flamingo. It stood near the monument to J. J. Carroll, an early naturalist who had sought protection for this small island on which birds had nested since long before his time. All eyes focused on the bird for fully half an hour before someone remembered the business they had come for.

While the men set about their business, Connie, in rubber boots, waded ashore and walked toward the flamingo, approaching within seventy-five feet before it flapped lazily and took to the air, long neck forward, long legs trailing. It circled over her and disappeared.

Quickly the zoo party gathered young herons, egrets, brown pelicans, skimmers, royal and Caspian terns, white ibis, and moved to a second island for laughing gulls, the parents screaming overhead, the fledglings squalling at being caged. They were back at the Cottages by noon, and they placed the captives under the oaks until sundown, when they were loaded for the night journey to San Antonio. Connie studied the young birds to learn all she could, but was glad when they were gone.

Stark advised her promptly that no flamingo was missing from the zoo and that the young birds from the coast were adapting well to artificial feeding. He, too, wondered if the storm in the Gulf had anything to do with the flamingo's appearance.

Oberholser encouraged her to publish the report, which appeared in the *Auk* of April, 1944, and also to write a report on the harlequin ducks she saw in January, 1945, which appeared in the October issue. The birds, male and female, were with a raft of twelve common goldeneyes near the foot of the Copano Bay causeway. She had seen them as she drove up the coast, and they were still there when she returned three hours later. Dr. Ralph Friedmann of New York notified her later that he, too, had seen a harlequin that month near Aransas Refuge.

Still other species were to be reported; black-tailed gnatcatcher, Brewster's warbler, and others, for by then not only Connie but a growing group of bird observers elsewhere in the state made discoveries that added bulk to the biologist's "monument."

Dr. Oberholser retired from the Cleveland museum in 1947, "to devote full time and energies to the Bird Life of Texas," he wrote. Thereafter his letters were handwritten; he had no secretary but still asked for details on the Cape May warbler, lesser black-backed gull, Hudsonian godwits, and—as late as 1957—for all particulars concerning the fall hummingbird migration Connie had found on Live Oak Point, "one of the most remarkable and unexpected movements in Texas, or anywhere else, for that matter."

He died on Christmas Day, 1963. He was ninety-three years old and still updating his massive manuscript, inspired at the last by acceptance for publication. Frank Wardlaw of the University of Texas Press achieved what no other publisher had; he persuaded the author to abridge the work and have Edgar Kincaid edit it. The monument would at last be erected in print.

Chapter 5

Rockport's population always doubled for Labor Day, and the holiday weekend of 1938 was no exception; although more tourist courts had been built, there were not enough for the throng that came for a last fling at summer. Vacation homes of Dallas, Houston, and San Antonio people were filled with guests, and luxurious motor launches were common in the little harbor. Hours before the crowd took over, Connie drove along the beach and turned back to the Tules, first to enjoy again the beauty of the roosting birds in the oaks reflected in the still water and then to count as they awoke, stretched, and spread their wings to sail down to breakfast.

The holiday over, the town shrank to less than normal size; natives took their vacations then; fishing guides and bait vendors closed shops and went fishing themselves. Some restaurants and motels also locked up. No strangers in outlandish costumes were seen on the streets, only decently dressed natives. It would be like this until December when middle-aged Midwesterners came down to fish away the cold months in their home states. For Connie it meant a new schedule of bird talks to clubs and schools, some perhaps fifty or seventy-five miles distant. Various publications also solicited stories, for which she neither expected nor received payment; she did it to spread the word about Texas birds.

On a mid-November evening so warm that doors and windows were open, she wrote in longhand a piece for one of the journals while Jack listened to the radio. At the end of the newscast he flipped the switch and his wife stepped outdoors to look at the stars. The telephone rang and Jack sang out in a nasal twang, "Long distance for Mrs. Haaa-gah." She took the receiver, and a cultured "Eastern" voice came on.

"Mrs. Hagar? This is Guy Emerson of New York. I am at a banking convention in Houston and have two days to spare, and our friend Harry Oberholser tells me that to learn the birds of Texas I can do no better than to get your help." She would be pleased to help, she said.

"Do you know where the whooping cranes are?" She thought she might find them. Emerson, then, would take a midnight train after the convention dinner, catch a bus out of Corpus Christi, and, as Connie advised, ask the driver to drop him off at Rockport Cottages on the way into town.

"Can we rent a car in Rockport?" he asked. She had a car. Then "Can we hire a chauffeur?" Her musical contralto changed abruptly to an unladylike snort. "I do my own driving!"

"I'll be there at eight," he promised.

Turning away, she then recalled that Emerson was on the board of the National Audubon Society, the treasurer—as one would expect a banker to be.

Next morning she returned from the Cove before eight. Jack strolled out to the cattleguard to assist the guest with his luggage. The bus did not stop. Muttering about uncooperative drivers, he quickly drove to the bus station, but no passenger got off. Crestfallen, he knew something had happened; no banker and businessman would disregard appointments. "You sit by the telephone," he told Connie. "He will call and explain."

Half an hour later a hideously orange Houston taxicab rolled into the driveway, and from it emerged a tall, handsome man in a satin-lapelled dinner jacket, satin-seamed trousers, black tie, and patent shoes. "I'm Guy Emerson, and I'm truly sorry," he began and went on to explain that the dinner went on too long, he missed the train, took the taxi, and then the driver had gone to Refugio instead of Rockport. No apology was needed, the Hagars insisted, already warming to him. His speech indicated and Jack quickly confirmed that he really was Boston and Harvard, and Connie recognized her husband's ready acceptance of a

[86]

fellow Bostonian when, as he led the guest to no. 2, Jack glee-fully poked fun at his formal attire. "Well. We got a waiter! We didn't need a waiter, but we got one anyway." For years he would sometimes refer to Emerson as "the waiter who came in a taxicab."

Soon their guest reappeared in starched khakis and bat-tered soft felt hat and was fortified with coffee and toast for a day in the field. By the time Jack waved the birders on their way, they were all using first names. Guy was rather dismayed that Fuzzy went along and that his hostess, in blue chambray, seemed to be dressed for a tea party, but he discreetly kept silent and was forever glad he did—Fuzzy proved to be a valuable snake spotter, and as for Connie's field costume, he would come one day to say vehemently, "It's utterly ridiculous for women to get themselves up in trousers for the outdoors. Why don't they dress respectably, like Connie Hagar?"

With others of Audubon, Emerson had pushed for the ref-uge on Blackjack Peninsula, not only because it was the chosen winter range of the remnant flock of whooping cranes, then only fourteen in all, but also because of the vast waterfowl population it served.

His life list of birds was the envy of Eastern birdwatchers, yet he had never seen the whooping cranes, tallest of America's wading birds. He had birded most of the United States and probably knew more birdwatchers in remote places than anyone else. His vice-presidency with Bankers Trust entailed much travel, to member banks far and wide, and he arranged his visits to coincide with the best bird season in each locality, usually giv-ing himself an extra day or so for field observations. Thus, his job, to him, was the choicest the company offered, one he would trade for no other, not even the presidency.

Connie had no need to explain Guy Emerson at the Refuge. Mr. Beatty, assistant manager, waited with a pickup to give them a guided tour. Connie offered her new blue, six-cylinder Packard sedan, but Beatty insisted on the pickup because the whoopers were in a brushy area that could damage her car. So she squeezed into the single seat between the two men, her knees against the gearshaft, which was shifted often as they plowed through sand

and slough. The knob left black and blue mementos of the adventure on her legs.

Rough going failed to daunt their spirits; there was so much to see: javelinas in sweetbay motts, white-tailed deer leaping from oak scrub, a flock of turkey hens foraging tall grass, and a majestic gobbler challenging the pickup's passage. Guy was awed and delighted by the gobbler, inflated to look twice its normal size, iridescent feathers gleaming, great tail fanned, gobbling loudly. "Is he really wild?" he had to know. "Somehow I always thought I'd have to crawl on my belly through underbrush to get a glimpse of a wild turkey."

It was past noon when the pickup pushed through waving sea oats to stop on top of a sand ridge. Before them a broad pasture descended to a swale in the middle distance. Hundreds of sandhill cranes stalked the pasture, and among them, but apart from them, were two larger cranes, gleaming white with long necks and long scapular feathers extending over the tails like graceful bustles. After a long, long look, Guy stood straight up in the cab, bumping his head hard but not caring, and shouted for joy.

The watchers then stood on the ground to study the birds at length, admiring every movement as the cranes strode here and there, picking at things in the grass, raising their heads high to look around, their regal bearing impressive even at a distance. But there was sadness, too, in seeing them, members of a dying breed, possibly doomed to extinction. The habitat demands of whoopers were so specific, the encroachment of civilization so relentless, it might be too late for them already.

"Oh, what birds," Guy sighed as they drove on through groves of blackjack oaks, over trackless prairie, to still another pair. Beatty knew the territories of each pair and that of lone cranes without mates. Only one pair had offspring this year. Late in the afternoon they came to the range of the family, the young crane still wearing rusty gold feathers on its neck. It fed between the watchful parents, a chick that had hatched only last summer somewhere in the Northwest Territories but had flown with its parents more than two thousand miles to this winter refuge on the Texas coast.

[88]

Near dark, it was time to start home. But Guy, before re-entering the pickup, suddenly gave vent to the excitement that he could no longer contain; throwing his hat into the air, he let out a loud whoop and leaped around, yelling at the top of his voice, "Hooray! Hooray! I came to see the whooping cranes, and I have seen them!" Connie had sudden doubts; was this nice man some kind of nut?

At half past nine the Packard homed in on the Cottages, and though his wife had been out for more than twelve hours with an utter stranger, Jack's sole concern was that she must be tired. "Go to bed," he ordered. "You must be worn out." She was, but it had been a fine day.

Jack heard the details at breakfast. The Hagars almost never offered meals to their guests, but Guy was different, from the very first. He always ate with them. His invitations to dine out were declined because Jack could not leave the Cottages, and Connie, though it was quite all right for her to roam all day with Guy, thought it improper to leave her husband and go to a restaurant with a gentleman from New York.

That morning he was still euphoric about the whoopers. They were more than a new species for his life list—they were the whooping cranes. Connie would deliver him to the train in Corpus Christi, but they had time to visit the two burrowing owls so politely curtsying from gopher mounds in the shipyard and to bird along the way. Guy told Jack to expect him again and often, and at the railway station he told Connie he hoped to get back in the spring.

As the train pulled away he settled in his seat and mentally castigated himself. The truth was, he had gone to Rockport reluctantly, not expecting much of Mrs. Hagar. He thought few women were really good birdwatchers, but Oberholser had so insisted that Guy had promised. He had made this trip simply to discharge that promise, and now he was ashamed. He wrote within the week, still rapturous about his new friends, new birds, and Rockport. In Houston he had urged Joe Heiser, also an Oberholser correspondent, to acquaint himself with the Hagars without delay. In Washington he had given an exuberant account to Oberholser and an associate, Ira Gabrielson. He also

[89]

sent books, *Birds of New Mexico* and *Birds of Minnesota*, which would be useful since many birds of these states also came to the Texas coast.

The Minnesota book helped her pin down her first pine warblers, one male and four females near Moore's Pool in December. "Always associated with pines," the book said. Connie was amused. Pines had to be carefully cultivated here; her pine warblers were in mesquites. In the same tree were eastern bluebirds, orange-crowned warblers, American goldfinches, and golden-crowned kinglets. Winter birds were coming in.

Sparrows were coming, too, but not so many as would appear in January and February. George Williams was with her one February day when they found the white-crowned sparrows near Sparks Colony, her first in Rockport though she had known them in Corsicana. Williams helped band a loggerhead shrike and a field sparrow. "This sparrow will show up in North Dakota next summer," she told him. Returns on her birds had been scant except for field sparrows—all from North Dakota. For two successive summers her birds had been trapped on a college campus at Fargo, and the following winters she had retrapped them at Rockport. She and George listed seventy-five species that day.

Connie banded fewer birds now, only those trapped in her yard. Arthritis had swollen her knuckles and stiffened her fingers. She had difficulty manipulating the tools and would retire from banding soon.

Winter's most severe norther was blowing the afternoon she set out for the school with a basket of bird skins mounted on ten-inch sticks. This was for the PTA, whose president had said, "Our children have learned so much from you, we felt we just had to hear you, too." Despite the weather there was a good turnout, and Fuzzy's presence beside the speaker surprised no one. The meeting opened with the Lord's Prayer, led by the principal, Mr. Weldon Smith. All stood with bowed heads, and murmuring voices filled the room. Halfway through Mr. Smith became aware of sounds not quite human among the voices— low grunts and guttural sighs from Mrs. Hagar's direction. Without a break in the devotional, he cast his eyes that way and verified his suspicion—Fuzzy sat with lowered head, wisps of wiry hair dangling over his face, jaws chittering and emitting small "prayerful" sounds. The principal glanced up to catch the twinkling eyes of the speaker but managed to bring the prayer to a proper end. Fuzzy relaxed and throughout Connie's speech kept adoring eyes upon his mistress.

The Hagars' guest list that spring was evidence that Oberholser and Guy had been telling others about Rockport. John H. Baker, executive secretary, and a Mr. Dabney, a board member of National Audubon, registered in March. They came to arrange sanctuary leases on Second Chain of Islands, where roseate spoonbills still maintained a viable colony, though they were becoming scarce elsewhere. The men gave themselves an extra day to bird with Mrs. Hagar.

Dr. Perkins and Mr. Hall of Cornell University came for wild flowers for the university herbarium, collected many plants, and counted reddish egrets, long-billed curlews, horned grebes, and brown and white pelicans, "the best birds of the trip." Mr. and Mrs. Theron Wasson of Chicago were so entralled by the wealth of birds that they promised themselves annual vacations there—and kept the promise for many years. For them, the sight of great egrets arrayed in bridal dress—exquisite capes of glistening, threadlike aigrettes blown into airy fans by the breeze—was breathtaking.

In mid-April the skies opened and poured forth seven inches of rain, flooding low places and bringing herons, yellowlegs, and egrets to the doors of the Cottages. Wilson's phalaropes spun on a pond in the yard. Two male vermilion flycatchers preempted perches beside the pond, and a house finch flitted in the oaks. It was to be the only house finch Connie would ever see in Rockport, and it remained for Joe Heiser's visit. He reported having seen house finches at Sinton and Beeville. Some freak of weather, he opined, had blown them off course. One day in Rockport convinced Heiser that the Coastal Bend produced species not found in Houston, and he too would return often, bringing with him members of the Houston Outdoor Nature Club.

Guy had only one day for the spring migration, but a long and bountiful day. From the Cove at sunrise they worked up the beach to Live Oak Point, dashed home for a bite of lunch, then made for Rattlesnake Point, and still counted birds in the oaks after supper. Guy's ears were as good, if not better, than his eyes. Notes from deep in the brush sent him stalking after a species he had already identified by voice, often a mere suggestion of a sound that Connie had not heard. Voices would never be her forte because migrating passerines sang very little as they rushed past her in the springtime. Guy was intrigued by the cadence of the eastern meadowlark; it was "not quite right."

"These," Connie explained, "are the Rio Grande sub-species, our nesting race. Both eastern and western meadow-larks move out after winter when these come in. My sister Bert and I think the Rio Grande has a more melodic song."

Guy challenged her separation of migrant and white-rumped races of loggerhead shrike, and Connie was pleased to recite the lesson learned from Dr. Oberholser. "Why, that's simple," Guy exclaimed. "Roger should put it in his book—I will tell him." Connie was stunned that anyone, even Guy Emerson, should tell Roger Tory Peterson, author of the birder's bible, anything, but, she learned, Guy loved "the boy" and had encouraged him to do what he most wanted to do—gave his life to birds. "I will bring him down sometime," he promised. It was a dizzying prospect.

Guy, in his turn, was stunned by the buff-breasted sand-pipers. In a wet field, feeding placidly, marching about with heads up and unafraid within a stone's throw of the car were more than forty buffbreasts, far more than the total number seen by birders on the East Coast in his lifetime. Nobody up there was going to believe this.

However, the bird that topped the day's list of 111 species was new to both. Beside a pasture of mesquite and blackbrush catclaw they heard a little aria like none they had ever heard before. It was repeated. Guy guessed it was a sparrow, but what kind? Then a very plain, small brown bird flew to the barbed-wire fence and sang in their faces. The song had a descending finale. Guy memorized it, whistling softly. The bird left the fence and rose into the air, still singing. A sparrow singing in flight? Whatever it was, there were many of its kind scattered

[92]

over the field, all singing. It wasn't in Peterson's book, so must be a western species. At home they searched other books and found it—Cassin's sparrow. Connie was to enjoy it every spring and summer thereafter, a common breeding bird that sometimes remained with her through winter. She would always find it associated with catclaw. They would share other discoveries in the years ahead, but this drab little sparrow with the lovely song remained a highlight.

Wild flowers were outstanding in May, and when Connie unexpectedly found some Eve's necklace in the sandy soil, she wrote to Ellen Schulz in San Antonio. The next week Ellen and her husband, Roy Quillin, were at the Hagar door. Connie took them along a shell-topped road winding behind the schoolhouse and across a sandy field fraught with grassburs and brilliant with paintbrush, gaillardia, widow's tears, winecups, scarlet pea, and others to a fringe of *Sophora affinis*, Eve's necklace, or velvet-leaf sophora.

"This is my secret garden," she said. "Almost anything may be found here, and this is the only patch of this sophora I have seen in the whole area." It was a beautiful spot, and Ellen, the authority of Texas flora, found other plants of great interest, too.

Quillin, an oologist with a notable collection, was more interested in nests—but not, he assured his hostess, in taking treasures from any of her pets. To find a Bell's vireo they went to Moore's Pool, and skirting the edge, which was grown over with rattlepod, they heard the question-answer, question-answer phrases of the bird in a willow, but at a low mesquite she pointed to a deep, compact pocket of woven stems and leaves containing four faintly speckled eggs. The owner fluttered anxiously nearby, so they looked and left quickly. Then they went to another nest, a curiosity to Connie. She had banded four fledgling mockingbirds from it, and now a lark sparrow sat on eggs laid in it. Lark sparrows, she had thought, always built their own cradles. It was a curiosity to Quillin, too.

For his gift to her, Quillin had copied notes pertinent to Rockport from his out-of-print *Life Histories of North American Birds* by C. E. Bendire, published in 1895. Specifically, the notes were "Remarks of H. P. Attwater of Houston, Texas, on birds of Rockport, Aransas County, Texas." Connie devoured the typed sheets, thrilled to think of Attwater exploring her territory more than half a century ago. He wrote of lesser nighthawks, which she had learned only this spring, and of Merrill's pauraque. "That bird I must see," she exclaimed. He had noted a nest of horned larks in a pile of dried cow droppings. "The ones I see prefer the cow's tracks," she said. Attwater had found orchard orioles nesting near St. Charles Bay, but to her those orioles were strictly migrants.

The lark sparrows hatched, and in July she returned to band the fledglings. On reaching the tree she heard Fuzzy's snake bark and turned to see him in front of the car dancing around a coiled rattler, its tail up and buzzing, its forked tongue flicking in all directions. Gripping the snake club, she circled for an approach and saw the snake strike. The dog screamed. She kicked him aside and swung hard, severing the snake at its midsection.

Then she ran for her dog; on his nose were two bright beads of blood. With him in her lap she raced home, disregarding speed limits and her own safety. Jack heard the horn and was at the steps. "A rattler bit Fuzzy," she cried. After alerting the maid, he slid behind the wheel, gunned the Packard, and was off on the Corpus Christi highway, shouting, "Don't worry, dahling. The vet will do something." It was fifty miles, and if the bascule bridge over the port entrance was raised, they might have to wait as much as an hour. Fuzzy's face was swelling; Connie whispered reassurances all the way. They tore over the long wooden causeway across Nueces Bay, and, thank heaven, the bascule bridge was clear. Jack slowed at the city limits. "No time to dicker with a cop," he said. The veterinarian's waiting room was full of people with dogs and cats, but the cry, "Snakebite," gave them priority, and the vet coolly took over.

"He will be all right," he said, injecting a shot of antivenin. "Could have been worse. The strike on the nose was lucky. The swelling will get worse before it gets better. Just keep him quiet."

Fuzzy fell asleep on the way home, and later, he crawled under the house to lie behind the bed of maidenhair fern Connie had transplanted from her mother's garden. For three days he lay there, his head nearly double normal size, barely able to open slits of eyes when his folks visited him. On the fourth day he emerged to a hero's welcome, hungry and wagging a happy tail.

The Gills proposed a trip to the Rio Grande Valley over the Labor Day weekend, picking up Connie on the way. She would see Lonnie Ring, a member of the Nature Club in Corsicana who had since moved to Alamo, and have a chance to see some Mexican species that occurred on this side of the river but nowhere else in the United States.

Lonnie led them to a densely wooded area along the Rio Grande and only seven miles south of her home. It was in many places impenetrable, a tangle of subtropical growth of trees and shrubs—anaqua, tepehuahe, retama, huisache, and scrub palms often matted with vines and teeming with birds. The visitors hardly noticed known species, so many others were new to them —green jays, great kiskadees, hooded and Altamira orioles, seedeaters, white-tipped doves, and long-billed thrashers. They were enchanted, despite the suffocating heat, the thorns, stickers, and cockleburs they were constantly picking from their clothes. Terry had an idea for Maurine to consider. "When I retire, why don't we move down here?"

Leaving the thicket, Lonnie turned grim. "You see those acres of cabbage?" she said, pointing to both sides of the road. "Two years ago they were woods like those on the river. Even then we had too much cabbage, but now we have more cabbage, half of it rotting in the fields. And now we have dust storms." She drove on. "See all these cotton fields? They were woods and wild flowers. Now we have more cotton, and more dust storms. The thickets I have shown you are all that are left of a vast tract of habitat that lured Mexican birds across the river, and they are left only because Valley nature lovers are fighting to save them."

Irby Davis, in the forefront of the movement to save the area, had more to say that evening. Valley birdwatchers hoped to give the tract to National Audubon Society for a sanctuary. Thousands of acres more suitable for agriculture were still available; there was simply no sense in taking wooded land. He wanted to prohibit collecting, too, which was diminishing the

[95]

native and visiting species. "You did not see rose-throated becards today," Davis said, "because a greedy collector came down and took all we had—six birds and three nests. We have not seen a becard since."

That made Connie so indignant that when she got home she wrote to the collector, a noted ornithologist, giving her opinion of his activities. He replied that "perhaps she did not understand the requirements of teaching."

A note from Guy told of his seeing ninety skylarks, his first Sabine's gulls, as well as auklets, murrelets, and others in Victoria, British Columbia. He would be in Rockport in early October.

During the night before his arrival Connie had awakened to the wild honking of geese, flock after flock going over. So she and Guy set out in the morning for the Hartman Ranch. In her Nature Calendar she wrote: "Grand day. Saw several thousand white-fronted geese, five snows, 1,000 Canadas. Also 9 avocets, 1 golden plover, 22 black-bellied plovers, thousands of mixed blackbirds—redwings, grackles, cowbirds. Also hundreds of pintails, few baldpates, shovelers. Roseate spoonbills still here, burrowing owl back in same place. Four little brown cranes." Oberholser insisted on calling sandhills little brown cranes.

This grand day also had its moment of sadness. As in the Valley, "progress" was changing Rockport. Connie took Guy to the little harbor across from the post office to see what was to her a scene of disaster: dredges pumping away the sand for a new yacht basin. A channel would connect it with the Intracoastal Canal, now creeping down the coast between mainland and barrier islands. The yacht basin, to be round within concrete bulkheading, was already dubbed the "million-dollar fishbowl." Financed by government money, it wasn't costing the community anything, they said, and so most citizens were jubilant, including Jack. He could see only benefits from it. But Connie mourned the loss; never again would she see clapper rails stroll across to the post office. Guy shared her regret, but like her, refrained from saying so in front of Jack.

A week later the Nature Calendar noted, "Geese and ducks

going over all night. Brown pelicans and cormorants in huge droves feeding at the Cove. Most I ever saw together."

The long freeze of January, 1940, challenged previous state records. Like a swift, young ice age it set in at the first of the month in the Panhandle and day by day moved southward; before it was over, most of Texas lay under a blanket of ice. Birds moved ahead of it. On January 5 Rockport was cold but not yet freezing, and Connie began to see enormous flocks of robins and bluebirds, as well as Sprague's pipits and water pipits. By the fourteenth robins and bluebirds had increased to unprecedented numbers. "All the robins in the world must be here," she told Jack. There were also more goldfinches and orange-crowned warblers, and ruby-crowned kinglets plus red-shafted as well as yellow-shafted flickers. Shorebirds, however, were scarce.

A hard freeze gripped Rockport on January 19 and held on for a week; the thermometer hit sixteen degrees two days, with sleet and snow. School was dismissed, and Connie was unable to venture far from home. The burrowing owl left the shipyard, and more sparrows arrived daily—vespers, white-throated and white-crowned, field, lark, savannah. More cardinals and yellow-rumped warblers came in. Through it all a lone black-crowned night-heron huddled miserably at the Cove.

When at last the sun broke through, Connie went farther afield. Except for dowitchers and long-billed curlews, shorebirds were still scarce, but hermit thrushes were everywhere; they even came to her doorstep for handouts. By January 30 it was warm and bright, and on Goose Island she found a real bonus left by the storm—western bluebirds and a fox sparrow. The sparrow was the dark western race, not as pretty as the reddish ones she had seen in Corsicana. She would never see western bluebirds again.

She marveled at the vitality and hardiness of the wild creatures; after three weeks of such weather she found only one dead bird—a young red-tailed hawk.

February was springlike. Irby and Anna May Davis came one weekend, and two carloads of Houston Outdoor Nature Club members, whom Connie would always call "the Houston bunch," came another weekend. In a brief replay of winter on March 12, another red-necked grebe rode the surf at the point, and in April there were whimbrels among the long-billed curlews, heralding another fine spring migration that later in the month produced a black-billed cuckoo among the yellow-bills, a new bird for Connie, as well as lazuli bunting at Paradise Corner. Most amazing, however, was the long-crested (Stellar's) jay in late May, and in her own yard. What could have brought this bird of western mountains to the Gulf Coast?

In June the Cottages were filled with 4-H Club boys from all over the state; Jack had extra water pipes laid to accommodate those camping out among the oaks. Meetings were held under the trees, and Connie gladly helped the leaders—game wardens, county agents, and others—with the nature studies. She welcomed chances to instruct and, she hoped, inspire young people, for in their hands lay the future of all wildlife.

She had agreed months earlier to give a talk for the long Fourth of July celebration to signal opening of the new yacht basin, but as the time drew near she feared that for once she might default. Something terrible was happening to her eyes; birds wore colorful halos, bright pages of magazines made her dizzy—the reds jumped backwards—big red letters on roadside billboards behaved like dancing dervishes. Soon the yellows began to recede; women in yellow dresses looked disembodied, their faces near, their bodies remote. Pages in the Nature Calendar were left blank.

She said nothing to Jack; her part in the festival meant much to him, and besides, he was in the midst of it all, planning, stewing around, complaining, fussing, and having a great time. By dawn of the big day he was at the beach supervising a battery of frying kettles for the thousands of pounds of fish that had been iced down for the occasion. And thousands of visitors came to consume it. Everything went well; Connie gave her talk on birds and seashells, received compliments from listeners, and then quietly slipped home to rest her eyes.

She gave her husband a few days to savor the success of the celebration—and to help clean up—then casually mentioned that she was having trouble and would like to see Dr. Atkinson

[98]

again. Jack was not alarmed; he had business in San Antonio anyway. They could go at once.

Jack left her in the doctor's waiting room and went about his business. The examination was longer, and more complicated, than previous ones, Connie thought. At last Dr. Atkinson laid aside his instruments and placed his hand gently on her shoulder.

"My dear," he said, "you have cataracts in both eyes."

Gripping the arms of her chair, she lowered her head as the doctor turned to greet Jack, who blustered in gaily. During their exchange she steadied herself; cataracts usually meant blindness, but she would not borrow trouble. If it did, she would manage somehow. She lifted her head and said softly, "Tell Jack."

Devastated, Jack sank into a chair, trembling so much his wife thought he might collapse. "What can you do?" he pleaded to the doctor.

"We can watch it," the doctor replied. "And treat her for malnutrition. Her general condition leads to this. Her indifference to food and a proper diet have kept her undernourished all her life. Malnutrition encourages other diseases and often shows up in the eyes."

Jack sought other causes. His wife was always reading; did that harm her eyes? And what about squinting through binoculars all the time?

"Reading never hurt anybody in good physical condition," Dr. Atkinson asserted firmly. "And she can look through binoculars all she wants to. Malnutrition is the villain here."

His answers lifted the patient's spirits; she could read and see birds as long as she had vision. And she would have vision. Already she believed that Dr. Atkinson would work still another miracle for her. And she would do exactly as he advised; although she had felt well enough weighing ninety pounds, she would, if he said so, resume those despised malted milks with gusto. But it would not be malted milk this time. With twinkling eyes the doctor said he was prescribing beer—three bottles a day—and he went on to explain in detail the need for nourishing foods and fluids, an abundance of fluids.

"I could give you yeast, or barley, or hops and order eight glasses of water a day, but you would forget because you would

[99]

not be thirsty. Beer works better anyway; in beer you get food and the fluids so essential to your eyes."

So reasonable, so simple. Feeling better, Connie recalled and related to Dr. Atkinson a tale she had been told of her babyhood when she was a frail infant who repeatedly reacted adversely to milk. Her Grandmother Yeater had slyly and secretly made a substitution for the milk, giving her substantial sips of beer, which had agreed with her. Her grandmother may have saved her life, the doctor suggested.

"Come back in October," he advised. "Meanwhile, three beers a day: midmorning, midafternoon, and bedtime." That was all. Leaving the city, they stopped at a drive-in for the patient's first dose of medicine. "It's good," she avowed. Jack put a case in the car.

She resolved to stay at home until colors quit jumping around. She read most of the time, about birds, shells, wild flowers, insects, antique glass, mammals—and always poetry. When callers asked for her, Jack liked to warn them, with an impish gleam in his eyes, "She's drunk. Dead drunk." Finding the dainty lady sipping beer jarred some callers, but others were pleased to accept a bottle.

Her eyes improved within weeks. In August, notes in the Nature Calendar were resumed. In October Dr. Atkinson found the cataracts no worse, perhaps better.

"Just keep up the beer," he ordered.

L. Frey,

CORSICANA, TEX.

102 BEATON STREET.

Bert and Conger

Jack and Connie

The Rockport Cottages

Connie and Fuzzy

Dr. Oberholser, Connie, Mrs. "Wrongway" Corrigan, and Jack

Trapping and Banding

Connie and Patch
Courtesy of the Aransas County Public Library

Rescuing a Pelican, with Nellie Teale
Photograph by Edwin Way Teale

Eisenstaedt at Work
Photograph by Jack Baughman

Connie at Home
Courtesy of Maynard Abrahams

Honoring Connie

The Bird Woman of Rockport
Photograph by Alfred Eisenstaedt, TimePix

Chapter 6

Weatherwise, the winter of 1940–41 was a contrast to the previous one. "Warm and fair," appeared often in the Nature Calendar, sometimes the notation, "Still dry." In late December and early January it recorded "starlings by thousands." Until then, starlings had been uncommon in Rockport. February notations listed western species usually associated with dry years: "Large flocks of lark buntings, pyrrhuloxias, and lesser goldfinches."

Often on her rounds Connie was joined by the Theron Wassons or the Raymond Hills of Cleveland, Ohio, who were regularly spending winters with the Hagars. Often, too, she now had birding friends from Houston, Dallas, and Corsicana. Rockport friends were becoming more interested, too. One brought her a presumably injured least grebe in breeding plumage. Not injured, it was "just an exhausted migrant," she said, delighted to handle it and snap a band on its leg. She kept it quiet for an hour and then took it to the Tules, where it left her hands with an indignant squawk. Others brought a dead shrike they had seen hit a utility wire and fall. It wore a band that Connie had applied two years earlier not a mile from the place where it fell. The bird had made at least three round-trips from here to some distant summer home. She made a specimen of it, singing over the task and sipping beer. She had gained three pounds and felt great.

Rockport friends also had recently supported Mrs. Hagar in an effort to gain protection for the brown pelican. She had learned that ignorant fishermen, believing that the big birds competed for their livelihood, made a practice of going to the breeding islands during nesting season to destroy eggs and young of the pelicans by dragging long, heavy seines over their nests. Appalled, she asked her state representative to introduce a protective bill. It passed with no opposition.

That the war in Europe threatened to involve this country was evident in Rockport. Rob Roy Rice had enlarged his shipyard and was building subchasers; a U.S. Coast Guard unit was stationed on the channel; the new U.S. Naval Air Station at Corpus Christi was commissioned; and soon strange, huge "birds," the Navy's amphibious PBY trainers, were regularly landing on and taking off from the bays. Every night Jack was glued to the radio for the final newscast, and frequently, as he switched it off, he remarked sadly, "We will be in this war." Connie noticed that he looked older, and grayer.

But the birds, oblivious to human troubles, pursued their atavistic ways. Tree swallows on March 2, soon followed by purple martins, came first in a migration that was, she thought, earlier than usual. And it proved to be one of the most exciting she had experienced. With a wave of blue-gray gnatcatchers March 15 came parula warblers, and five days later more parulas, many more, plus black-and-whites, prothonotary, hooded, pine, and yellowthroats, as well as waterthrushes. Their numbers increased, and they were joined by yellow-throated and blue-winged warblers. A flight of Franklin's gulls went over before the first scissortails arrived on March 24. Upland sandpipers led the parade of shorebirds. Exhilarated by it all, Connie wrote another piece for the *Rockport Pilot*, as she was constantly urged to do, extolling the wonders to be seen in their small community.

More migrants were on the way. In mid-April the peninsula was flooded with warblers—Kentucky, blackpoll, Nashville, yellowthroats again, and black-throated greens. More yellow-rumps and orange-crowned arrived, the winter residents of these species having long since departed for points north. Brown thrashers were numerous. A big push of eastern kingbirds, northern orioles (Baltimore race), and dickcissels moved through on April 20, when nighthawks arrived.

Vireos came next, with catbirds, indigo buntings, eastern pewees, orchard orioles, and more warblers—redstarts, chestnut-sided, and yellows (still "summer warblers" to her, as she had first learned them). A vast mixed migration on April 23 brought summer and scarlet tanagers, painted buntings, western king-birds, eastern phoebes, both black-billed and yellow-billed cuckoos, yellow-headed blackbirds, rose-breasted and blue grosbeaks, and Lincoln's sparrows. A flight of anhingas was fol-lowed by sharp-shinned hawks and several merlins. Black terns swept along the coastline. Winter's scant population of green herons grew to dozens.

The next day, April 24, Connie wrote in her Nature Calen-dar, "Largest mixed migration I ever saw." Irene Covarrubias, the housemaid who "had caught the bird bug" from her, called Mrs. Hagar to the back steps. The Calendar continued, "Irene and I watched Baltimore and orchard orioles, indigos and tana-gers, pass for 35 minutes without stopping. Saw my first golden-winged and first Cape May warblers. Tennessees very common, chestnut-sided, one prothonotary, magnolias, Blackburnians, black and white, summer. Painted buntings common, dicks nu-merous, kingbirds, blue and rose-breasted grosbeaks, cuckoos. Cold, damp, windy."

Birds were fewer but still passing next day when she went to Woodsboro to give a talk on wild flowers. And all the next day, a Saturday, it rained, with thunderstorms and gusting winds. Sunday Connie awakened to find the backyard full of puddles and the puddles full of shorebirds: pectoral, spotted, solitary sandpipers; dunlins; dowitchers in reddish plumage; black-bellied plovers with very black bellies; and again, Wilson's phal-aropes spun in the water.

Mr. Blanchard, the Audubon warden for Lydia Ann Island, came that afternoon with a bag of dead birds killed at the old lighthouse on the channel in the previous night's storm. She sorted them—Philadelphia and red-eyed vireos, summer tana-gers, indigo buntings and warblers—cerulean, Blackburnian, and magnolia. But live birds were still working the oaks. Blan-chard counted fifty-two indigo buntings in one tree, and Connie spied her first bay-breasted warbler of the season.

The warden was staying overnight to meet Mr. Alexander Sprunt, Jr., the next day. Sprunt, supervisor of Audubon sanctuaries, "had something up his sleeve," Blanchard said. She knew Sprunt only from his articles in *Bird-Lore* and was pleased to meet him. After his inspection tour of the Audubon sanctuaries, he revealed what was "up his sleeve." Audubon Society proposed to establish a summer education class for adults on the Texas coast, and John Baker, executive secretary, thought Rockport Cottages would be ideal headquarters. Connie thought so, too, but the decision would be Jack's. Sprunt would run the camp, but Jack would be in charge of accommodations. He was enthusiastic; meals could be served in the large no. 9 cottage at the end of the row.

During the discussion Sprunt's eyes kept wandering to the window, noting that the ground outside was almost solid blue with birds, and his business finished, he made for the door. "Never," he asserted, "never have I seen so many indigo buntings." He was not an effusive man, Connie had learned, but he was visibly impressed. She led him around to the oaks, remarking that the first bay-breasted warblers had shown up yesterday.

"Bay-breasts?" he exclaimed. "I have never seen one."

"Then," said his hostess, pointing, "I have the honor to introduce Alexander Sprunt to a new species." He studied those foraging in the leaves and, stalking on through the grassburs, soon returned the favor, announcing, "Palm warbler." She rushed to his side to see two yellow-breasted, rufous-capped birds twitching their tails under the yaupons.

"That's a new one for me," she said. "Thank you."

Sprunt would return in two weeks, and soon reservations for the camp were coming in from distant states as well as from Texas. Meanwhile, Connie helped a National Geographic Society photographer locate certain species and went with Dr. Emmet R. Blake and Dr. Melvin A. Traylor of Chicago's Field Museum of Natural History to study nesting shorebirds. On Frandolig Island they took photographs and made plaster of paris impressions of nests of least terns, willets, Wilson's plovers, and horned larks.

The atmosphere of the Audubon Camp turned sour by the end of the first week. Sprunt was informative and interesting during his scheduled group sessions but at other times remained aloof from participants. The disappointed visitors crowded around Mrs. Hagar, who took them on extracurricular field trips to see snowy plovers and red knots in brilliant plumage, foraging on Mustang Island beach, late-migrating Baird's and white-rumped sandpipers, and sanderlings at Rattlesnake Point. Purple gallinules at the Tules and magnificent frigatebirds drifting overhead satisfied the most exacting guests.

The problem was solved in early June when Sprunt departed and Audubon sent in his place their thirty-six-year-old research director, Robert Porter Allen, fresh from his lengthy study of roseate spoonbills in Florida. Buoyant, outgoing, avid to learn and share sights and sounds of this new region, Bob Allen soon had the camp guests happily spilling all over the area in their eager nature studies. The Hagars loved him instantly and forever.

"Connie, it's your territory, will you help me?" were almost his first words on arrival, and she knew at once she would enjoy helping him more than anyone who had come her way. Together they arranged the boat trip to Grass Island in Mission Bay as a climax to the camp.

Grass Island was a scene of incredible productivity: hundreds of white-faced ibises tended eggs or young, tricolored herons and Forster's terns flew in with fish for their nestlings, the red bills of white ibis arched over the rims of nests, mottled ducks and fulvous whistling-ducks coached rafts of downy ducklings in nearby waters, black skimmers on scrapes at the sandy edges covered eggs or young, and big pink spoonbills hovered over pink-skinned begging babies clothed in thick white down. The grass and low trees were likewise covered with down and feathers shed in the busy colony. The noise was deafening.

Allen stayed an extra day so that Connie could introduce him to the whooping cranes; three adults had remained on the refuge this summer, apparently healthy birds but incapable of the long migration to their Canadian nesting grounds. She also introduced Bob to the song of the Cassin's sparrow. Bob Allen really cared for birds more than anyone she knew. Others loved them, enjoyed them, but Bob cared—about their welfare, about individual birds, their ways of life, and, most of all, their future.

Again, golden-plovers, two individuals on separate dates, passed in the fall migration; they were not supposed to be there in the fall, Connie knew, but there they were. On October 12 with a visiting birdwatcher on the Tivoli road, she watched a migration of swallows. Barn and tree swallows mostly, but also cliffs, banks, and rough-winged. "Drove through five miles of swallows," she wrote in the Nature Calendar. The month was also remarkable for great flights of southbound monarch butterflies.

Rain was sorely needed, but the warmth of December drew tourists to the coast earlier than usual. Jack fussed about, busily attending to the wishes of his guests. On the first Sunday of the month Connie, in short-sleeved navy blue with matching high-heeled slippers, gathered her sheet music from the piano where she had been practicing and stepped out into the sunshine to wait for friends who would take her to the Christian Science church in Aransas Pass for the morning service. A red admiral butterfly probed a mallow blossom. On the ten-mile drive kestrels and harriers were seen.

On the marquee of the Aransas Pass theater they saw that *Snow White and the Seven Dwarfs* was showing, and, since "everybody says it's darling," the party decided to return that afternoon for the matinee. It was darling, Connie thought as she watched in the dark theater, rapt as any child lost in a dreamworld of witches, poisoned apples, good deeds, and magic kisses. The dreamworld was shattered when a man ran wildly down the aisle toward the screen. He turned and ran back and threw himself into an empty seat beside her, breathing heavily. She saw he was shaking violently, gripping the arms of the seat, staring at the floor. Then he gasped and blurted, "They've bombed Pearl Harbor. We are at war with the Japs!" He left as abruptly as he had come.

She sat for long minutes, the reality dawning on her, and half wished that the movie would never end. She did not want to go out and face another war. She had come into this dark hall without a care, but while she was absorbed in a fairy tale, everything had changed; everything would be different now. Nothing would ever be the same again.

[106]

She found Jack pacing the house, their guests crowded around the radio in the small office. Hoarsely, he repeated all they had heard, raging at the sneak attack.

How bad it was nobody then knew, but new horrors unfolded day after day. The Hagars volunteered for Red Cross, bond drives, giving whatever service they could render, earnestly wanting to help. The Nature Calendar was neglected for a time, but then Connie turned back to the birds; in birds, at least there was sanity and order. There was, after all, something unchanged.

The Houston bunch came for the Christmas holidays, and Estelle Fiser returned for the winter. She and a new couple, the Fred Stearnses of Toledo, Ohio, joined Connie for the count on New Year's Day. They listed 93 species, goldeneyes and vermilion flycatchers being the bright spots and 250 marbled godwits the most numerous species.

National security required that everyone in the coastal community carry an identification card. The U.S. Coast Guard set up an office in the *Rockport Pilot* plant, where Jack Blackwell, owner and photographer, could snap ID photos while applicants were being fingerprinted. When the Hagars applied, Connie innocently carried her binoculars and was at once suspect. The Coast Guardsman did not know them or anything about birdwatching; to him, binoculars were devices for spying. He would have to relieve her of those for the duration of the war. Connie tried to explain, but Jack simply walked down the block to Johnson's Drug Store, where the mayor and county judge were having coffee with their cronies, and hauled them back to the office to vouch that birdwatching was not a subversive activity. Her ID card was issued.

Coastal communities also were required to "dim out" at night. Windows were draped or blackened where night work was done, lest a glowing outline become a target for enemy submarines allegedly prowling the Gulf. Practice blackouts, throwing the entire coastline into darkness for many hours, were held, occasionally on such short notice that more than practice was suspected.

Food rationing posed no problems for the Hagars, but gasoline rationing made a difference. Connie combined her surveys with necessary errands and took fewer excursions into other counties. She pooled birding trips with the Stearnses and other guests, who also wished to see birds in the Valley.

March came in like a lion—raw, blustery, and wet—but when the Tattons of Salt Creek Ranch sent word that the eagles were nesting, Connie set out with Fuzzy beside her, oblivious to the weather. A giant white-headed, white-tailed bird with an immense wingspread soared over a pasture and planed down to perch on a dead branch jutting above the fresh green crown of a pecan tree. Something limp dangled from the eagle's talons. Atop the green was a platform of sticks and limbs, as big as a piano, she thought. A burst of rain dimmed the picture, but she saw the big bird leap to the edge of the platform and spread its umbrellalike wings over it. The rain ceased, the eagle tore at the prey it held, and to the watcher's delight, a dusky white eaglet with black eyes lifted its shoulders above the rim and waddled to the parent, beak open, impatient for lunch.

Birds took second place the next week when Dr. and Mrs. Knott of Ann Arbor came. Botany was his hobby; he had all but memorized Ellen Schulz's book and had marked it with his "most wanted" species. One by one they were found and admired. Connie had often said that those she helped usually did something wonderful for her, and Dr. Knott kept up the tradition. In the Rockport Cemetery he found the black flower, *Aristolochia longifolia*, also called pipe vine and swan flower—a plant she had sought for years. It grew against a gravestone, bearing a long tubular, purplish black blossom with yellow throat spots. Several buds would open in a day or so. When they returned to photograph the black flower, it was gone. The caretaker had zealously cleaned the cemetery of all "weeds."

The sickening loss was the only blight in a "great week" noted in the Nature Calendar and described by Dr. Knott as "one of the most profitable and fulfilling" in his experience. Not until they were leaving did Connie learn that Dr. Knott was a lexicographer and editor of the G. and C. Merriam *New International Dictionary* on her shelf. He was pleased to autograph it.

On a March morning Connie rose at half past four and prepared breakfast while Jack readied the car for her. Wrapping a
bottle of beer in newspaper to keep it cool, she drove north in
the dark. Only she and Fuzzy and shrimpers departing the harbor were awake at this hour, but an early start was mandatory for
seeing the prairie-chickens reportedly booming on Highway 35
south of Tivoli. The sun would not rise for another hour, but
daylight came on as she slowed the blue Packard to a crawl on
the shoulder of the road. Something moved; she cut the motor.
On a narrow, cleared stretch across the fence six brownish forms
strolled the bare ground. They were indeed prairie-chickens,
remnants of the Attwater race of the greater prairie-chicken,
once an abundant species in the state but now approaching
extinction.

As the light improved, a cock marched stiffly into the center
of the clearing, tail up and fanned, head down, with a pair of
feather horns pointing forward. His step quickened, his feet
beating the earth in the same spot; the bird was going nowhere
except around and around, his stiff wings brushing the ground.
Bright orange puffs inflated his cheeks as he danced on. Suddenly the orange puffs deflated with a low, hollow sound like the
distant horn of a tugboat; the cock relaxed into indifference
matching that of the several hens before which he paraded.

The display, however, inspired another cock, and as he
danced, more birds appeared in the clearing. Two strutting
knights came together head-on a foot above the ground in a vigorous thrashing of wings; when they dropped, unhurt, they
strolled apart, again indifferent. Hens moved in, and more cocks
took up the display. One claimed center stage while others beat
tattoos with their feet on the sidelines; low booms were mingled
with chickenlike squeaks and chuckles. Except for these sounds,
the scene was enacted in total silence. Connie was unconscious
of passing time until the sun's first rays touched the treetops, and
suddenly, as if one bird, the whole flock of prairie-chickens flew
over a low embankment and into the brush. In less than a minute
the clearing was empty.

Whenever she was to give a program, she would leave

early, and one morning, on her way to speak to the Corpus Christi Garden Club, she saw beside a marsh a small black bird stalking from a patch of salicornia onto the sand—a black rail, new to her. With two young men from the Naval Air Station, Lonnie Ring's son Darrell and Lieutenant Berry, she found two other species new to her in Rockport: a small flock of bobolinks on the Rincon and a woodcock at Moore's Pool. The boys were more excited about Hudsonian godwits and white-rumped sandpipers. Darrell, who fancied bugs over birds, introduced her to the black witch moth, found in her own carport.

Many of her everyday birds were new to Mr. and Mrs. Laurence Grinnell of Ithaca, New York—reddish egrets, mottled ducks, black-necked stilts, gull-billed terns, and the scissortail on a nest behind a transformer on top of a utility pole—but they could not become excited by the oldsquaw that spent a week in the bay. The Grinnells, too, returned her favors; they found the black *Aristolochia longifolia* growing behind no. 9. "In my own yard," Connie exclaimed. It would be guarded carefully.

Guy Emerson came in June, after too long an absence, they all agreed. He had volunteered full time for the Red Cross war fund, traveling widely out of the national capital, but these travels were less adaptable to birding than his banking trips had been. The fund had easily passed the $50 million goal and was going for $75 million, but he chose not to think about anything but birds in Rockport. It was his first break in a long time.

He didn't care if there was nothing unusual; he just wanted to see birds, and the song of the Cassin's sparrow was "worth the trip," he said. The scissor-tail babies fledged, and Connie pointed out how the parent bird had cunningly built a "porch" to her nest, a six-inch extension of grasses on one side, on which her tail rested while she incubated the eggs. "It keeps her tail from being conspicuous to predators," Connie explained. A nighthawk had eggs in a box of rusty nails in the carport.

Despite gasoline rationing and travel restrictions, a surprising number of bird people found their way to Rockport that summer and fall. The Hagars especially welcomed opportunities to entertain servicemen. One they particularly enjoyed and who came often was stationed at Fort Sam Houston with the Army Signal Corps. On a Saturday morning in July Connie returned from her drive to find Jack chatting by the steps with a young woman and a young man in uniform, wearing corporal stripes on his sleeve. Jack introduced them: "Dahling, this is Miss Woods of San Antonio and 'General' Richard Philip Grossenheider. They are birdwatchers, and they want to see yellow-rumped, shirt-sleeved Hagar birds. Folks, this is my wife, Pure Nuts."

"We'll settle for passenger pigeons," the corporal said, taking the hand she extended. "It would be interesting in connection with my duty at Fort Sam, where I happen to be a pigeon trainer."

"The best I can do in that line are Inca doves, ground-doves, and mourning doves," Connie offered, "and I'm ready to start when you are." Inca doves and ground-doves were new to both, as were other birds they saw during the delightful weekend.

In civilian life Dick Grossenheider was an artist and assistant curator of birds at the Saint Louis Zoo. He had already painted several Texas birds but was equally interested in mammals, snakes, insects—all wildlife. He had illustrated a forthcoming book on Michigan mammals. Rockport's main street with its quaint, he thought, false-fronted buildings posing as two-storied stores fascinated him, and he proposed to bring his sketch pad next time and work on that subject.

Before the next time came, the facades were changed drastically. August was hot, as always, and at midmonth the air turned still and humid. Clothes felt sticky, and even mild-tempered people were irritable. On August 25 a frigatebird drifted lazily along the shore, and old-timers shook their heads. "Storm coming," they said. Next day a square red flag flew above the Coast Guard station—gale warning. The winds blew harder in the night, and the next morning the red flag was centered with a black square—hurricane.

For two days the storm played tag in the Gulf, aiming now at the upper coast, then at the lower, and finally at the middle coast. Jack asked his guests to leave. Against the beating gale

Connie drove the shoreline and found it empty; presumably all birds had gone inland—somewhere. Stores and homes were boarded up, and many residents followed the birds inland. Those who remained stored water, food, and fuel. Many took their supplies and candles and flashlights to the stone county courthouse. Rain fell intermittently, and on the afternoon of the twenty-ninth, winds gusted to hurricane force. At sundown Jack made final rounds and was literally blown through the front door that slammed behind him. "All battened down," he announced cheerfully. Connie stood at a back window, partly open to relieve pressure; the atmosphere was electric, fraught with mystery, strangely fresh smells, and ominous sounds.

She washed the supper dishes and went to the piano. Jack sat beside her and struck a few chords but soon returned to the radio. Rockport was directly in the path of the hurricane. Rain poured in torrents, the wind shrieked louder and louder around the sturdy white cottage, which trembled at times but stood. Then came that droning hum, an unremitting undertone to all other sounds. It neither rose nor fell but droned on and on, bespeaking an element of power and terror against which humans were helpless. Connie left the piano and cuddled in Jack's arms.

A flying timber struck the kitchen window, tore the screen, and shattered a corner of glass, admitting a gush of rain. "Stuff a pillow in it," Connie advised, and then she was convulsed with laughter. She remembered, she explained, the houses of the poor she had visited in Corsicana when working for the Charity League. Many of them had pillows stuffed in broken windows, and she had said disgustedly, "Only poor white trash would do that." The device worked very well.

Shortly after ten o'clock the house went dark, the radio silent; power lines were down. Jack lit candles, and they prepared to retire. Another crash sent them to the living room window, and a flash of lightning revealed a crumpled mass of lumber that had been the windmill. "Time we tied into the city water lines anyhow," Jack said lightly. The Hagars went to bed.

Before they slept, the wind abruptly ceased; all was still except for that dread undertone, the hum of havoc. The eye of the hurricane was passing over Rockport. In the lull they fell asleep. There would be a backlash, but the worst should be over now. The hurricane moved up the coast to Matagorda and there turned inland, cutting a swath of destruction to and beyond San Antonio.

Jack was up early to assess the damage, which was minimal at the Cottages; the windmill pump still worked and would tide them over until city water could be piped in. He went downtown, skirting debris in the streets; small frame buildings were flattened, others unroofed. Boats had sunk in the yacht basin and at Fulton had been torn from their moorings and tossed up on the shore, some across the road and into trees. Water was high in low places and ran like rivers in some streets, and on the business street, wind had carried away the false storefronts, overhangs, and doors. The old red corner grocery store was demolished. Since no one had been killed, the more progressive citizens opined that the storm had done them a favor, forcing them to improve the looks of the town.

Some families, however, had spent a harrowing night. With the rising tide on Copano Bay, a shrimper had tied his family together with ropes, his youngest child on his back, and led them through ankle-to-hip-deep water to higher ground, where they had tied themselves to a tree and huddled there until dawn.

Disaster relief teams were at work by noon, and late in the day, with most streets and roads passable, Connie drove out to check on birds. They were few and scattered but none dead that she could find. A flight of pintails, the first ducks of the season, flew in next day, and on Labor Day, the quietest the Hagars had known in Rockport, black terns and swallows migrated in and the usual species occupied the bayfront as if nothing had happened. High water stood for a week, forcing snakes of all kinds from their low hideouts, but snakes were less troublesome than the hordes of big marsh mosquitoes that swarmed in, "big enough to saddle," Jack said.

By October the Hagars were engaged again in Red Cross and bond drives, and Connie went often to entertain servicemen and -women at the USO in Corpus Christi. Another subchaser was christened with due ceremony, and it slid down the ways at the shipyard. From San Antonio, where Dr. Atkinson pronounced her eyes much improved, Connie went on to Corsicana for a short visit.

Witte Museum gave a one-man show of Dick Grossenheider's bird paintings, and the *San Antonio Light* chose one of them for its Picture of the Year Award. Dick gave the Hagars photographs of several of the paintings, "expressing the essence of the creatures," Connie thought. They had a "hawk weekend" together, seeing the usual kestrels, harriers, white-tails and the not-so-usual merlins, caracaras and ospreys; ferruginous, Swainson's, and rough-legged hawks; and a long flight of Mississippi kites. At Little Bay they watched a peregrine dive into a raft of pintails, scattering the frenzied flock and harrying one out of sight.

"I have taken pintails from hawks," Connie told Dick, "but learned how foolish it is. Hawks sink their talons in the bird's breast, and it's a goner anyway; they die in my hands. Besides, it is nature's way, and we should not interfere. And—we eat ducks, don't we?"

On another weekend she sat with Grossenheider at Aransas Refuge while he sketched whooping cranes from a distance, using binoculars. A small spotted skunk ambled from the brush and was quickly impressed on the artist's sketch pad.

Nature's way was exhibited again for Connie and Guy Emerson at Port Bay in December. They saw a merlin plummet into a thicket and rise as a wisp of feathers drifted to the ground, yellow and black—a Maryland yellowthroat. "I never mention these things in my nature talks," Connie said. "People just do not understand." They listed eighty-eight species that day, including American bitterns, and at supper they realized that the next day was the first anniversary of Pearl Harbor Day. A year of war had gone by with no end in sight.

Guy's customary compliments indicated that he had not, nor had anyone else for that matter, noticed anything different in her appearance. Connie was gratified because she was wearing a full set of dentures. Since midsummer she had gone twice a month to Corpus Christi to be relieved of her always trouble-some teeth, troublesome, she presumed, because of an indul-gence in sweets going all the way back to the ice cream parlor in Corsicana where she had had a charge account. It had been no great ordeal; having learned to live with arthritis and cataracts, she knew she could live with false teeth. Nor did it hurt her pride; indeed, the dentures were a pleasure, so much cleaner, so much less trouble than her own teeth had been.

The war had hurt the Hagars very little personally, but they ached for the young men in battle. Jack had to scrounge for sup-plies; linens were hard to come by, and sometimes little things like matches could not be found. But people understood short-ages, and such things were not real hardships.

Grossenheider brought her a tear sheet from the *St. Louis Post-Dispatch* of Sunday, January 17, 1943. It was a full-page color spread of five watercolors he had done in Texas. The text cited him as a native son and mentioned his exhibit in San An-tonio and the display at the American Museum of Natural His-tory of sixty-five of his drawings for the Michigan mammal book.

Not until the end of their birding weekend did he tell Con-nie and Jack good-bye—for a long time. He was off to Australia soon. The Hagars had come to love him like a son and were deso-late. He wrote of painting and exhibiting in Australia, and Con-nie answered his letters promptly, as she did for several "boys" overseas, who, she understood, yearned for mail—and that she could provide. Then they learned that Dick was missing in ac-tion, presumed to be a prisoner of the Japanese. Not until the end of the war in the Pacific did they hear that he had finally escaped and was safe with his family—and that a visit to Rock-port was at the top of his agenda. For many years he continued to correspond and send beautiful Christmas cards done with his talented brush.

Soon after Dick left for Australia, they had another service-man for a long stay. Lt. Ralph O'Reilly, a paratrooper in training at Fort Hood, had fractured a leg while scaling a broken concrete wall and, facing convalescence, had written to his friend Dr. Oberholser, asking where in Texas he might see birds while healing. The answer, naturally, was Rockport. Despite the heavy cast on his leg, he was able to see birds in abundance with Connie's help.

At the same time John Baker telephoned that he was bringing Ludlow Griscom, a director and soon-to-be board chairman of Audubon, to see the coastal sanctuaries. Captain Dawson of the Texas Game and Fish Commission would be with them, and they all wanted one day in Rockport.

Baker and Dawson were always enjoyable guests, but Connie was uncertain about Griscom, research curator for the Museum of Comparative Zoology at Harvard, generally regarded as the ultimate bird authority in the East, keenest and most accurate at field identification—often by flight alone, oftener by voice alone. His perceptions amazed his colleagues. He knew birds, he knew he was the best, and he demanded that others subscribe to his autocratic decisions. They did. Nobody argued with Ludlow Griscom, not even Guy. Guy had at times claimed out-of-place or out-of-season birds, which when reported to Griscom and analyzed by him in the light of his unquestioned knowledge, were pronounced "impossible," and Guy had meekly deleted them from his list, though he felt sure of his sighting. If "Ludlow wouldn't allow it," it was out.

Connie was certain that there would be nothing new for him in Rockport. Griscom already knew every bird north of the Mexican border and probably knew more of Mexico's species than anyone else at that time. He had traveled the continent from Labrador to Panama more than once and had birded the West Indies and Europe. As a youth he had been schooled in several European countries, and he spoke several languages fluently.

Baker rented a car in Corpus Christi and brought his party over just before dark, in plenty of time for a long evening of bird talk in the Hagar living room. Griscom was so agreeable that Connie wondered if she had been misinformed. Rather short and stocky, broad of brow and square of jaw beneath close-cut hair parted down the middle, his face looked rather cold, even supercilious, in repose, but when he talked, it became animated and friendly. And he talked a great deal, charmingly. She encouraged his delightful tales of travel and birds. Perhaps he was more than a bit pompous, but it was forgivable in one so learned, and she was learning things just from his casual remarks. She was always glad to learn.

Now and then he made a comment, apparently deferring to her and indicating that he knew her Rockport reports well, but obliquely slanted to suggest that possibly, just possibly, they could have been somewhat glorified. Did he question them? she mused, or was she unduly suspicious of him? At any rate, he made it clear that he expected nothing unusual here; he had come just to see some good birds that he had not seen in a long time. Maybe a ladder-backed woodpecker? "Of course," she promised, "but I still call it the Texas woodpecker." As the party broke up Griscom stepped to the piano and struck a few bars of Chopin, a bit hungrily, his hostess thought. She knew that he had given up a promising career as a concert pianist to devote himself to birds, but he declined to play that evening.

The morning dawned warm and sunny, and with Ralph O'Reilly included, the party was off early for a long, zestful day marked at times by sharp competition, much laughter, and stimulating discussions. Mid-February was no season for a spectacular show, but the abundance and variety of shorebirds on beaches and mudflats was always impressive. A flight of tree swallows went over. "First of the year," Connie told them. They drove up Highway 35 for white-tailed hawks and got a Cooper's for a bonus. White and white-faced ibis were at Salt Lake and pied-billed grebes were on every pond, some already behaving amorously. "Eared grebes will be at Oystercatcher Point," Connie said. Griscom's eyebrows went up. "Eared grebes in Rockport?" They were common in winter, she assured him, and there they were, romping in the waves. She added that she had seen all the grebes here, though of course the western and red-necked were very rare. Griscom gave her in icy look. "Not the least grebe? Certainly not so far north."

"That's what I call Mexican grebe, isn't it?" said Connie. "Let's go to Moore's Pool."

Silently they scanned the pool with binoculars, noting ducks of many species, pied-bills again, and then Connie spoke. "What's that out there beyond the three coots?" The small bird went under, came up, and submerged again as Griscom focused on it, and then he answered her question. "Unmistakable," he asserted, looking both pleased and chagrined.

"Good for you, Connie," Baker exclaimed. "You are keeping your record clean." He patted her shoulder, not displeased to have the star taken down a notch or two although this outing was plainly for his benefit, and, like a visiting potentate, he accepted it as his due.

On the Port Bay road they slowed to a stop, and she said, "The Texas woodpecker should be at one of those posts, or perched on the barbed wire between."

"Perched on a wire? A woodpecker?" Griscom was half-teasing now. Woodpeckers did not rest on wires. A small red-thatched woodpecker emerged from a hole in a post and flew to a wire where it sat facing them.

"Just like a trained seal," was the dry comment. "Do you call him Butch?"

Grasshopper sparrows at Rattlesnake Point were no surprise, nor were seaside sparrows. By imitating their voices, Griscom made them pop up on the tall weeds for all to see. He was, however, more interested in sparrows with yellowish faces. Sharp-tails, he was sure, but what race? He stalked into the marsh, pausing to utter various buzzy notes that fetched the sparrows to the top stems of ironweed—but not for long because the birds quickly dropped back into cover. He returned to the car to announce triumphantly, "Mrs. Hagar, you have the Nelson's sharp-tailed sparrow here."

"That," she said sincerely, "I am very, very glad to know. I could never be sure. Tell me your secret." He was happy to do that, and she added, "Maybe you will help me with savannah sparrows. I know I see different races, but I cannot pin them down."

The request restored Griscom's good humor; he relished the role of instructor, and thereafter they studied every flock of savannahs, some dusky, some pale, others in between, the authority pointing out the sometimes obscure differences in subspecies. He named three races that had traveled from as many different and distant regions to spend the winter in Rockport. Connie was very impressed; such knowledge did not come easy. He had worked for it and deserved all the credit he claimed.

After supper they added up their score: 136 species plus five additional races. It had been a good outing; even the star was enthusiastic. He wished Mrs. Hagar would send him her migration list—just migrants—telling when, where, and how many of each. She agreed. Still, he had some doubts about her. She had not produced snowy plovers, which he did not think should be there anyway. Also, he was skeptical about the buff-breasted sandpipers she had so persistently reported.

"You do not see them every year, Mrs. Hagar?" Every year, she affirmed. His eyes turned cold as he looked straight into her face and proclaimed: "Mrs. Hagar, in my lifetime I have seen three buff-breasted sandpipers, and I am the envy of the East Coast."

"Come during migration," she invited. She would not argue with experts; just let them come see for themselves.

"I want to come back," he assured her grimly.

Baker had been looking through a pile of hand-colored cards on the dropleaf table. It was Valentine's Day, and the schoolchildren she had lectured to about birds had remembered Mrs. Hagar lovingly.

"You must be everybody's sweetheart," Baker smiled.

"I am to Miss Katie Clark's room. I give her pupils a bird talk every year. They work for weeks on these valentines."

She would be giving a nature talk to the nurses at the U.S. Naval Hospital the next day and could not go to Aransas Refuge with them; she was sorry and they, disappointed. Did the service people appreciate the nature talks? "They eat them up, and it's the least I can do," she answered. Baker nodded approvingly; it helped the Audubon cause, too.

He also explained why Audubon had turned down the offer of the Valley sanctuary. There were no funds for upkeep, but he was delighted that the Interior Department had accepted it and would establish the Santa Ana National Wildlife Refuge there.

Within the week of their departure Connie and O'Reilly saw snowy plovers at the Cove and on Live Oak Point. "That's birdwatching," they agreed. "You can't win them all." Another good spring migration came on before Ralph, quite recovered, returned to duty.

Chapter 7

Griscom gave them three weeks' warning of his next Rockport trip, his return visit coming even sooner than he had expected, and his letter was more cordial than Connie expected.

Museum of Comparative Zoology
at Harvard College
Cambridge, Massachusetts   March 23, 1943

Mr. and Mrs. Jack Hagar
Rockport Cottages
Rockport, Texas

Dear Hagars:

This is to break the bad news to you that I shall probably arrive in Houston, Texas, on Friday evening, April 16 with my intimate friends, Mr. and Mrs. G. W. Cottrell, Jr. I have decided that I do not dare wait until the conclusion of the war and possible feebleness and old age [he was fifty-three] and I am now going to try and realize the ambition of years to study the spectacular migration on the coast of Texas and to see all the local birds around Brownsville that one cannot get there in winter.

I am trying to persuade Captain Dawson to come along for part of the time at least, and shall hope that I can manage to dig up a car for transportation purposes. Approximately half the time will be spent in Brownsville and half the time will be spent in the Rockport Cottages at Rockport, owned and operated by Mr. and Mrs. Jack Hagar. Everything seems so nice in the way of locality and personnel that I cannot keep away.

I am much indebted to Mrs. Hagar for expert leadership and a superb day's birding last February and I admire Mr. Hagar for his firmness of character in remaining normal and not succumbing to the lure of colored feathers. May he always remain so.

Regards to both,
Ludlow Griscom

Jack had not taken to Griscom and was not mollified by the oblique compliment. He noted that the letter did not request reservations—they were taken for granted—and at the writer's convenience since no exact date for Rockport was mentioned. But they were his wife's friends and as such would be given the best he could offer.

Connie welcomed the next encounter. Griscom was a challenge on a par with Dr. Oberholser but was more fun, especially when his complacence was jolted. She and Jack had been delighted by Guy Emerson's quick note, scribbled after hearing from Griscom an account of his visit. "Congratulations! You survived," he wrote.

Captain Dawson was persuaded and arrived Saturday in time to meet the afternoon bus bringing the party from Houston. George Williams also had been persuaded to come for the weekend. Connie asked Dawson to bring them around by the shipyard to see the yellow-headed blackbirds; they might be gone tomorrow. Hummingbirds swarmed at turk's cap blooming in front of every cottage.

The guests insisted on sitting out by the oaks through the warm twilight. The Cottrells called it a "Texas treat"; it was still chilly back home. They were a congenial couple. He belonged to the Linnaean Society, and both were good birdwatchers. An afternoon shower had washed the earth, which now smelled as fresh as the day of creation, and soft breezes mingled the scent of honeysuckle with that of huisache daisies. A gibbous moon climbed toward the zenith, and a black-crowned night-heron flapped from the trees, squawking hoarsely.

"Sh-h-h-h," whispered Griscom, leaning forward and listening. A plaintive "Ker-WEE—oo" was heard in the distance. He whistled the same notes and had an answer, then again, and the answer was closer, and still again, closer. "Pauraque."

Connie was thrilled. This was the resident bird on Attwater's list that she should have known by now. "You have found a new bird for me, in my own territory," she told her guest.

Many migrants were in the oaks Sunday morning, including some first arrivals of the species—blue grosbeaks, dickcissels, and redstarts among them. The hostess went, as usual, to play and sing for the church service but joined the party in the afternoon. A long flight of Franklin's gulls fed over the Rincon pasture, and in the short grass, water pipits chased insects. They looked alike to everyone except Griscom, who, to his own amazement more than that of the others, found at least one Rocky Mountain pipit among them. "I'm dumbfounded," he confessed. "This is a Colorado bird, not at all well known. The boys will be glad to know about this."

The swale back of the Fulton Mansion was a pan of shallow water bordered by sedges and cordgrass. "Should be short-billed marsh [sedge] wrens here," Griscom said, getting out of the car and gathering a handful of pebbles. Connie followed him to the rim of grass, where they sat on a fallen log as he made kissing sounds on the back of his hand and skittered pebbles across the water. She had hoped for but never found sedge wrens and quickly recognized the tiny birds that jumped up in the grass, scolded, and dropped again into the depths. A charming new bird for her. One thing she most liked about Griscom was that he tried to show his finds to everyone in his party, and she gratefully told him so.

"Oh, sure," he said complacently. "Everybody wants to bird with me."

The day's list matched that of his previous visit, and the next morning brought in a larger mixed migration and additional species, including a flight of Swainson's hawks, followed by a stream of broadwings. Flycatchers arrived en masse: pewees, empidonax, and Wied's flycatchers. "But no ash-throats yet," Connie remarked. Dawson and Williams had left; she and the Cottrells and Griscom were sitting in the backyard.

[123]

He tapped the arm of his chair, wondering aloud, "Ash-throated . . . Ash-throated . . . Now where would an ash-throated flycatcher be going from here?"

"Up into the western part of the state, where they nest, I guess," Connie replied.

"Orient yourself, Ludlow," Cottrell suggested mildly. Ash-throated flycatchers appeared the next day.

The visitors went on to the Valley but were back the following Sunday, which was Easter. "Beautiful day," the Nature Calendar recorded, and a long list of buntings, sparrows, fly-catchers, grosbeaks, orioles, cuckoos, warblers, and shorebirds followed. Most of the birding was on home ground, since Connie was again involved in church services.

Monday she took them to the Bayside prairies. She did not mention buff-breasted sandpipers, but they were what she hoped for, in vain, although long-billed curlews, upland sand-pipers, and other expected species were plentiful.

Griscom proposed "night birding" for the evening, a new experience for Connie. The idea appealed to her, and she was willing, she said, provided Jack could spare the stamps for rationed gasoline. It was nearing the end of the month, and he might be running short. She knew perfectly well that Jack would manage somehow, but she chose to remind the visitors that they were consuming "Jack's gasoline" as if he had no other use for it.

At dark they drove toward Salt Lake, away from habitation and traffic, stopping from time to time to listen. Griscom's imitations of the birds' voices produced responses from both pauraques and chuck-will's-widows. He also located several resting on the roadway; their eyes reflected the beam from the headlights. The chucks, of course, were in migration, but pauraques, she realized, must be fairly well distributed over the peninsula. She had learned something new and was having a good time. But still no snowy plovers, no buffbreasts. Why were these birds eluding her when she most needed them? She took her guests to Rattle-snake Point and on a high shellbank surrounded by marshy growth, stopped and turned off the motor.

"Snowy plovers should be here," she announced. Other plovers and waders were abundant. Griscom eyed the terrain covered by sea lavender, ironweed, and salicornia and turned to Cottrell, asking, "Bill, did you ever see a more unlikely spot for snowy plovers?"

"What's that?" Connie asked, before Bill could answer, indicating the edge of the marsh. Binoculars were not needed to see the small pale bird trot from behind a clump of salicornia and make for the water's edge, pausing a time or two to raise its head and look around.

"It's a snowy plover," Griscom affirmed. "How often does this happen here?"

"Believe it or not, we have a few all year round, more in spring and fall, of course."

"Irregular, very irregular." Disgruntled, he repeated, "Irregular."

Turning back, Connie drove slowly beside the Rincon, scanning the prairie carefully. She stopped and focused on a group of small birds in the short mesquite grass. "In the middle of the field," she told the others. Griscom aimed his binoculars and gasped.

"Let me out of this car, I'm coming out." He opened the door gently; no noise must disturb those birds. The Cottrells followed as he stalked the flock, glasses leveled upon it as they walked. Connie and Fuzzy remained in the car, she contentedly whistling a little tune under her breath.

The birds flushed, displaying the silver linings of their wings as they moved to a more distant feeding ground. The observers rushed back to the car, Griscom agitated and exultant.

"Mrs. Hagar!" he almost stuttered. "Those are buff-breasted sandpipers! Ten buff-breasted sandpipers. Ten!" In one glimpse he had more than trebled his life total of the species.

The Cottrells were babbling, life birds for them. When they came down to earth, Mrs. Cottrell turned to Connie, saying, "I shall tell you something now, Mrs. Hagar. When Ludlow heard about your seeing buffbreasts he said, 'That's impossible! Utterly impossible.'"

They all had a good laugh, and Griscom had the grace to say, "It really is impossible. I am not sure I believe them myself."

[125]

Although they had three more days in Rockport, everything thereafter was anticlimactic. Connie, secretly and wickedly gleeful, enjoyed her triumph; Ludlow Griscom had at last seen the light, though it did not occur to him to apologize for his doubts. The visitors contented themselves with revisiting special birds of the area—purple gallinules, roseate spoonbills, and many others. On the day of departure they were reluctant to leave. They were taking a bus to Corpus Christi to catch a plane, but Griscom, still the visiting potentate, had an idea: If Mrs. Hagar could drive them to the airport they would have two more hours to bird in Rockport.

"If Jack does not need the car," she said sweetly, but intentionally reminding Griscom of the obligation. "I shall be delighted." Jack accommodated, as expected. She saw them to the plane, agreed again to send Griscom her lists, then drove home and went to bed. It had been exhilarating but exhausting, and she did not protest when Jack hoped out loud that "we never see *him* again." Jack had taxied the party to meals, "feeling like a peon," he said, and though the proper appreciation had been expressed and he liked the Cottrells, he had derived no pleasure from Griscom.

"Hot and dry" was a frequent notation in the Nature Calendar; ponds were drying up, but Moore's Pool still held water, and on it a pair of least grebes were assembling a raft of dead vegetation. For a week Connie watched them working steadily every morning in the middle of the pool, open to the hot sun. These small tropical grebes nested regularly in the Valley, but except for a nest found many years ago south of San Antonio by Roy Quillin and others, they were not known to breed as far north as Rockport. She got permission from the landowner to enter the pool; she wanted to be sure.

Early on a mid-May morning, wearing a black bathing suit and tennis shoes, she waded in, sliding her feet along the slippery bottom and skirting the spread of American lotus with creamy yellow blossoms standing high above the huge green pads floating on the surface. Gallinules stepping lightly on the pads moved away from her, and coots plunged out of sight. Cattails screened her approach from the grebe sitting on a little mound in the middle of the soggy raft, but as she neared it, the golden eye of the slaty bird spied her movements and with a shrill "Beep," it leaped from the raft and under water. Moving closer, Connie looked down on two grayish white eggs, studied them briefly without touching, and quickly got away. So Mexican grebes *were* nesting in Rockport.

There should be more eggs, then the incubation—how long she did not know—but she kept the nest under observation for almost a month. One bird was always on the mound, the other nearly always in grassy cover nearby. Then one morning Connie thought she saw a tiny form beside the sitter, and early the next day she waded out again, carrying a butterfly net.

Drought had shrunk the pool, but water was still knee-deep. Crouching low, she inched ahead; the cattails were denser now, and she was almost at the edge of the raft when again the parent grebe beeped and dived. But in the same instant, the butterfly net came down, imprisoning two small, dark, wriggling downy chicks. Gently removing them from the mesh, she turned them over and about to examine them thoroughly; she was surprised to see bare red skin on top of the head and white streaks on the throat. They peeped their objections to this indignity, and the parent bird, having surfaced, also protested. Two eggs remained in the nest, begrimed by the rotten vegetation—and one of them suddenly trembled. Then the shell came apart in jagged pices, and a wet wisp of a bird fell out. Immediately the tiny head struggled forward, and stubby appendages that would be wings stretched from the sides. The rapid transformation that followed seemed like a miracle. "A little bird that looked like nothing," she would say, "in an instant seemed to dry in the warm sun and become fluffy and independent."

The birds must not be disturbed any longer. She felt guilty to have stayed so long, but she was enthralled. She laid the infants back in the nest, and instantly they slid off and submerged. She watched them swim expertly away, just under the surface, "like butterflies sailing underwater."

At the car she turned her binoculars on the nest and saw that the fledglings and a parent were snugly nestled upon it. She donned a smock, put a towel over the car seat, and drove home.

[127]

Coots, pied-bills, and gallinules also were nesting on the pond, but it was the day of least grebes; she did not want to confuse the issue. Her sister Bert would call it her one-track mind at work.

Visitors from afar were fewer that summer, travel restrictions being more severe, but young servicemen and -women from nearby military posts filled the vacancies. Lieut. Lloyd Ingles and his wife from the Corpus Christi Naval Air Station came to photograph birds. A biology teacher from California in civilian life, Ingles shared his hundreds of photographs of Rockport birds with Connie. Others came just "to get away from the base," and the Hagars sought to make their holidays happy. For one lonely Wave who came frequently, Connie learned to make kidney-bean salad after the girl confessed that it was what she most hungered for; Connie kept the "fixings" on hand thereafter, though she did not care for the dish herself.

It was, however, a glorious summer for Connie, most fruitful for learning more about nesting birds by often hitching a ride with Pug Mullinax on his regular patrols of bays and islands to check on illegal netting and possible violations of hunting and fishing regulations. They left the yacht basin at 6:00 A.M. and usually were back before noon. Pointing north up the Intracoastal Canal, Pug might course along the mainland shore then across to shellbanks and islands, noting the activities of other boaters and fishermen, most of whom he knew. At the same time, his passenger was watching for the activities of birds. From time to time he turned to look at her and smiled, though she might not be returning his glance. She sometimes wore a pink-flowered cotton dress, trimmed with tucks at the waistline, and short sleeves. Breezes ruffled the light brown hair of the pilot but not the silver crown of his passenger. He thought the big binoculars looked too heavy for her small hands, which in reality were strong and firm. Although she spent a great deal of time outdoors, her skin was not browned or roughened.

His eyes were straight ahead when he felt a hand on his sleeve, and he leaned to try to hear her above the roar of the motor.

"Pug, please slow down and pull in as close to that spoil bank as you can." He cut the motor and swung inshore. Dredging for the Intracoastal Canal had destroyed ancient breeding habitats but at the same time had created new ones, which many birds, though perhaps a different species, were quick to preempt. A multitude had taken over this spoil bank. As the boat nosed in, a screaming cloud of wings took to the air, protesting the intrusion.

"They don't like us, Mrs. Hagar," Pug shouted above the din.

"We won't stay long," she promised, keeping her glasses fixed on the reef. It was covered with hundreds of eggs. In shallow scrapes so close together, the mystery of how the gulls and terns could know their own was a fresh wonder. Black skimmers and royal and Sandwich terns occupied the near rim; Caspian terns were attached to an outer flat of sand; and in the center where sea ox-eye and ironweed grew were hundreds of laughing gulls. Willets rose, flashing black-and-white wings, to join the cacophony.

"And oystercatchers," she said enthusiastically, telling Pug where to look so he might learn the species. The warden was interested; there was not much anyone could tell him about waterfowl and game birds; they were his business. But other feathered fauna had been mostly "sea gulls and snipes and cranes" until he had started learning from Mrs. Hagar. She had also helped him with mourning doves, then being studied by the Game Commission.

It was time to go because those eggs must not be exposed to the blazing sun for too long. As the boat backed away, the nesters calmed down and returned to their duties. Passing a beacon tower with one side open to the canal, Pug remarked that it was the winter roost of a duck hawk. He had often seen it perched inside its retreat.

Ahead was Second Chain, a string of islets supporting thorny shrubs; granjeno, agarita, and brasil with mats of cow-itch vine and bindweed covered many of the islands. Birds were on most of them, but Pug pointed to Carroll Island, still favored most by spoonbills and brown pelicans. That day the elongated island, scarcely an acre, looked like a jeweled brooch: a narrow beach of white sand bordered the mound of greenery, which in the center rose to the height of scrubby trees and Spanish daggers. The green mass was sprinkled with pink spoonbills, white egrets, blue herons and gray ones, and dark chocolate white-faced ibises. Shrubs and prickly pear were weighted with nests, the heads of sitting birds barely visible above the foliage; in some, half-grown heron nestlings sparred with siblings and neighbors with huge, sharp beaks. Spaced about the colony were the big platforms of brown pelicans, owners sitting in regal solemnity upon them.

The boat drifted around the island, creating little disturbance, but though the scene was not so noisy, it was far from quiet. The low hum of squeaks, groans, and hisses was constant. Pug asked if she would like to go ashore.

"Not here. These birds do not return to their babies and eggs so soon as gulls and terns do, and it would not do to expose them too long."

Another islet was occupied exclusively by brown pelicans, and another, with scant vegetation, by royal, Sandwich, and least terns. On still another, black-crowned night-herons were nesting, and from the opposite sides, olivaceous cormorants flew up. Their nests she would like to see. Pug drew as near as he dared and threw out an anchor as his passenger kicked off her oxfords and slipped into rubber boots. Pug tucked his uniform trousers into boots and stepped into the water—still too deep for Mrs. Hagar. He held out his arms and lifted her over the side, "light as a feather," he assured her, waded in, and set her down in shallow water. Night-herons squawked and flew, and cormorants took to the water.

The cormorant nests were among a stand of reeds around a swampy depression; they held sets of chalky bluish eggs, brown and dirty from the wet, dead grass lining the cavity. "Probably the ugliest eggs in bird-dom," she chuckled. "When fresh they are smooth, but the chalk builds up to protect them from dampness."

They turned the boat toward home. Pug had reached the limit of his patrol, but there was no hurry. They had time to pass slowly by the pelican rookery and watch adults feeding their waddling young. It looked more like a fight than a feast. The young plunged their bills deep into the great pouches of parents, gobbling so eagerly they seemed to be wrestling the provider who, in turn appeared to be swallowing its own offspring.

Passing Third Chain of Islands, a smaller group, Mrs. Hagar became excited again and called for a stop; on a low grove a vulture perched and another flopped on the ground. "Black vultures," she exclaimed. "Can they be nesting here?" Pug anchored and steadied the boat; she searched the scene with binoculars. "They are! Those babies are beautiful, like lumpy powder puffs with shoebutton eyes." Pug found them in his glasses; the big black birds stood guard over four awkward, lurching bundles of white down surrounded by debris. "This is all new to me," Mrs. Hagar said.

"I don't think buzzards are as ugly as most people do," Pug offered. "They are scavengers, yes, but that makes them very useful."

At the yacht basin Jack stood by the blue car, Fuzzy dancing wildly. Fuzzy never went on boat trips; they made him seasick. Tossing a rope, Pug grinned as Jack, catching it, made gratuitous remarks about the kind of company the pilot kept and wasting the state's money on birdwatching.

"Good birds, dahling?" he asked, lifting his wife to the pier with an affectionate peck on her check. She thanked the warden again.

"Any time, Mrs. Hagar," he assured her. "You're never any trouble, and I'm patrolling anyway. We will pick another pretty day soon."

With Benny Earp, another game warden, Connie occasionally stowed away on patrols of the southern section of Aransas Bay. Both Pug and Benny had been along when the flamingo was discovered, and afterward she had learned that the bird might have been in the vicinity for a month. Dr. Gordon Gunter, marine biologist, told her that G. A. Rattisseau, a veteran hunting and fishing guide, had seen what he believed to be a flamingo around Copano Bay.

By mid-August hatchlings from the islands were following their elders to the mainland: young spoonbills in white plumage, reddish egrets minus reddish manes, and tricolored herons so much more colorful and handsome than the parents. Yellow-crowned night-herons appeared with long-legged young, and she wondered if they, too, could have been hatched nearby. Hot and dry weather continued into autumn.

Black terns were most conspicuous in the fall migration, flights going by daily for a month, and one afternoon when Connie drove to Corpus Christi, black terns were in sight every mile of the way. Equally conspicuous that day was a migration of snout butterflies, so thick that when she crossed the wooden causeway over Nueces Bay, clouds of them flew ahead of the car, and the roadway was slick with their crushed bodies.

Hummingbirds again concentrated at the Cove; beginning in August the numbers grew, and in late September the Nature Calendar mentioned day after day "hundreds of hummers in the tangle at the Cove." Many were still present when Guy Emerson came October 8. He looked tired and worried. The war weighed heavily on him and he was grateful for "two whole days" at Rockport.

A large flock of sandhill cranes foraged in a swale near Copano Bay, where he sat for half an hour just listening to their throaty, conversational voices. On the Fulton Beach road they got out to stroll around the pool surrounded by cattails, looking for rails. Connie turned toward the beach and stood for a while before asking, "Guy, what's wrong with that heron's head?" He studied the big bird, a great blue heron, except for the head, which was all white, including the occipital plumes. He had seen such a bird in Florida.

"Nothing wrong. Just a Wurdeman's heron, that's all. And another new bird for the bird lady of Rockport." The stranger was gone the next day, but another new bird for the bird lady was seen on the Hartman Ranch—a Harlan's hawk. Again the ranch hosted thousands of ducks and geese.

"You and the birds are great therapy," Guy told the Hagars at the end of his stay, much restored in spirits.

Harold Mayfield of Toledo, Ohio, spent a November week in Rockport seeing birds and sharing the Hagars' Thanksgiving dinner. Another guest, a short-eared owl, arrived that day on the vacant field in front of the Cottages and remained the rest of the year. Connie thought the long dry spell was somehow responsible for the owl's visit. It was still there when she and Jack returned from a Christmas trip to Corsicana, but it departed on January 1 when at last a long and abundant rain began to fall.

January, 1944, was cold and wet, the kind of weather that aggravated Connie's arthritis. She could no longer grip the snake club firmly, and playing the piano was agony, but she practiced persistently until her fingers bent to her commands and the pain abated. And for the first time, arthritis was affecting her joints. Walking was uncomfortable at times, but with the return of warmer weather, that trouble eased. No one heard her complain. Some days her bird outings were curtailed in favor of obligations to Red Cross, bond drives, clubs, and service organizations.

Dr. and Mrs. Robert Gammell of North Dakota came in February with a "want list" of South Texas specialties, and they appeared to enjoy the benign weather as much as they did the birds.

Ralph O'Reilly returned, again to recuperate from an accident. In the year since he had left them, he had been in Italy with the Allied invasion and was wounded when a bomb exploded in the jeep he and three companions were riding. His father telephoned to prepare the Hagars; his son had suffered a broken jaw and broken leg. He had been unconscious ten days in the camp hospital, was transferred to another hospital, and finally sent home to recover near his family and be discharged. The young man's appearance was heartbreaking to Connie and Jack, but they forced a cheerful welcome and arranged for his comfort in the cottage next to their own.

"I just want to get warm," Ralph moaned. "I've been cold to the bone forever. It was cold in Italy and cold in Michigan. Just let me get warm." The weather was blessedly warm, as if making a special dispensation for the soldier, and a male vermilion flycatcher at his back door gave him a warm glow. He stayed nearly three weeks, going daily with Connie on her rounds seeing again the familiar species he longed for, seeing the beginning of the spring migration, hearing the songs of Cassin's sparrows. When he left in March, he was so nearly restored that he was ready to go back to his old job with General Motors.

In late March a push of blue-gray gnatcatchers in the oaks

included one that was different. She followed it around, noting field marks until she was sure it was a western species out of its range—a black-tailed gnatcatcher. It would happen again, but at four- to five-year intervals. The great kiskadee that arrived a month later with Joe Heiser and the Houston bunch—but from the opposite direction—would happen again, too, also at long intervals.

The European wigeon she found off Fulton Beach April 11 would, however, be her only sighting of that rare species in Texas. It had come just ahead of a norther, which next day brought a flight of thousands of Franklin's gulls, the first of several big migrations of them that spring. "Flycatching" over the grassy lots in front of the Cottages, the gulls were so noisy that a guest thought her radio had gone haywire. Whimbrels probed the grass beneath the gulls.

The Gulf of Mexico was so stormy on May 1 that shrimpers made for port early. Headers were waiting at the fish house, lined up on both sides of long wooden troughs through which conveyor belts and running water carried shrimp emptied from the boats. At the side of each header hung a large bucket; they were paid by the bucketful. Adept hands snapped off and discarded the heads of shrimp and dropped the edible tails in the bucket. Men, women, and children headed shrimp. For some it was a living, for others, pin money, to be paid at the end of each day.

That day, amid the furious activity, a big white bird had trailed a trawler into the harbor and to the fish house, where, confused, it had flown inside and perched on a trough—to the consternation of the headers. It was as white as a snow goose and had black wingtips, but it was no goose—it had a long, sharp beak. Nobody knew what it was. A buffy wash covered its head, and the eyes were sharply delineated by black lines. The manager came to investigate the commotion, saw it was indeed a strange one, and telephoned Dr. Gunter, the marine biologist, who called Mrs. Hagar.

They arrived at the same time, and both at the same moment exclaimed, "Gannet." The bird was in trouble. Connie wanted to take it, and the exhausted creature was easily captured and placed in a tow sack. At home, being cautious of that dagger bill, she examined the bird; it had very thick feathers. It was her first gannet, and by reading, she determined that it was fully adult, at least three years old. And it was covered with vermin; perhaps that was its trouble. She dusted it with Fuzzy's flea powder and made it as comfortable as possible in a covered tub. The bird seemed to be all right, so late the next day she carried it to the end of the long pier at Hunt's Cottages and dropped it in the water, where it floated for a time and then swam to deeper water. It was gone the next day, to find its own kind and habitat, she hoped.

Guy Emerson came again in late May, this time as president of National Audubon Society, "obliged," he said with a twinkle, to inspect the Society's coastal sanctuaries. Gordon Gunter took them the first day south to Lydia Ann Island, where two hundred "pinks" were nesting among laughing gulls and great-tailed grackles. Seaside sparrows were on territory, and magnificent frigatebirds floated above the launch both going and returning, as if they were flying an aerial escort.

Frigatebirds were overhead the next day as well when Benny Earp and Pug took them to the Second Chain. The breeders on Carroll Island that year included white ibises. All nesters appeared to be doing well, but great-tailed grackles were far more numerous than in previous seasons—a serious threat to eggs and young. Four gull-billed terns were among other terns on a sandspit. Their eggs Connie had never seen, but the party decided against going ashore for fear of undue disturbance.

Cruising homeward, Pug told Guy how Mrs. Hagar helped him with his job: "On her early morning rounds she sees violations and reports them to me. She can always describe the spot, usually gets the license number, and sees how many people there are, what they are shooting at and with what. One man, when confronted by Mrs. Hagar's statement that he was shooting ducks out of season, confessed and paid his fine. "In fact," he added, "when the young boys around town see violations, they call Mrs. Hagar oftener than they do me."

Connie heard that and said, laughing: "The children think I have authority, but all the authority I have is the authority to tell Pug." Most cases concerned senseless killing and meddling with songbirds.

Stupid people, Pug went on wrathfully, still abused the big birds. He had found eight spoonbills beaten to death on Hog Island, the sticks still lying among the birds, and spoonbill nesting had been poor on that island the following year, perhaps also because fishing shacks had been built on Hog Island and birds were unwanted. It would be watched more closely from now on, Guy was assured. Another problem was that often when fishermen used live bait, gulls would dive for the bait and get caught, and too many fishermen simply snapped off the heads of the gulls. Then there was the story of the brown pelican, which Pug told with relish.

Mrs. Hagar was on the seawall one day when she saw a man trying to hook a pelican; she knew the man, a broker from upstate who claimed to be a sportsman. Politely, she asked if he knew that pelicans were protected, and his reply had been that he "wished all pelicans were dead." Furious, she went for Pug. When the warden appeared, the man was tying a rag on the pelican's feet while a boy held it down with a dip net, but on seeing Pug they let the bird go. Nevertheless, Pug took him before the justice of the peace, who ruled that without a dead pelican he had no case.

Pug and Connie were disappointed, but the case was not closed. Pug saw the bedraggled pelican three days later waddling awkwardly in front of his own house. Unable to fly, it had wandered around hungry those three days. He untied the rag and took the pelican to water, but half an hour later it was dead. Now he had a case. He took the bird to the justice of the peace and filed charges. Mrs. Hagar testified at the hearing, telling what she saw and quoting the man's wish that all pelicans were dead. The offender paid a fine of twenty-five dollars plus costs, for a total of forty-two dollars.

Chapter 8

Painted buntings tended nestlings in a yaupon thicket behind the Cottages that first week in June, 1944, a tense period the world over, for everybody knew that something was about to happen in Europe. Like everyone else, the Hagars pored over newspapers and listened to radio newscasts, and when Gen. Dwight Eisenhower launched the Normandy campaign, they fervently hoped it was the beginning of the end of the dreadful war.

But the war and Dr. Oberholser sent them another birding companion destined to be a lifelong friend. Dr. Locke Mackenzie, a New York surgeon serving in the Navy, was sent as a consultant on a program at the Naval Hospital in Corpus Christi, and, having a weekend free, he arranged to spend it with Mrs. Hagar, whom Dr. Oberholser had recommended highly.

They covered Live Oak Peninsula the first day and went to Aransas National Wildlife Refuge the next. They saw an osprey fishing a bayou, and under little bridges on Highway 35 they found cliff swallows nesting. The heads of nestlings peeked from mud cups attached to the bridges' undersides, but above them, rough-winged swallows were still in migration. In a brush thicket on Goose Island they found olive sparrows, "Texas sparrows" to Connie. They were new to Dr. Mackenzie and known to Connie only from Valley sightings. Long-billed marsh wrens, commoner in winter, appeared to be nesting at the Tules.

Sparrows were of special interest to the New Yorker; he had made a definitive study of Gambell's white-crowned sparrow for the American Museum of Natural History and was knowledgeable on other species as well as other birds, having traveled extensively in pursuit of his hobby and attained an enviable life list.

"Fine day," began her list in the Nature Calendar, a phrase which often meant, among other things, that it was a day filled with laughter, her kind of outing. For Connie, birdwatching was not a grim pursuit.

"I want my wife to meet you," Dr. Mackenzie told the Hagars in parting. "She is beautiful but wouldn't know a hummingbird from a pelican."

In July Connie and Jack watched a splendid sunset from their front lawn, and at dusk the incessant buzz of cicadas was louder than ever—a sure sign of dry weather, old-timers said. Nighthawks quartered high above them, uttering their single-note calls, but a small flight of other nighthawks passed low over their heads, turned, and passed back—trilling. They were lesser nighthawks, never common there.

Cicadas proved to be true prophets; August was searing, and no rain fell. All pools dried up, except Moore's Pool, down to a mere puddle where waders crowded in to feast on dying fish. Among them was a Virginia rail, also less common there than in Corsicana. In another week Moore's Pool also was dry, and birds dispersed.

Drought, however, did not deter hummingbirds. The population at the Cove grew to hundreds and then thousands through September, and there were still hundreds when Locke Mackenzie returned in late October. He saw them in late afternoon, competing for choice red blossoms, squeaking and hissing, and he marveled at the numbers. This, he ventured to say, was a movement few bird authorities knew about.

Mackenzie had come with a rented car and a "brilliant idea." He had never birded the Valley; would Connie go with him tomorrow? Jack made a mock scene of resistance but was happy for her to have the outing. Then he asked, "Who is Mrs. Jade Hagar?" He handed Locke his telegram addressed to that name.

"Oh," the doctor winced, "that's my terrible handwriting. I wrote it in a hurry at the airport." Thereafter, his special name for Connie was Jade.

[138]

They left before daylight and did not return until almost midnight, having had a "helluva delightful day," Mackenzie said. Despite his long life list, he had added eleven to it among the sixty-two species seen on a grand sweep of Valley "hot spots."

While driving home in the dark, he had confided to Connie that he planned to abandon his surgical practice after the war; he had seen so many mangled bodies during his Navy career that he thought he could not go on when it was over. He had told no one else.

Blanche and Bob Bush came from Ennis to spend Christmas. The day was springlike at seventy degrees, but there was still no rain. Before breakfast Connie took Blanche to the beach to see the daybreak rites of the black skimmers. Rising in groups of hundreds, the skimmers sailed out over the water, circled, and banked, forming a pattern of black dots against the early sky. Then, like a sudden fall of snow, they turned their white undersides to the viewers, circled again, and went out of sight, only to skim back and settle on the sand, and to repeat again and again. "I've seen this only on winter mornings, and very early," Connie said.

January, 1945, was warm and dry, and very windy on the fourteenth when Connie set out alone for Aransas Refuge; Fuzzy had been lethargic of late and averse to riding. It was the day she pulled out beside the Copano Bay causeway and saw, among the goldeneyes, the harlequin ducks, a dressy drake and his plain brown companion with white cheek spots, still there when she returned from the refuge.

At the end of the month, after she had sent her report to Oberholser, Williams, and the *Auk*, Dr. Ralph Friedmann and Dr. Edward Fleischer, on a tour of South Texas, came to Rockport for a day. They arrived in late afternoon and spent the evening with Connie planning the next day's trip. When she happened to mention the harlequins, the men turned to one another and shook hands in mutual congratulations. Dr. Friedmann explained. "We saw the drake at Aransas Refuge two days ago! We felt sure it was a harlequin but decided it was just too fantastic. We didn't know what to think." Their day in Rockport produced no rarities, but the visitors were happy with seventy-three species they saw and called it a great day.

The Nature Calendar contained a sad entry for January 29. "Put little Fuzzy to sleep in Corpus Christi. He had a tumor. Was nearly 15 years old. Great dog."

Despite summer weather in winter, or perhaps because of it, February birds included mountain plovers on the Bayside prairies, Sprague's pipits at Rattlesnake Point, and another black-tailed gnatcatcher in her yard. On a morning when she went again to see the prairie-chickens dancing, she counted 141 sandhill cranes in a pasture, and they, too, were dancing. Spring could not be far behind.

Norman Hill of Boston, a friend of Ludlow Griscom's, also visited that month, and Hill's account of the birds, together with the periodic reports Connie sent, inspired an enthusiastic letter from the star birder of the East Coast.

> Dear Hagars:
>
> Many thanks for a series of interesting bulletins from the ever active Texas firing line! Congratulations on your latest astonishing addition to the fauna of Texas in the shape of a Harlequin Duck. Such records show that heaven only knows what is going to turn up next and where, no matter how unlikely or improbable; and I have to devote a line or two on your Harlequin in the next Seasons Report to Audubon Field Notes. My young friend Norman Hill had a lovely time and it was apparent that you delivered the goods with your usual competence.
>
> How nice it would be if I could get to Texas again before I am too old!
>
> With warm and affectionate regards,
Always sincerely,
Ludlow Griscom.

My, how this man has thawed, Connie thought. Jack had a good laugh that he was included in the credits and was almost ready to admit that his fellow Bostonian was not such a bad guy after all.

A wave of parulas on March 2 signaled the start of spring warblers, and another wave a week later brought a pretty hybrid, Brewster's warbler. Sparrows had been less abundant that mild winter, but for a month they moved through in large flocks, including clay-colored sparrows, new for Connie in Rockport. Weather perhaps helped account for the lingering of western meadowlarks, which sang their brilliant melodies during a week-long return visit by Dr. Fleischer and for a Neblett reunion when Sonney and Alice May came from Schenectady and Bert visited from Corsicana.

Scissor-tailed flycatchers woke the Hagars long before dawn on Palm Sunday. The trees must be full of them judging by the clattering conversations, Connie thought. Watching them from the breakfast table as the sun rose, she remarked again as she often had that the Texas bird of paradise was her favorite of all birds.

She stacked the dishes while Jack went to back out the car. A momentary sadness swept over her. She still missed Fuzzy terribly, but she and Jack had agreed not to get another dog. It hurt too much to lose one. The front door closed behind her husband, and then she heard his cries, loud enough to be heard all the way to the post office, she thought.

"Connie, dahling, Connie come quick! Come see who is here to take little Fuzzy's place."

She dashed out, alarmed because Jack rarely made such a fuss and because she had not fully understood what he had said. He was still shouting when she stepped outside, and pointing to a miserable canine creature cowering in a canvas chair. It was a mere puppy, frightened by the furor and, she felt, ashamed to have been caught intruding but too scared to move.

"Why, little dog, good morning," she cooed. The pup shivered hopefully, then wagged all over but still made no overtures.

"Get him in the house and feed him," Jack ordered, his voice gentle and coaxing. The animal was black-and-white, but Connie saw that much of the black was alive—the pup was encrusted with fleas. Its eyes were mere slits, the eyelids so heavy with fleas they could hardly open.

"I'll get rid of those fleas first," she said. "Poor little doggie, come into this house." It crept from the chair uneasily but balked at the door. "Why, it has never been in a house before," she said, picking him up and carrying him inside. He was a trashy little animal, no doubt about that, but a dog—and hungry. Jack was right; a bowl of milk was first. The flea-bitten beggar lapped without lifting his head until the bowl was empty. Their resolution about no more pets was forgotten. Birds were forgotten, too; Connie went for tweezers and set to work on the fleas, all stick-tights, she noticed, no dog fleas.

"Little thing must have been living with chickens," she said. "Grandmother Yeater would say they are so thick you couldn't put the point of a cambric needle on him without touching one." Flea by flea she tackled the eyelids, and after a time raw pink rims were visible—and still half the fleas remained. But the pup needed a rest, so she put him in a box Jack had lined with towels. He fell into blissful slumber while his rescuer made a hurried tour of the beach. Man-o-war birds were hovering over town, perhaps signaling an approaching storm.

Several sessions with the tweezers convinced her that they were a useless weapon against fleas; there were thousands. So Jack went to Johnson's Drug Store for flea powder, carbonated Vaseline, and the makings of a creosote bath. The puppy was cooperative; human attention, the relief he surely felt, and gentle hands were too good to resist. Connie was certain of his gratitude. At last they could see what he looked like—white except for black ears and one patch of black on a cheek, covering one eye. Short-haired and trim, his appearance suggested a lineage of random canine liaisons, probably fox terrier predominating. Whatever he was, he slept that night at the foot of the Hagars' bed, clean but smelling of creosote.

They took him to Fuzzy's doctor in Corpus Christi for vaccinations. By then the dog's ears were peeling, and the Hagars explained the flea treatment, which the veterinarian said could have "cooked" the animal's ears. (It did not and must have been permanently effective since the dog never again had a flea in his ears.) The veterinarian estimated his age at three months.

As for the puppy's name, Connie said Jack should decide. "You found him, he's yours." No, he insisted, she must decide. "Well, if it's up to me, I'm going to call him Patch."

Her husband agreed, provided, he said, "You don't think

that's disrespectful to General Patch." Jack was a great admirer of the American military leader involved in the campaign in Italy.

"Well, he is a little tramp, but lovable and grateful. General Patch should not mind."

Patch was lovable and loving, playful and rollicking, and too boisterous for birdwatching, but Connie was patient. She taught him restraint in the field, not to bark at birds, not to dash ahead without permission. It took years, however, before she could say he was the equal of Fuzzy as a birding companion.

Easter and April Fool's Day came together in 1945 with strong winds and the first good rain of the year. Water ran in ditches, and the pools filled. Flocks of white pelicans moved north, five hundred in one flight that Connie counted. Another wave of clay-colored sparrows came and went. Some hawks went over, mostly falcons and red-tails, but no broadwings. More hawks went over the next day but still no broadwings, and she wondered about them until the afternoon paper, the *Corpus Christi Times*, arrived with a story that infuriated her.

THOUSANDS OF CHICKEN HAWKS FLY
OVER SHELL ROAD NEAR NUECES BAY

Thousands of chicken hawks today flocked over Corpus Christi and the region to the west and north of the city in a phenomenon that proved mysterious to virtually all the city's nature students.

The birds of prey were first noticed over the Shell Road sector adjacent to Nueces Bay, shortly after sunrise.

Residents of that area thought them to be gulls and paid scant attention to them. Later, Ernest G. Dimond of 2518 West Broadway, an employee of the Missouri-Pacific Lines, observed them swooping over chicken farms and went for his shotgun.

Dimond knocked down several from these flocks and warned residents along Shell Road after discovering what they were.

Dean Edwin L. Harvin of Corpus Christi Junior College said he had observed them through the morning but was unable to identify the birds at such a height. He was unable to explain their flocking.

"The sky was literally black with the hawks," Dimond reported. He said he had never seen such a spectacle in Corpus Christi.

"Damn! Damn!" Connie exclaimed, throwing the paper to the floor. Chicken hawks indeed! Such ignorance, such stupidity! She marched at once to her desk and wrote a letter to the editor, "putting the record straight," she explained. The letter was published immediately, while hawks were still migrating, and Byron Buzbee, farm editor of the *Caller-Times*, telephoned for more information, then pursued the subject in his regular column.

> Mrs. Jack Hagar of Rockport, one of Texas' leading ornithologists and certainly the best versed in birds peculiar to this section, advises that the hawks which have been flying over South Texas this week are Broadwing Hawks and not chicken hawks.
>
> Hundreds of them have been flocking over Nueces and Aransas Counties since last Sunday, when their numbers became noticeable, and sent many residents scurrying to closets for shotguns and shells.
>
> The movement of hawks takes place every spring, Mrs. Hagar said. They gather from their winter homes and start north, breaking up into smaller flocks through their flight till they reach as far as Manitoba and New Brunswick.
>
> Their main food consists of rabbits, mice, weasels, small snakes, grasshoppers, thousand-legs, ants, spiders, earthworms, and a few small fish. There is little evidence that broadwings ever attack poultry—but try to tell that to most people. A hawk to them is a chicken hawk, always. Cooper's and sharp-shinned are the two hawks that may go after poultry.

Connie was pleased, thinking that in the farm column the truth might do some good.

Rains continued, and cold fronts throughout the month grounded thousands of songbirds, which was witnessed by not only Connie but also many of her friends in the birding fraternities of the larger Texas cities. With the Houston bunch one day, Joe Heiser estimated a thousand dickcissels in one flight. When Guy returned at the end of the month, the migration was in full swing, with a lazuli bunting and Wilson's phalaropes again spinning merrily in backyard puddles.

"Just imagine having phalaropes at your own back door," he marveled at breakfast, watching them through the kitchen window. Orchard orioles and northern orioles of both the Bullock's and Baltimore races hung in the oaks like small Japanese lanterns. Purple gallinules and moorhens were at the Tules, sharp-tailed sparrows and a hundred Hudsonian godwits on the Rincon.

Guy was in excellent spirits; seeing the Hagars and fine birds was part of it, but it was also the prospect of peace, at least in Europe. Hitler's empire had fallen apart, and the archfiend himself was probably dead. A week later Rockport along with all America, indulged in a shouting, horn-blowing, kissing, and laughing celebration of the enemy's capitulation.

The Nature Calendar made no mention of the victory; it listed birds daily, as always. The Gills were there in June when Ralph O'Reilly came again for a week. Pug took them to Second Chain of Islands, warning them that the spoonbills were having a poor season. High tides had destroyed many nests and high winds had not helped. The winds, however, might explain the unexpected but unmistakable sight of two white-tailed tropic-birds apparently following a male frigatebird out over the Gulf. The streaming tail feathers and pretty pattern of black on the mantle were clearly visible. They were a first for Connie but not for Rockport. She knew that Clint Murchison, who with Toddie Lee Wynne owned and ranched on Matagorda Island, had obtained a permit to collect species for Southern Methodist University and that among them was a white-tailed tropicbird. (The SMU collection was neglected and eventually stored in a basement, from which it was exhumed in the early sixties by Billy O'Neil of Falfurrias, a student at SMU and friend of Connie's.)

In July Connie went again to Second Chain, this time with Joel Hedgpeth and Jack Baughman from the Game and Fish Commission's laboratory on the yacht basin. They found a new spoil bank, created by maintenance dredging for the Intracoastal

Canal, which had become a giant nursery for terns—Caspian, Sandwich, royal, gull-billed, and least terns. On a broad sandy flat the Caspians herded their collection of fluffy progeny in a long column several feet wide, which moved back and forth under the guardianship of a dozen adults, who kept them from getting too near the water or from scattering. All the while, parent terns flew back and forth from the sea with shrimp or minnows in their bills, each bird apparently seeking a specific chick before delivering the catch. From time to time a feeding parent would settle down beside the column and one of the chaperones would take off to the sea.

Bluebirds and orchard orioles made a pretty picture in the oaks as Connie and Jack sat at breakfast and a solitary sandpiper dipped in the edge of a puddle. It was August 5 in Rockport but a day later on the other side of the Pacific, where an atom bomb was dropped on Hiroshima, ushering in the nuclear age and ending the war. Connie sat most of the day with Jack, listening to radio broadcasts. They did not feel like celebrating then or soon after, when the peace treaty was signed; they simply felt a great sense of relief and hoped never to experience another war.

They did feel like celebrating, though, when word came from Dick Grossenheider, so long a prisoner of war but alive and well and on his way to Rockport. He arrived in September, a week after another major hurricane had made landfall near Rockport, leaving in its wake a multitude of birds, nearly two hundred anhingas, whimbrels, vermilion flycatchers, and thousands of purple martins going south.

Dick gloried in the birds but his real objective was to see the Hagars again and catch up on their doings. He mourned for Fuzzy but predicted that Patch would make a worthy successor. Patch adored Dick, a playmate who ran and romped with him and waged tugs-of-war with him over old shoes.

The fall migration was prolonged, and in the next month Connie saw more fall warblers, hawks, and brown thrashers than ever before at that season. But most intriguing to her were the least grebes breeding so late in the year. She had been alerted by the male bird, swimming around a clump of reeds out in Moore's Pool. Every day she saw him there, circling the reeds and piping an odd little whistle. The pool was too deep to wade, but she believed the mass of gunk inside the cattails supported a nest, and she was sure when one day she saw a second grebe slide off the mass, feed around a while, and return to it. On October 13 both adults were towing a little flotilla of dark and downy grebelets. A Couch's kingbird hawked from the willows.

At home Connie found Jack studying the guest register. "Nobody's coming for a few days" he said. "Why don't we go somewhere?" It was wonderful. They had been tied down forever, it seemed, by guests and war restrictions; for four years neither of them had spent more than one night away from Rockport Cottages. They chose the Hill Country, and Mountain Home, a place that was little more than a name, and for four delicious days they did nothing but ramble aimlessly. Connie loved every Carolina chickadee she saw, and she saw many. Rockport had nearly everything, but no chickadees. They went home refreshed, and early the next morning she was at Moore's Pool to check on the least grebes. An adult swam about with two tiny hitchhikers on her back, but as the car stopped, the bird slowly submerged, and the chicks slid off. The water was clear, and through binoculars the chicks could be seen swimming inches below the surface.

Jack was waiting for her to return with the car so he could do his errands. Patch went with him, and Connie went to the piano to practice for Sunday's service. Pausing to turn a page, she heard a knock on the office door and hurried to it, hoping she had not impolitely played on while someone stood there.

A big man, broad-shouldered, gray-haired, and gentle-faced, wearing loose-fitting outdoor clothes peered at her through rimless spectacles. "Good morning," he said in a pleasantly deep, drawling voice. "You're Mrs. Hagar, I'm sure, and I have been wanting to meet you for a long time. I am Roy Bedichek." Connie beamed, extending her hand. He was a friend of the J. Frank Dobies about whom she had heard much, an unashamed nature worshiper who cared about wild things, flora and fauna.

"Dr. Bedichek, I am delighted, for I have been wanting to meet you, too." She led him into the living room and inquired about their mutual friends, but soon the conversation turned to birds and what she had been seeing lately. Any birds of interest?

"They are all interesting to me," she assured him, "but most interesting right now are Mexican grebes with young just out of the nest." Reciting the progress of the little family, she saw eagerness tinged with polite skepticism in his face.

"Mexican grebes," he intoned slowly. "I've never seen one. Think you could show them to me?"

"Let's go," she invited, hearing Jack drive in. She introduced her husband, who recognized from her manner that this man was a valued new acquaintance.

Bedichek gazed at the grebes through his glasses a long time before leaving the car, fearing to disturb them. Then he slipped out and leaned over the fence for closer views, half disbelieving what he saw; it was just too easy, getting a bird like this that he had long wished for. Not just a bird, either, but a whole family. He studied the nest, too. Other birds were around, but he looked only at the grebes.

"Great. Simply great," he rumbled happily, getting in the car and adding, "Think Mr. Hagar would put me up for the night? I want to stay over and see what else is going on in this enchanted country."

The tide was low that afternoon, and the new friends walked far on the wet sand to get closer to birds. The bay was still, mirroring a pale blue heaven and flocks of avocets resting in the shallow edges, half of them standing on one leg with heads tucked back over their shoulders. Marbled godwits, dowitchers, yellowlegs, and other sandpipers woke from siestas and began probing for hidden marine life. At Fulton Beach, Franklin's gulls, behaving like laughing gulls, swarmed around the fish house. A small bird stepped along the water's edge on yellowish feet and legs. Bedichek sat up alertly. "What's that?" he asked. Piping plover. A smile as wide as his face could accommodate appeared. "Is it, now?" he drawled happily, wiping his glasses with a wrinkled handkerchief. "That's another new one for me."

A few hummingbirds lingered at the Cove, where a shock was in store for Connie. A fifty-foot lot, from bay to marsh, had been scraped clean and stakes driven in the outline of a small house. She wanted to cry. One of the best tangles on the ridge was gone. Bedichek was thoroughly sympathetic and little consoled by four Bonaparte's gulls flying over. Arriving back at the Cottages, they heard the muted, jingling hissing of cedar waxwings. The setting sun gave the trimly tailored birds the look of burnished copper.

After a restaurant supper, Bedichek presented himself again at the door and in an oddly humble manner inquired if he might come in and talk to Mrs. Hagar a while.

"Why, Dr. Bedichek, I would be honored to talk to you any time." In the living room again he stood for some moments fingering the array of seashells on the bookcases, then blurted sadly, "I want to make a confession. I hope you will take it the way I mean it."

"Of course. But you need not tell me anything you don't want to." He wanted to.

"You see," (he seemed to be fumbling for the right words), "I have heard people in Austin talk about you, and the people in the Valley, and all, all the wonderful discoveries you make. And I have said 'That woman is a faker. Nobody is as good as people say she is.'" That woman was laughing, but he went on confessing. "To tell you the truth, I came down here to prove it. Now I am ashamed."

"Dr. Bedichek, you are not the first to doubt me. This has been going on ten years. I am used to having to produce proof for everything I report. You have been far kinder than some who doubted me."

At that the big man bristled indignantly. "Well, you just send them to me, now. Any time anyone questions your reports. I can tell them, and I will!"

Connie turned the conversation to the visitor himself, birds he had seen in Europe as a youth on a bicycle tour, other adventures. She was surprised and delighted that he had known George Finlay Simmons and had learned so much from the author of *Birds of the Austin Region*. Taking down her own old copy of it, she said she, too, had learned much from his book.

Rising to leave, he mentioned that Orion should be crossing the sky about then, and Connie suggested they go out the back

[149]

way for better visibility. Jack joined them, saying he was always willing to admire "that great Irish hunter."

Few people rose earlier than the Hagars, but this guest was one who did. He had made coffee and jotted down some impressions in his notebook by the time they were stirring.

Connie took him to the Hartman Ranch, detouring at his request to pay their respects to the venerable giant oak on Lamar Peninsula, believed by some to be the largest in the country, certainly the largest in the state. Geese had arrived on the ranch; Bedichek estimated ten thousand—Canadas, snows, blues, and white-fronts.

Bidding farewell, Bedichek declared himself forever in their debt and wondered what he could do for Mrs. Hagar in return. "That's easy," she replied promptly. "I have never seen your Austin specialty, the golden-cheeked warbler, and I very much want to see it."

"Well, that's sure 'nuff easy," he boomed cordially. "That's it. You come to Austin any time between March and August and we will find golden-cheeks, plenty of them. We'll get Old Tawm, too, to go along." Old Tawm, she learned, was Dr. Thomas P. Harrison, Jr., professor and doyen of the English department at the University of Texas, distinguished scholar, and devoted naturalist.

Connie saw him off and went to her desk. She had a piece to write for the *Pilot*, a thank-you letter to her community for the big free-standing sign out in Little Bay proclaiming the CONNIE HAGAR WILDLIFE SANCTUARY, so designated by legislative act at the request of appreciative fellow citizens.

Other visitors enjoyed a December redstart traveling with orange-crowned warblers, hooded mergansers, a small flight of mountain bluebirds, far out of their range, and the first bronzed cowbird for Connie at home.

The Nature Calendar for January 2, 1946, listed only one bird—little gull. Connie was at the beach very early to see again the winter ballet of the black skimmers. Patch nosed a small crab, and a small bird flew past her, over him, and out to sea. Certainly a gull, but it was so small, with such dark wings and back. At home she pored over the books: Peterson's, as well as

[150]

Bent's *Life Histories* series. Her bird fitted descriptions of the immature little gull, a rare European straggler to the East Coast. But in Rockport, Texas? She decided she had not seen enough to defend the sighting, though she was sure of it in her own mind. She would say nothing about it.

Dr. Dillon Ripley of Yale stopped by for a day in early March and two weeks later returned for a longer stay. He was most interested in Inca and ground-doves but could not ignore fifty golden-plovers at Nine-Mile Point and Bonaparte's gulls on the bayfront. Ripley also was intrigued by waves of blue-gray gnatcatchers. "This I have heard Griscom talk about but could not take it in," he said. "By the time they reach us they are singles or in pairs, and we assumed they migrated singly. But you *do* have them in bunches," he added wonderingly. How long did such movements last? All through March, becoming scarcer in April, Connie told him. "Think of that," Ripley said, shaking his head.

Another early March visitor was Lieut. Fred M. Packard from Corpus Christi Naval Air Station. He had studied with Griscom at Harvard and gone on to the National Parks Association before joining the Navy. He especially wished to see the bald eagles nesting near Tivoli but was even more gratified by Sprague's pipits and cinnamon teal.

Packard returned whenever his duties permitted, often sharing outings with other guests: the Fred Stearnses of Toledo; the Gills, who had now moved to the Valley and lived in Harlingen; the Charles Hamiltons; as well as George Williams and others from Houston. Another lazuli bunting was found "in the same old weed patch where I've always seen it," Connie said, and bobolinks mingled with dickcissels on the Rincon, "the only place I ever see them, and not often at that." Baird's sandpipers were identified, another green-tailed towhee, and another first for the hostess—hepatic tanager.

A huge hawk migration, mostly broadwings, attended by many anhingas, preceded a sharp norther in late April and was followed by an electrical storm that brought down thousands of songbirds. People telephoned from all over the peninsula saying they had yards full of "Mexican canaries." A teacher said her schoolroom was invaded by them. Thrushes, catbirds, buntings, orioles, and flycatchers were listed plus eleven species of warblers, including cerulean and golden-winged. The storm also killed many birds, whose bodies were brought to Mrs. Hagar to prepare as specimens for her bird talks.

One evening when the party was gathered on the Hagar steps comparing their day's lists, Packard asked why Connie had never published a checklist of birds in her territory. She raised both hands in horror. "Too much work! Too much paperwork. I'd rather be outdoors, or indoors studying the paperwork of somebody else who knows more than I. Besides, I can't type."

Joe Heiser chimed in, endorsing the idea, as did others. Guy had also proposed a checklist, saying, "It's all in your head. Just get it on paper." Her answer had been the same, but Packard was insistent.

"You give me the information, and I'll do the typing. I will do all the work. You just provide me with the records." When he left that night, he carried a stack of her Nature Calendars.

Three weeks later Packard sent her a preliminary list for appraisal and enclosed a letter to Roger Tory Peterson, if she approved, for her to send him. He thought Peterson would benefit from knowing about western species that came her way, and through him, they could help other birders visiting her territory.

He also reported seeing an unmistakable California gull and was sending a note on it to the *Auk*. His letter concluded: "For a person working entirely alone, these are the most amazing series of records I ever saw. They will develop into a valuable article."

Connie did not regard writing letters as "paperwork." Her correspondence grew as friends, acquaintances, and strangers wrote for help, to thank her, to tell about their birds, or simply to say they had read about her and thought what she was doing was wonderful.

"Dear Jade," began a long letter from Locke Mackenzie. He had, after all, resumed his practice in New York City but had arranged for more time on his own. His "no. 3 son," Michael, was showing interest in birds and going with him on field trips. Also, he was recommending Rockport to birding friends and at a meeting of the Linnaean Society had told Eleanor A. King, editor of *Audubon*, that the magazine should do a profile on Connie, which, he had also told her, would not be complete without a full face of Jack.

To his wife's response Jack appended: "Have Mrs. King warn me in advance so I can have Pure Nuts sober for the interview."

Packard was with her often through the summer, asking questions as they watched the buildup of wood storks through July and August and the start of fall migration. His questions often concerned numbers for only now and then did the Nature Calendar give numbers of given species, nor did it always show that birds seen were on a trip outside the areas she covered daily.

The answers came easily. Connie simply glanced at the date in the Calendar, scanned the list, and like a crystal gazer in reverse, looked back to that day and described it in detail, recalling exact numbers if few birds were involved, estimating larger numbers. Packard was astonished by her memory. "A lifelong habit, inherited from both parents," she laughingly explained. She could still recite long poems she had memorized years before.

"How about these Derby flycatchers?" That was Live Oak County. "And Say's phoebe?" Kleberg County, though stray individuals of both species came to Aransas County occasionally. After much debate they decided to include in the checklist all the seven counties she had closely observed since coming to the coast, although she no longer made the weekly extended trips. She did, of course visit other counties on speaking engagements and always observed birds en route. Meanwhile, she had added another new bird to her own and the area list—a swallow-tailed kite on the Market Loop June 27.

Packard was released from the Navy in late August. "Just in time," he said happily, "to get to the AOU meeting in Urbana, Illinois," then on home to Passaic, New Jersey.

The checklist would go on, however. He wrote from Urbana, where he was enjoying conversations with other birders. "Charming" Dr. Oberholser wanted a copy of the lists. "Only four days and the Navy seems far behind me, but Rockport seems very close and warm in my heart," he wrote. "I can't tell you how much knowing you and working with you meant to me while in Texas. You made me feel that Texas is a home away from home, and I loved it. . . . Professor Williams has written corroborating some of our facts that drew screams from Griscom; notably the early eastern phoebes, the brush-inhabiting Le Conte's sparrows, the many whimbrels, and others."

Packard wrote again from Passaic, having stopped at the Field Museum in Chicago and found a number of specimens that had been taken at Corpus Christi in early years, including a few not on the checklist but which could now be included. Dr. Emmet Blake sent his regards, and "would the Hagars please remember Fred to Patch with a kiss on the nose."

Chapter 9

The year 1947 would be one of headlines for Connie and her birds and for Rockport, but it began with severe cold in January, the temperature dropping to twenty-three degrees. The landscape was frosted with ice, and there came unusually large flocks of Brewer's blackbirds, starlings, and snipes. One day Connie counted two hundred common snipes feeding on the grounds of the Cottages. A sharp-shinned hawk fed on the blackbirds. A solitary vireo and a vermilion flycatcher occupied the same oak—a pretty combination in the winter scene.

The year also introduced more birders from afar, many of whom would become lifelong friends of the Hagars. So many came in February that Jack had to find places for the overflow in other Rockport motels. There was, however, a cottage reserved for Jack and Edith Stevens of Plainfield, New Jersey. They were new to birds, they hastened to explain. Stevens's physician had advised him to take up a regular outdoor recreation; golf did not appeal to him, and his wife had hit upon birdwatching—their friends in the Audubon Society seemed to enjoy it so much. The same friends had sent them to Rockport. They were eager and quick to learn, and to Connie, a joy to teach. Jack had studied law at Harvard then gone into the family textile business, which had been founded by his grandfather in 1813, and he was now president of the company. He embraced his new avocation with the same ardor that he gave his successful business, and as Connie had predicted, both Jack and Edith became experts. Thereafter, their travels all over the continent and foreign lands were focused on birds. Jack would also become a director on the National Audubon Society board, and for more than twenty years their travels would always include a week or two at Rockport in April for the spring migration.

The Cottages again overflowed in April, but Connie gladly helped those who had to stay elsewhere. A series of cold fronts "pushed everything down so everybody could see," the Nature Calendar said of the thousands of dickcissels, big migrations of Franklin's gulls, shorebirds, chuck-will's-widows calling through the nights, and sometimes a whip-poor-will. The usual waves of warblers included the Connecticut, cerulean, prothonotary, blackpoll, mourning, and one Cape May at the Cove.

Harold Mayfield sent the May issue of the Toledo Naturalists Association's newsletter containing his article "Mid-Winter on the Texas Coast," based on his January visit. It was a long piece, describing the area in detail, beginning, "An incongruous sight as I stepped off the plane in Corpus Christi was seeing a flock of starlings fly up into a palm tree."

Observing shorebirds there, he explained, was facilitated by

> The shallow waters [that] reach back into the land through innumerable estuaries. There is no lunar tide, but a change of wind sweeps the water back as it does on our own Lake Erie shore, revealing vast mudflats. However, the shell-built subsoil is so firm one may walk confidently across a sea of mud that he would hesitate to venture upon in Ohio. . . . The water's edges are lined with diving birds and waders. The whole heron tribe struts the shallows only a few yards from human promenaders on the village street . . . almost every piling has its brown pelican or cormorant . . . raptors are like those we have in Ohio but incomparably more abundant. . . . This section gains interest in that here is a mingling of eastern and western species wintering together but migrating to summer territories widely separate.
>
> It is significant and typical that the interesting variety of birds is not the only factor attracting nature students to Rockport. Probably the most important single factor is the presence of Mrs. Connie Hagar, who is not only remarkably well informed about birds, flowers, marine life, and other

natural features of the locality but who is a gracious hostess interested in advising visitors, scientists, and amateurs alike.

Dr. Robert Lockwood, radiologist at an Army hospital in Alexandria, Louisiana, wrote for mid-May reservations. He explained that he had persuaded his bride-to-be that they should have a birdwatching honeymoon, she having adopted his hobby. His parents' friend, Carl Buchheister of National Audubon, whom he had consulted for the trip, had advised, "Go to Rockport, Texas, and stay with the Hagars."

The doctor would fly to Philadelphia, claim his bride, fly back to Houston with her, and drive on down. He hoped, too, that the accommodations would be air-conditioned. Jack hooted. What kind of birders were these? But, they were honeymooners, so they should have no. 2, with the family furniture. He confirmed, explaining that the cottage was "air-conditioned by nature."

Their first glimpse of the coastline convinced the honeymooners they had chosen well. At the foot of the Copano Bay causeway Lockwood hit the brakes and pulled off; two tall, immaculately black-and-white birds stepped lightly on the crushed shell on fantastically long red legs. Black-necked stilts! Gloating, he started the motor—and turned it off. A large hawk flew in front of them and perched on the dead branch of a tree. White head, black crown, rosy face—caracara. Two new birds already.

Slowly they drove into town, detouring to make sure that the onion-domed courthouse was real and not a mirage. Hearing their car, Jack was on the steps when it stopped. Any qualms he might have had about air-conditioning evaporated at the sight of the beaming faces of the dark-haired young man and the fair-haired girl. Lockwood introduced himself and turned to his wife, but Jack, possessed by the imp that made him tease anyone he liked, beat him to the draw. He opened the door for the girl, shouting "You are Maggie-off-the-Pickle-Boat, I know." She laughed at the nickname taken from an old sailor chanty, and Ann Lockwood was always Maggie-off-the-Pickle-Boat to Jack Hagar.

[157]

Helping with the luggage, he took them inside and addressed Dr. Lockwood, "You turn on the air-conditioning this way," and then he opened the windows to let in a stream of fresh, cool air.

"Got it," the guest grinned, guessing rightly that he would never be let off that hook. Without fail, whenever the Lockwoods came thereafter, Jack would inquire at least once if the air-conditioning was working.

Connie, too, took to the young couple at once. Ann had to learn the common birds, Bob wanted more on shorebirds, but both would be content with "just birds." They were out every day, often all day. Wilson's phalaropes flocked in wet meadows, acting like other sandpipers, and only rarely removed themselves to ponds to perform their typical spinning capers. Many pectorals, a few stilt sandpipers, yellowlegs, and ibises were in the same wet meadow. White ibises with their bright red sickle bills delighted them, and both they and the white-faced were new to Bob. Green-backed herons nested at the Tules; clouds of black terns swept along the shoreline. Cedar waxwings lined up on a utility wire, all facing the same way, while eastern kingbirds occupied other utility lines.

Ann loved the roadrunners galloping drunkenly beside the road and the roseate spoonbills—they were easy, but all those sandpipers confused her. Bob asked for oystercatchers and other species and was directed to specific habitats. He was "utterly astounded" that Connie knew exactly where to go for whatever he sought.

The Lockwoods spent many evenings outdoors with the Hagars listening to cicadas and watching nighthawks hawk around streetlights. He had grown up on the campus of Haverford College, where his father was librarian and professor of Romance languages and where both parents had taught him about the wildlife around them.

"Haverford College" rang a bell in Connie's head. She went to her bookshelves and found a slim volume published in 1912: *The Birds of Texas*, an annotated checklist by John K. Strecker, Jr., curator of Baylor University Museum at Waco. Embossed on the flyleaf was "Haverford College Library."

[158]

Bob examined it curiously. "An extra volume Dad disposed of in later years," he speculated.

"Well, I'm glad he did," Connie said. "It was out of print and I wanted it. I found it at a rare book dealer's."

She forsook her guests one morning to deck herself in a sheer frock, a wisp of hat, and high heels to drive to Corpus Christi to tell the assembly of Texas Garden Club ladies about "Coastal Fauna." She carried a basket of bird skins.

Wolf whistles from Lockwood, lounging on the steps of no. 2, were echoed by Jack standing by the idling blue Packard as she tripped lightly out the door. Patch half rose from the floor, looked at her feet, and dropped back to rest; he didn't go when she wore high heels. Ann came out to admire. "You look like a Dresden doll," she declared.

"Just hope I don't cuss a line and ruin everything," the doll chuckled as she took the wheel.

The luncheon tables on the Plaza Hotel's deck were decorated with seashells of many kinds arranged among draped fishnets and beach flora: sea oats, goat's-foot morning glory, and others. Penny Peckenpaugh, housewife, botanist, garden editor of the *Corpus Christi Times*, and longtime friend of the speaker, introduced her. Connie pushed the microphone aside; she spoke clearly and from long practice as a soloist could adjust her voice to reach the corners of the hall. Though she could be heard, she could not be seen by all; standing as tall as she could, her head was barely above those seated in the audience, but with the bird skins mounted on little sticks everyone could see what she was talking about. She spoke without notes and with only a vague outline in her mind, preferring to say what came to her on the occasion. Her audience listened in amazed and eager silence. Finishing with the birds, it occurred to her to say something about the shells on the tables. From the head table she moved out among them, lifting specimens here and there, relating lore about each. She tried to stop more than once, but the fascinated listeners kept her talking, how about this one, that one, and others?

On the final day of the garden club convention, a motion was passed unanimously that the federation should have a state bird chairman, who should be, of course, Mrs. Hagar. She did not want the job; she had given many years to club work and wanted no more of it, although she did pay dues and give programs for several organizations. The Corpus Christi Garden Club, among others, had made her an honorary member rather than give her up. But the federation insisted; the board had decided to try this year for national honors and saw in Connie Hagar one chance, at least, of a trophy. The president, Magnolia Green, clinched the matter with the plea, "This is for Texas, Connie." She consented.

Soon she realized this was a good thing. Garden clubs stood for parks, preservation of natural areas, highway beautification, and conservation of wildlife and natural resources—all the things that mattered to her. And the clubs had influence. Legislators might ignore the voices of birdwatchers calling for protection of nesting areas, but few would dare flout the united voices of rose growers. She bought a scrapbook and began clipping her "press." She outlined programs to distribute to the clubs, articles about birds, and more speeches. Press notices were plentiful. Her talk to the Southwest Writers Conference at Corpus Christi in June was quoted in the *Caller*. When John Baker, president, and board members of National Audubon came to inspect the sanctuaries, the newspapers sent a reporter along and produced a Sunday spread with photographs under the headline "Rich Heritage of Bird Life Found on Gulf." On Baker's advice, reporter Johnny Brown quoted Mrs. Hagar for his story.

Reporter Bess Stephenson and a photographer from the *Fort Worth Star-Telegram* accompanied Hamilton Hittson and his party from the city's Forest Park Zoo on a collecting trip. Bess Stephenson found Mrs. Hagar "the one to ask if you want to know anything about birds" and the most interesting feature of the expedition. She wrote an ample background on the "bird woman" and described the island rookeries and their inhabitants, saying "Mrs. Hagar knows exactly where to look and on which island for whatever bird is sought."

From her desk in the bedroom, Connie was puzzled by a sad little avian drama she could not explain: A female cardinal repeatedly tried to feed nestling mockingbirds and repeatedly was driven away by the annoyed parents. It took two days to discourage her.

For the fall issue of the *Lone Star Gardener*, the federation's magazine, she wrote a long article suggesting club activities related to birds, which concluded: "Nothing is more fitting than that the women of Texas Garden Clubs should work with and for preservation of our birds, for what a sad spot a garden would be without their bright presence. . . . As your bird chairman I am willing to help in any way I can."

Requests for help poured in, together with more requests for personal appearances than she could possibly accept.

The crown jewel among press clippings was the article "Lady with Binoculars," which appeared in the July, 1947, issue of *Audubon* and which was written by the editor, Eleanor Anthony King.

Eleanor King had been making the rounds with Connie in February, taking notes, studying birds, and collecting photographs, including some of Patch. Her story ran several pages, telling of the subject's childhood and the influence of her parents, about Jack, their daily routine, and the Nature Calendar. "Few amateurs," the story continued, "have upset as many preconceived notions about migration routes, added as many species to a state list, or entertained as many ornithologists as Connie Hagar. . . . She is not the khaki and boots breezy type but a tiny 93-pound package, dainty and delicate as a sandpiper, fastidiously dressed in color schemes carefully chosen down to the earrings. . . . She dances Put-Your-Little Foot, sings, plays piano, discourses eloquently on literature, quotes poetry, collects shells and antique glass."

Distinguished visitors were named, and most had been separately interviewed—Oberholser, Emerson, Grossenheider, and Griscom, who was quoted: "I have never been afield with anyone who knew a territory and its possibilities better. The evening before a trip Connie predicts about what the day's list will be, and what species of interest to the visitor she can produce. Things turn out just about that way." George Williams was cited as one who, Connie had told her, "pulled me out of a number of pits I had fallen into."

The *Audubon* article inspired several big city newspapers in Texas to obtain and publish effusive stories about the achievements of a native daughter. The *Rockport Pilot* pulled out all the stops for her on the front page of the July 24 issue, and the *Corsicana Sun* no less lovingly and lavishly ran columns about the famous birdwatcher, reminding readers that she was a Neblett of Corsicana and still their own.

Jack walked on air, he was so inflated with pride. Connie was gratified mainly because the publicity should make more people aware of what Texas had to offer and would encourage bird conservation.

A telephone call from the Gammells in North Dakota, who had been with Connie again in the spring, was the first of a flood of calls and congratulatory letters about the *Audubon* story; they came from friends and from strangers all over the country.

One stranger was Rebecca Mallory of New York City, who wrote, "As a Sealy from Galveston, I am always particularly proud of any achievement by one of my own sex in Texas . . . I miss the Gulf breezes, the prairie stretches, and the great spreading live oaks. . . . I started the National Tribute Grove for Redwoods and have often discussed with John Baker the bird sanctuaries in Texas."

From Toledo, Fred Stearns said, "Gosh, I wish we were with you now." His wife was pleased that Patch was included; Dillon Ripley expressed the same sentiment. Mrs. Theron Wasson from Illinois said, "Well do I remember that night I phoned from Corpus Christi and you identified those birds in winter plumage as fast as I could describe them." The story made Mrs. J. L. Hooks in Beaumont "want to hit the road for Rockport. After all these years you have changed so little. I have thought many times of you and your sister and wished we could have another visit together."

From Schenectady Sonney offered his compliments in a left-handed way, as younger brothers are wont to do: "My Sweet Sister: Why didn't you warn us about the *Audubon* article? A vice president brought it to my office and said, 'Until now I thought you were a big shot at General Electric but after reading this I decided that gal Connie is really something and you just work here.'"

Letters kept pouring in for weeks. And Connie Hagar thanked every single one who wrote, friend and stranger alike. Also, she periodically apprised Eleanor King of the response to her story, realizing that few of the people who wrote to her would also thank the author.

The summer continued hot; shallow pools dried up, and birds typical of arid habitats increased in numbers—golden-fronted woodpeckers, Harris' hawks, caracaras, pyrrhuloxias, and others.

Construction began on a new marine laboratory beside the yacht basin for the Texas Game and Fish Commission, and the general contractor, W. D. Anderson of Austin, brought his wife Agatha to live with him at Rockport Cottages for the duration of the project. A congenial couple with many interests, they wanted to learn about birds but felt too ignorant to consult one so knowledgeable as Mrs. Hagar. So they bought binoculars and a field guide and quietly began naming species on the grounds.

Discovering their activities, Connie took them in hand. With Connie as their teacher, Bill and Agatha proved to be bright students. For nearly a year she often had one or both with her on her rounds. Georgie Belle Getzendaner, wife of another engineer then in Rockport, went along frequently. On September 3 they found a fall migration of buff-breasted sandpipers on Rattlesnake Point. This species had not often been seen in fall.

Two hurricanes threatened that month, and one came near enough to drop some rain, but the drought—and the heat—continued. On September 20 the community sweltered under 102 degrees, but two days later the first norther shivered the shirt-sleeved population. It brought a vast migration of swallows, hawks, and both eastern and western kingbirds.

The swallows, however, were in reverse migration—flying northeast. With Agatha and Georgie Belle, Connie went afield to see how widespread this movement was. It was the same everywhere, thousands of swallows and some hawks moving back over the paths they had traversed in recent weeks. The north wind blew two days, shifting to the northwest, and the reverse migration held throughout. When it abated, birds resumed their normal flight patterns.

Driving to Victoria for a garden club talk, Connie passed

[163]

under thousands more swallows, as well as geese, in one great formation after another. Cooper's and sharp-shinned hawks occupied tall trees by the Guadalupe River.

The Victoria meeting initiated a long schedule of personal appearances the state bird chairman would make in the next nine months. One trip took her to San Antonio, where Dr. Atkinson pronounced her eyes in good condition. "Just keep up the beer," he said.

That fall the U.S. Fish and Wildlife Service and National Audubon together undertook a three-year research program on whooping cranes to be done by Robert Porter Allen. Soon after settling on Aransas Refuge, Allen brought his family to meet the Hagars, who quickly extended to them the affection they felt for Bob. Evelyn Allen, they learned, was a fine pianist who had made her debut at Carnegie Hall and could have had a concert career but chose to share her husband's career instead. Music was a lasting bond between her and Connie. She was elated at the prospect of having Bob Allen nearby for three whole winters, not only for his great knowledge but also for his warm personality. His friendliness was offered to anyone she took to the refuge, including Ann and Bob Lockwood, who were awed to think of birding with Robert Porter Allen but seized the opportunity gladly.

House wrens in unprecedented numbers migrated to the peninsula, and one afternoon on Fulton Beach a California gull was conspicuous among the herring gulls. Connie was now "up with Fred Packard," she gloated. Shortly thereafter in Galveston, George Williams reported seeing a California gull, always rare on the Gulf Coast.

Like the Cove, Fulton Beach was becoming more and more attractive for summer and permanent homes. Fulton Beach owners, however, cleared only the site necessary for houses, leaving most of the leaning oaks intact. Drilling for oil on the peninsula was also destroying some favored habitats, but roads built by the oil companies opened areas not previously penetrated by Connie, and she was welcome to use the roads.

One November morning at the Cove she was astonished to see feathers covering the remaining brush thicket at the outer tip of the sandspit; feathers everywhere, as if someone had emptied a down pillow there. She wondered if many birds could have molted there. She went back that afternoon and was even more mystified to find the feathers gone. Patch at her heels, she walked around the spit and found something new. On the thorny outermost fork of a granjeno bush was a bundle of leaves and grasses and feathers! Mostly feathers, sticking out all over it, "looking like the wrath of God," she thought. Not at all like the neat verdin nests she knew, but surely a verdin's winter retreat. Cactus wrens, too, provided themselves with warm shelters against cold winter nights, but this was too small for a cactus wren. Urn-shaped, it lay horizontally on the branch, the neck facing her, and under a tiny awning of feathers was a doorway no bigger than a nickel. All this had been put together in one day by one small bird.

The owner was nowhere in sight; perhaps it would not return until bedtime. The wail of sirens interrupted Connie's inspection. Looking north, she saw great billows of black smoke in the direction of Copano Village. Whistling for Patch, she hurried home; Jack would want the car to go to the fire.

Fire trucks from Aransas Pass screamed past her on the highway. This was no ordinary brushfire, Jack told her. Brush was burning all across the upper end of the peninsula. Men from three communities were fighting it, but the woods were bone dry, and the wind was scattering firebrands to start new blazes. The only water in the area came from wells, and there was little the firefighters could do except beat the burning weeds with sacks dipped in water brought in barrels from town, where water pressure was low, at that. Scattered dwellings were already lost. Jack went downtown to help with food and drink for the firefighters.

At dusk a red glow extended all across the northern horizon; the wind had died down, but the fire raged on. Before bedtime, Connie borrowed Jack's flashlight and drove back to the Cove. With the headlights beamed on the granjeno bush, she walked over to it, eyes on the nest, unmindful of where she put her feet. She found herself sprawled face down in the weeds. "Damn. Should have looked." She just hoped she had not frightened the bird—if it was at home.

It was at home. Aiming the flashlight from under her chin,

she peered into the tiny hole and straight into two jetlike little eyes. In the dark she smiled, contented. The verdin did not move.

By morning the fire had jumped Highway 35 and invaded Fulton. Efforts were now aimed at saving threatened homes. It was Sunday, and Connie played as usual for church services, where the congregation included few men, only old ones. That afternoon the fire was controlled and soon extinguished; a light north wind had helped turn the tide.

Monday, Darrell Ring came to take Connie to the Valley. She gave a program at Alamo for the Valley Federated Garden Club then remained several days to bird with Lonnie Ring, Terry and Maurine Gill, and Irby and Anna May Davis. They covered the Upper Valley from roads lined with tall palms marching away to the horizon in rigid, straight rows. Later they did the Lower Valley all the way to the white Gulf beaches of Boca Chica. At Port Isabel five black-shouldered kites perched on utility towers. Connie saw her first Botteri's sparrows and renewed acquaintance with Altamira and hooded orioles, great kiskadees, chachalacas, green jays, and others.

The Gills brought her home and stayed over to dine Sunday on a goose Jack had shot. It had first been carefully measured for Dr. Oberholser.

The verdin's nest was the centerpiece of Guy Emerson's visit in December—five days in Rockport, a vacation he had long promised himself. In late afternoons they drove to the Cove and waited for the little bird to retire. It would perch, preen, perhaps feed around, then suddenly at dusk shoot like a bullet straight into the small entrance. "Must have good brakes," Guy opined.

Mountain plovers were on the Bayside prairies; there was also a good raptor show, including a merlin. Geese gathered at the Hartman Ranch, pyrrhuloxias in the brush, sandhill cranes in the pastures. Guy's last day they spent on Aransas Refuge with Bob Allen and Julian Howard, refuge manager. Of the six pairs of whooping cranes that had returned from their still unknown breeding range in the Northwest Territories, each with one offspring—a heartening and exceptional crop—they saw four, plus six other adults. Bob Allen knew the families by sight, their movements, and the territories they defended.

The winter remained dry and turned cold around Christmas. Among holiday guests was Dr. Thomas Harrison, the "Old Tawm" whom Bedichek had promised to bring but who had decided not to wait and to come on his own instead. He wanted a vermilion flycatcher, but the bright fireball that had haunted the yard for a month had departed. Connie took him to other likely places—no vermilion. He was, however, charmed by black skimmers skimming the shoreline, their grotesque red bills barely touching the water. They were new to Harrison.

Black-throated sparrows arrived the next day, a rare treat for Connie, and a short-eared owl, but Harrison had to leave minus his most wanted bird. "Never mind," he said. "It's a good excuse to come back."

The bird was very much in evidence a few days later for Mary Belle Keefer and Lena McBee, "deans" of the El Paso bird club. On a clear, warm Christmas afternoon they and all other Hagar guests piled into cars to visit the geese and sandhill cranes on the Hartman Ranch.

The year 1948 would be another of landmark events, the first coming very early with a visit from Roger Tory Peterson himself. He wrote from his home in Glen Echo, Maryland, the day after Christmas, saying he was to give an Audubon Screen Tour in Corpus Christi on January 2 and could have two days with her and Bob Allen before his next show in Houston. He would arrive on the train at 5:00 A.M., go to the Plaza Hotel, and then have the afternoon free. He was "looking forward to seeing you at last, also the Sprague's pipits and the whooping cranes."

Bill and Agatha Anderson took Connie to the Plaza Hotel early that afternoon; the Allens were already there. It was more of a reunion than an introduction. Towering a foot above her, Peterson took both Connie's hands in his, declaring the occasion one he had long anticipated. Connie told him, as she would tell many others later, that it was "one of the greatest thrills of my life."

They had much to talk about while driving along the shoreline that afternoon and at dinner with Frances Naismith, president of the local Audubon Society, and her husband Jim. The conversation never strayed from birds, and Jim, a civil engineer, having little to contribute, listened with amused interest. Next day he told his associates that "birdwatchers are the most single-minded people in the world."

Connie sat entranced that evening as Roger narrated his film, *The Mystery of Migration*, to his audience in Wynn Seale Junior High School's auditorium, and she was tempted to stand and cheer when he asserted, "You on the Gulf Coast are inclined to take the brown pelican casually, but those from the north coming here probably want to see this bird more than any other fowl." She wished all fishermen on the coast could have heard that.

The weather next day, a Saturday, was all Connie could wish for, warm and bright, when Peterson and Allen joined her for a day in her own territory. It was a fun time, intense birding with teasing and laughter and yarns of previous birding experiences. They examined verdin nests and glimpsed the small owner of one. Pine warblers and pyrrhuloxias were on Goose Island, a vermilion flycatcher at Moore's Pool, a host of ruby-crowned kinglets at Redbug Corner, "where they always congregate in winter," Connie said. Little Bay and the shore produced all the expected species.

But about the Sprague's pipits? They would find them, she assured. Cruising a back road, she eyed all likely prairies and spied a small flock of birds fly up, twittering, and settle again in short grass. They got out, searching the pasture with binoculars. There were mostly water pipits, but among them were some with finely streaked backs and pale, pinkish yellow legs. Roger was first to call them. "You do have Sprague's pipits!" he exclaimed. "So far east of previous records." Connie waited, whistling a low tune, as the men stalked the field for closer views.

Sunday was devoted to the whooping cranes, with Allen and Howard introducing Peterson to nearly all the thirty-one wintering on Aransas Refuge. The six families were seen on their widely separated territories, each pair chaperoning a youngster in nearly white plumage sprinkled with coppery juvenile feathers. Thoroughly satisfied, Peterson returned to his Screen Tours.

Summerlike weather continued. The gas heaters stood unlit even in evenings, and it remained very dry. To that Connie attributed increasing numbers of black-throated sparrows, which favored stands of Spanish dagger. Also coming were more verdins and a scattering of the western form of the rufous-sided towhee.

But on January 16 at 2:30 P.M. Jack called his wife to the front. All across the northern horizon and reaching high into the sky was a wall of dark, slate blue—a blue norther. In minutes it was upon them, and by nightfall the temperature had dropped twenty-five degrees and was still falling. Ducks and shorebirds by thousands fled to inland ponds.

The norther ushered in a prolonged winter, with intermittent freezes, thaws, and rain, lasting into March. The Lockwoods arrived with a hard freeze on January 26 that robbed Jack's lemon tree of blossoms and leaves. Taking the weather as a challenge, Ann and Bob went out and were rewarded by sparrows of many species flocking in brush and grass. One, they decided upon lengthy consultation, was a Bachman's sparrow. "But it's a piney woods bird," Connie marveled, "I've seen it only in the Big Thicket." Perhaps it had been forced out because its food was frozen; if that was the case, it would not likely stay long. Nor did it; temperatures rose to forty degrees, and the sparrow was gone by the end of the month.

"Miserable weather," was recorded for weeks, but February visitors had no complaints; the Wakemans and Websters came from Massachusetts, the Hickmans from Buffalo. George Lowery and Bob Newman stopped by en route to Mexico, and Arly McKay came to see the whoopers.

Perhaps because of the miserable weather, raptors were more abundant. A burrowing owl took a lease on an old wooden drum in a trashy corner of the idle shipyard; a short-eared owl roosted behind the Cottages; there were Cooper's and red-shouldered hawks, harriers and a merlin, Harlan's and Krider forms among the many red-tailed hawks. Harris', rough-legged, white-tailed hawks, and caracaras excited the Wakemans and Hickmans. Bald eagles had a big fuzzy white eaglet at Hog Bayou in a nest "big as a barn door." Sandhill cranes and cinnamon teal were more numerous. Least grebes, tufted titmice (black-crested), verdins, and red-shafted flickers were new to most guests, and the black-throated sparrows new to all.

On a bright, almost warm, mid-February day the first tree swallows went over, but a few days later the Nature Calendar recorded, "Locke and I got 73 species in the rain." A sunnier day allowed Mackenzie to photograph the king rail, whimbrel among long-billed curlews, yellow-crowned night-herons, fulvous whistling-ducks, and the burrowing owl.

Among the Hagars' guests were Bishop and Mrs. William Scarlett of Saint Louis, and on a day when Connie and her neighbor Lucille Little were involved in civic duties, the Episcopalian bishop and Mackenzie set out on a dawn-to-dark birding marathon, working the coast from Corpus Christi to Tivoli and listing two hundred species, including thirty-six they had not seen previously in the area. The Scarletts canceled other stops they had planned for Texas to remain and see the beginning of the spring migration: purple martins, a great buildup of dunlins and other shorebirds, yellow-throated warblers scratching at a frozen birdbath. The state was frozen over March 12, but sedge wrens flicked in and out of cattails on a ditch beside the airport—a single landing strip. Robins started north, and sandhill cranes gurgled farewells from high above.

Connie had vowed never to leave Rockport during spring migration, but the Violet Crown Garden Club of Austin had set her program on a date that would enable her to see the golden-cheeked warbler. Bedichek sent clippings from the *Austin American* announcing the tea in the ballroom of the Driskill Hotel at which Mrs. Jack Hagar, "the remarkable woman naturalist who had brought the coast of Texas into prominence," would speak on marine life and show specimens from her large collection of seashells. The article included a lengthy and laudatory biography of the "61-year-old, energetic 100-pounder standing less than five feet tall."

Bill Anderson appointed himself her chauffeur and guide. The tea was on Maundy Thursday, March 25. Again Connie's accounts of the lives of creatures that had inhabited the shells held the audience spellbound. Many specimens, she explained, were rare ones from the Pacific, sent to her by servicemen with whom she had corresponded during the war.

Roy Bedichek and Dr. Tom Harrison called for her early on Good Friday. They headed for the hills. "No use looking for golden-cheeks except in cedar brakes," Bedichek said. On a dirt road beside a steep ravine they stopped. A sweet song rang out: "Tweeeo-tweoo-TWEETsy." A flash of yellow and black bounced up to a juniper branch only a few feet from the car—a male in full breeding plumage, his cheeks golden yellow. Triumphantly, the men found four more singing males, all at close range for careful study. For a bonus they introduced her to the black-capped vireo and the canyon wrens, their songs echoing from cliffs. Both were new for her.

Driving home that afternoon, Anderson told her that some of the Austin ladies planned to come to Rockport and wished to know what would be proper to wear going out with Mrs. Hagar. "I told them to dress as if they were going shopping, if they wanted to dress like you." Jack greeted her with the news that "half of Houston is here for the Easter weekend."

Milton P. Trautman of Ohio State Museum at Columbus arrived in April with his wife and a wish list headed by buff-breasted sandpipers. Connie was "speechifying" that afternoon, but she gave them directions to the Bayside prairies off Farm Road 881, unpaved but navigable, and advised them to take the side roads. "There will be fifty buffbreasts in short grass near the old tin barn," she promised. It sounded too fantastic, but her assurance gave them hope. That evening they came to report.

"You were wrong, Mrs. Hagar," Trautman said with mock severity. "There were not fifty buffbreasts out there." Then his expression changed to exultation as he added, "There were hundreds!"

Fred Gipson, longtime reporter on the *Corpus Christi Caller*, sent her a note and a clipping. Fred had interviewed and photographed her several times during his tenure on the newspaper but now was living in Mason, his hometown, and working on his second novel, *Hound Dog Man*. He was also "free-lancing for ready cash," the note said, using material he had saved from the past. The clipping was a full-page spread from the Easter *Denver Post* with his story, "Conger Hagar Born with Curse of Curiosity." The photographs showed her with brown pelicans, at her traps, and banding blue jays. Jack, as always, displayed the page prominently and liked to tell ruefully that for the banding picture he had tried to help by holding the ladder and had nearly been scalped by an angry blue jay.

The Cruickshanks were a highlight of the season. Allan, on assignment for *Audubon*, recorded photographic impressions, and Helen put hers on paper, impressions that would go into a book about Texas, *A Paradise of Birds*. Their stay was brief, too brief for the Hagars, but they were exploring the entire state on this tour. However, Allan warned that they might "pester" them again. The Hagars hoped it would be often; everybody liked ebullient Allan and gracious Helen.

In late May Charles Schreiner of Kerrville and Connie poled a skiff across the narrow channel between the beach and Frandolig Island to tramp the low, sandy tract densely covered by brush. The brush was laden with hundreds of nests tended by long-legged waders. Nestling great blue herons were like comic-book characters with their oversize beaks and untamed mops of head feathers. Nests were so close together that they could—and did—jab at neighbors. Tricolored and black-crowned night-herons and great, reddish, and snowy egrets had nests in all stages from fresh eggs to near-fledging chicks.

That evening Connie pasted the final entries in her garden club scrapbook and decorated the cover with a cutout of hibiscus blossoms. Next morning Jack mailed it to Lexington, Kentucky, where the National Council of State Garden Clubs would convene the next week. She hoped it would win some recognition for Texas, and if it did, Magnolia Green would be there to accept.

Connie was out when Western Union telephoned from Corpus Christi, but Jack took the message: "Congratulations. Won special award for special achievement in ornithology. Love, Nolia Green."

Jack met her at the cattleguard as the car turned into the driveway. "You won, dahling! You won! You won!" he shouted.

The morning *Caller* had an Associated Press story from Lexington headlined "Texas Woman Given Award as Ornithologist." It reported that the white ribbon for special achievement was one of thirteen national awards presented at the meeting. It went on to boast that Texas now had one hundred nationally accredited flower-show judges.

Connie had still another year to serve as bird chairman and two more bird talks to make in June, one in the town of George West, where she and Georgie Belle Getzendaner were guests of Joan Caulfield, who had birded with them at Rockport and who gave them a visit with brush country birds; then on to New Braunfels.

Rookeries were still very active June 25 when she went again to Second Chain with Raymond and Louise Hill of Cleveland as guests of Pug Mullinax. Red-winged blackbirds had taken over a swale, and black vultures were nesting again. They were turning toward home when a large brown bird flew past the boat and ahead; it rose, twisted, and made a steep dive, leading with a huge and sharp yellow bill and revealing a white body and wing linings. It flew back over the boat. A brown booby! Connie knew of a record from Matagorda Bay twenty years before, the only record that she knew of for the area.

Bert spent an autumn month with her sister, witnessing a prolonged hummingbird migration in which broad-tails were prominent, though ruby-throats and black-chins predominated. Connie had begun to report this fall phenomenon to *Field Notes*, and others were now coming to see it.

Hunters swarmed in at the Thanksgiving opening of the season; hunt clubs were filled to overflowing with sportsmen. One of them at St. Charles Bay Club hardly qualified as such. He brought down a long-necked "snow goose," which proved to be a subadult tundra swan. Les Sontag, veteran hunting and fishing guide who in his youth had known the swan as a regular winter migrant to Rockport, heard the moaning whistle that followed the gun blast, the "swan song," they called it, and pointed his boat toward the falling bird.

"This is no snow goose," he asserted, retrieving it and noting the grayish neck feathers. "It is a young whistling swan and Mrs. Hagar will want to see it." He had not seen one himself in many years.

Four days later another wounded but doomed swan was brought to her, and a third was killed before the season ended.

[173]

Sadly, but with great interest Connie examined the illegal trophies and wished that hunters were required to know their birds before being allowed to use a gun. Properly regulated hunting, she agreed, had its place. Certain populations benefited from harvesting, but ignorance she could not forgive. Just think, she mourned, these magnificent creatures had after many years returned to an ancestral range only to die. Would she ever see one alive and free?

Fine weather through the year-end holidays drew many guests, among them Bedichek and his wife and "Old Tawm." Dr. Harrison saw the vermilion flycatcher that time.

Chapter 10

The state bird chairman had a crowded schedule in February, 1949. From Kingsville, where she spoke at the 4-H Club Live-stock Show, she went on to Seguin, where, after her talk at the city auditorium, she was interviewed on radio. It was a new experience, but after a few leading questions she was at ease and chatted comfortably for half an hour. That the broadcast reached a wide audience was evidenced by the letters and calls from friends, most saying, "You sounded just like yourself."

In San Antonio she stayed with the Quillins. Her program had been well publicized in the newspapers, and the hall at Witte Museum was filled. Ellen, the museum director, introduced her friend with evident pride, and her letter of thanks a few days later said, "Connie, your lecture was grand . . . and your 'togs' most becoming. In fact, you were plumb perfect both in text and personal appearance."

In Connie's absence Dick and Idabel Klein had discovered a new bird for her territory—a great black-backed gull, not so special to the Ohio birders as to her. It remained for the winter for many others to see and photograph. Western grebes also made another visit.

Jack and Edith Stevens came in March, ahead of the spring migration, with a proposal—why not send for their plane and take the Hagars to Mexico for a few days to meet the migrants on their way and see some Mexican birds? Jack agreed promptly—for his wife, not for himself. Connie explained: They had gone to Mexico in 1928 after the presidential election; Jack, the only Re-

[175]

publican in Corsicana, had put his money on Hoover, taking bets coming and going from the "suckers" backing Al Smith. They had "bucketsful" of winnings, so they spent it on a trip to Mexico. They traveled until half the money was spent, then turned around and spent the rest coming home. But Jack despised Mexico, most of all the food blazing with hot peppers, and declined to visit there again. But he did want Connie to go.

They squeezed in a date between her commitments and flew to Victoria, Tamaulipas, rented a car, and explored two river valleys. Many birds were familiar, but more were strange, and the only help they had were notes and lists provided by Irby Davis. Using them and Peterson's field guides, both eastern and western, they were able to name a surprising number of the unknowns. "Connie made the deductions that counted much faster than we did," Stevens said. She called it a wonderful trip, fifteen new birds.

In April George Lowery, assisted by Bob Newman and his wife and Richard Miller of Philadelphia, set up moon watches on the spring migration: one at the Cottages, the other at Port Aransas, the teams alternating at the stations each night. Lowery mounted his telescope at the back of a carport between cottages and aimed at the rising full moon, counting birds that crossed it and often identifying them, at least as to family.

Connie described the birds they had seen in Mexico, and Lowery agreed that she had identified them correctly. On his return to Baton Rouge he sent her additional literature from the museum files and a box of bird skins for her to study as long as she needed them. They would help her, he said, "on her next trip to the land of the bat falcons."

Unusual features of that spring migration included many rough-legged hawks, twenty counted one day on the Sinton road; a push of hepatic tanagers (very rare at Rockport) that lasted several days; and meadows flooded and occupied by flocks of dunlins and Baird's, white-rumped, and pectoral sandpipers. Harry Darrow of New York reported a glaucous gull.

Rockport people, too, were helpful. Wherever she went they would stop to report their nesting birds or to ask why the mockingbirds were attacking their dogs or cats. Patiently, she explained the defensiveness of parent birds. The golf pro told her that woodpeckers were nesting in posts at the country club; a shrimper reported that gallinules hatched.

Truck drivers and delivery boys waved in passing, calling out their greetings, "Hi, Mrs. Hagar." Such democratic camaraderie did not amuse Guy Emerson on his visit in April. After she had waved and returned a "Hello, boys" half a dozen times one morning, he inquired icily, "Are you, by any chance, running for office?"

She chuckled. "They are my friends. They tell me things, usually nothing of importance, but sometimes it is. If I discourage them they won't tell me."

Adm. W. L. "Bull" Wright, retired and living in Aransas Pass, took Connie to see a breeding colony of least terns on a spoil bank off the ship channel, a new location and the largest concentration of least terns she had ever seen. She was most pleased to note that the site was unlikely to be disturbed.

One June evening while Jack was downtown, Connie sat outside to study stars and planets. Patch engaged in a nature study of his own, chasing the flashing, cool green lanterns of click beetles and never catching one because the elusive prey turned off the lights the second he snapped. His frustrated bark changed suddenly to a throaty growl—his version of the snake alert. She dashed indoors, found the long-idle snake club, and returned to find the dog dancing around a slender twenty-two inch reptile banded with red, yellow, and black. First making sure that it was not a milk snake but indeed a deadly coral snake—Jack had killed two in the yard that summer—she gripped the club as firmly as her arthritic fingers could, aimed true and broke the snake with one blow. "It's really a pity," she said aloud to Patch. "It's a beautiful snake."

Between the visits of Dale Zimmerman and Bryan Harris from the halls of academe in Michigan she helped George Crossette of the National Geographic Society with a photo-story. Her "children," Blanche and Bob Bush, came for Labor Day.

Geese were honking through the early October nights when Fred Packard arrived, full of apologies for lack of progress on the checklist; his work with the National Parks Association and UNESCO entailed considerable travel. Also, he had agreed to several writing projects, including a life history of the brown-capped rosy finch for the Bent's *Life Histories* series. He came, however, for further consultation on the checklist and to see autumn birds. On a trip to the Lower Valley they marveled at hundreds of wood storks along the way and spent a day on Laguna Madre National Wildlife Refuge with manager Luther Goldman. Thousands of ducks had come in, including more red-heads than either had ever seen. It was mainly for them that the refuge had been established. Fulton Beach again was chosen by California gulls, five of them, and another black rail was seen at the Tules.

Connie could not find the rail again later for Bedichek, but they found consolation near the shore of Copano Bay: an enormous raptor, dark brown with white in the wings and at the base of the tail. "Excuse me if I faint," Connie gasped, "but it is an immature golden eagle. Never did I hope for one at Rockport." The eagle haunted the area into December, and Connie escorted dozens of birders to see it.

After two years, the U.S. Fish and Wildlife Service reported on two ducks shot on Aransas Bay in the 1947 season. The hunter had given Mrs. Hagar the bands, which she sent in promptly, but the delay, it was explained, was in having to decipher them by chemical etching. No. 34-640652, a pintail drake, had been banded at Bear River Refuge in Utah in September, 1936—eleven years earlier. No. 42-635220 was from a redhead drake banded in Saskatchewan in June, 1945.

The Lockwoods came in November for a long stay, Ann to recover from a lengthy hospitalization, during which Bob Lockwood also had been hospitalized. Their one wish throughout was to "get to Rockport. We will get well there."

"You will. You will," Jack promised, bustling about to make them comfortable and to conceal his distress at how wan and frail Maggie-off-the-Pickle-Boat looked. He placed deck chairs at their back door, where Ann spent long days soaking up the sunshine of an Indian summer that lasted through Christmas.

She helped prepare the Christmas feast and next day went with her husband and Connie for a bird count—125 species.

[178]

Unusual was an influx of pine warblers, traveling with bluebirds and goldfinches, and most unusual were greater scaups in several locations.

Doubling back between the swales on both sides of Farm Road 881, Lockwood slammed on the brakes when Connie yelled, "Stop this car!" Something was different about a big white "egret" stalking a wet ditch. Lowering her voice she instructed, "Look at that bill, look at the legs." Bob looked. "Yellow," he stated firmly.

"You are looking at a great white heron," Connie said, "Years ago Annie Ruth and I saw a great white heron at Port Bay Club, not far from here. Birds have a way of showing up in the same places."

"You yelled like a house was afire," Bob teased.

"I know," she answered, contrite. "I am always yelling at people."

For the New Year Count, 1950, the list totaled 101 species.

Ann became more vivacious by the day, and for a time the Lockwoods and Connie had the birds all to themselves. Then other guests began checking in, and at the end of the month Connie wrote in the Nature Calendar, "Too many people for good birding." Four or five she could handle, but ten to fifteen crowded her. "Nobody sees anything," she said.

"Let us take some of them out," Ann volunteered. Thus, through spring they managed to keep "Momma" from having more birders at a time than she could enjoy. They had come to sense species in the way they had so envied their mentor—by flight, stance, and behavior—and they were instantly aware when unusual birds were present.

"That comes," Connie told them, "from observing the same species regularly at their various activities. I don't feel that I know a bird until I know it in any plumage and the way it acts. I cannot understand how some people are satisfied to have a bird pointed out to them, then just put it down on a list and go away without studying it."

Bob and Ann took her to the Valley in February for her bird program in Edcouch. That evening they crossed the Rio Grande to Reynosa to test whether those famous border dinners were all they were said to be. The Lockwoods, accustomed to seeing Connie pick listlessly at food, were dumbfounded at how much she ate, almost as much as they did. Unlike Jack, Connie relished Mexican food, especially with cold Carta Blanca beer. They spent the next day on Laguna Atascosa Refuge, again with Luther Goldman.

Not in the shape of a valentine by any means, but a sweetheart none the less, was a raptor found on the saint's day at Salt Lake—a goshawk! It moved to Rattlesnake Point and was missing the day Emerson arrived, but a thorough search on the eighteenth uncovered it again at Salt Lake. Guy all but held his breath to make certain of field marks as the giant of accipiters flew past, circled, and returned to its perch on a telephone pole, facing them. Finally he lowered his binoculars and said grimly, "That is a goshawk—and nobody is going to take it away from me." Connie knew "nobody" was Ludlow Griscom. Guy added, "This bird I will count." It was a life bird to him, too.

Life birds came rarely to Guy Emerson, who for ten years (and years to come) held the record for most species seen in one year—497. He was an ardent lister, but the list was only one aspect of the game; he was enthusiastic as well about the 87 other species seen that day, including horned grebes sprouting the golden ear plumes of breeding plumage, a large raft of common goldeneyes, and great blue herons on nests. They had gone into breeding plumage in December.

Sunday morning Connie and Guy went up Highway 35 to watch the prairie-chickens on the lek, returning in time for her to play for church and seeing three short-eared owls on fence posts on the way.

The owls, a fledging bald eagle, and the prairie-chickens had many birders trekking up the highway in the next six weeks. One morning Martin and Jane Paulsen of Milwaukee counted eighteen chickens, the highest total of the season. Maurice and Irma Braun from Hawk Mountain Sanctuary in Pennsylvania were equally intrigued by marbled godwits, also new to them.

The spring migration, led by black-and-white and yellow-throated warblers, proved so good that a number of guests extended their stay, thus displacing others who had reservations.

[180]

Among the latter was a party from Illinois, for whom Jack found quarters nearby and to whom Connie, not wanting to disappoint anyone, gave a full day on the peninsula.

Just how full and satisfactory for them she did not know until that fall when she received a copy of the September bulletin of Illinois Audubon Society and a note signed by John Bayless on stationery of the financial editor of the *Chicago Tribune* saying, "We will never forget the Rockport tour with you which helped make our Texas trip the best ever." The bulletin's lead story described their trip through Texas into Mexico, stopping at Houston with George Williams and his son Stephen, in Harlingen with the Irby Davises and Terry Gills, and Rockport—citing all for "Texas hospitality exceeding southern hospitality."

Of Rockport he said, in part: "Mrs. Hagar led us on a bird chase that for energy and good results equalled anything we have experienced. . . . We listed 92 species, adding to our life lists eared and Mexican grebes, lark sparrows singing, Inca doves, Mexican cormorants, black-crested titmouse, red-shafted flicker, golden-fronted woodpecker, roadrunner, and a reddish egret in the rare white phase. . . . We retraced Mrs. Hagar's route next day but were soon convinced that the birds knew she was not along. We got 64 species."

When Clarence Brown of Montclair, New Jersey, checked in for the month of March, Connie was promised to other guests, so Lockwood took the newcomer on his first rounds, discovering that they had several mutual friends in the East. That evening Bob assured "Momma" that "Brownie" was a birder she would enjoy. Recently retired from a long stint with Westinghouse, Brown was among the top birdmen in New Jersey, member of the Princeton group and the Urner Club, an exclusive band of men only; no woman was tolerated. He had known Roger Peterson as a boy and had helped him learn birds.

Lockwood was right. Connie found Clarence Brown not only a first rate birdwatcher but also a delightful companion. He was tall, thin, and narrow-faced with a prominent red nose attributable to a predilection for good whiskey. A shaggy wisp of graying hair matched gentle gray eyes that went with a gentle voice. He wore khakis and always had binoculars hanging from his neck. Skeptical of short-eared owls on Highway 35, he eyed the almost treeless prairie, saying that "short-ears don't come to such places." A few minutes later Connie slowed and indicated a bird. What was it? "It's a short-eared owl," he affirmed. "My apologies to you and the owl." He saw all three of the owls. "In such a place," he mused.

He was also skeptical of Patch, but after the dog trotted out and raised a flock of pipits, Sprague's among them, and gently flushed thrushes from thickets without driving them away, Brown became another champion of the mongrel.

"Dr. Lockwood taught him," Connie said. "He helped make Patch a good birding dog, but it took some doing."

Soon Clarence Brown was "Brownie" to all the house party at the Cottages. He would return every spring for eight years and share notable birds with Connie, but it was several years before he confessed that he, like others of the Urner Club, had actually gagged at the prospect of birding with a woman, and that on his first outing with her he felt somewhat condescending. "But," he added, "I minded my manners and am damn glad I did, for once."

Broad-winged hawks staged mass migrations March 19 and 28, both coinciding with mild cold fronts. All morning, birders watched from the Cottages as the raptors streamed past between them and the shoreline. Anhingas and a scattering of red-tails and falcons tagged along.

Fred Thompson of Austin, editor of *Texas Game and Fish* magazine, spent a day in the field with Connie, taking notes for a story that would appear in the August, 1950, issue. Her Easter holiday was spent helping marine biologist Jack Baughman with a seminar attended by scientists in several fields and by some of her Garden Club Federation friends. George Lowery, two from Purdue University, and an Illinois Wildlife Service man stayed over a few days to bird with her. Another weekend was devoted to her family—Bert, Sonney, and Alice May.

April guests included others who would be regulars thereafter, among them Dorothy Eastman Snyder and Kay Tousey from Massachusetts. "Dot" Snyder, curator at Peabody Museum and Audubon specialist with young people, was an observer after Connie's own style; she embraced all wildlife, including reptiles. A masked booby was discovered the day of her arrival. She saw a "fabulous" migration, but most exciting was a small bird she and Connie came upon one day at the Cove. It was near the end of Dot Snyder's visit, April 29; high tides had pushed shorebirds back behind the dunes, where plovers, long-billed curlews, and whimbrels were feeding. Among them was a smaller, shorter-billed curlew.

Definitely a curlew, they agreed. It fit the description of the eskimo curlew—a species then considered probably extinct! They stayed with the bird until dark and that evening hauled out the books to confirm or deny the meticulous notes Dot had made. If not an eskimo curlew, what else? Nothing they could justify. The bird was not found the next day.

Dot Snyder's notes were reviewed by Massachusetts authorities and found "very, very interesting, but too unlikely," she wrote Connie. So Connie marked it off her list, but she believed it to be an eskimo curlew. Fifteen years later another would come to Rockport.

Frank Watson of Houston, formerly of New Jersey and the Urner Club, came to bird a weekend with his friend Brownie. Neither ever passed up a D.O.R. (dead on road) bird, no matter how common, lest they miss learning something. The D.O.R. found that day was far from common—the Cory, or dark phase, of the least bittern. It had been hit by a car.

Dark had fallen and guests were assembled outdoors in lawn chairs, sipping their chosen libations from ice water to highballs and talking over the birds of the day, when Brown and Watson brought in their find. It was examined with interest; few had seen that plumage. "Some of the D.O.R.s that Brownie brings in stink to high heaven," Connie remarked. "But you see it pays off."

Young ladder-backed woodpeckers fledged from a fence post the first week in May, ground-doves hatched, and four baby road-runners, "little black nothings, all red mouth," broke through their shells at Rattlesnake Point in a nest built entirely of dung, pressed and packed tightly in prickly pear. "Ugliest nest I ever saw," Connie said, "but darling babies." Only a mother or another bird lover would agree to that description.

Still the migration was not ended; on May 12, after many birders had left, the peninsula was inundated with birds. Twelve kinds of warblers, chimney swifts, purple martins, wood-pewees, and thousands of swallows, eastern kingbirds, and Wilson's phalaropes came. Connie drove from place to place to see them all. She estimated five thousand barn swallows, ten thousand cliff swallows, two thousand kingbirds, five thousand phalaropes. There were white-rumped and stilt sandpipers, as well as thirteen buff-breasted sandpipers. The day was cloudy and cool, but nothing unusual about the weather.

And it was a one-day phenomenon. The thirteenth was clear and warm, and only a few straggling migrants were seen. On the nineteenth, after south winds in the night gusted to fifty-seven MPH, another great wave came through, mostly warblers, thrushes, and hummingbirds and swallows, but fewer.

Between these waves, Lonnie Ring telephoned and Connie went to see a show that had the Valley birders all excited—a hundred black-bellied whistling-ducks at Santa Ana National Wildlife Refuge, their dark plumage set off grandly by the blazing coral pink bills and feet. She also saw the jacana near Brownsville, stepping lightly among lilies on a resaca, while the Gills had white-tipped doves and groove-billed anis staked out for her.

Bob Allen returned for a month at Aransas Refuge, where a momentous event was anticipated. Crip and Josephine, the crippled whooping cranes that could not migrate with the flock, had built a nest and produced an egg. From a tower overlooking the large marshy enclosure occupied by the cranes, Julian Howard, refuge manager, kept watch on them through daylight hours. Allen joined him there. On May 25 the behavior of Crip and Jo, both guarding the nest vigilantly, indicated hatching, but not until the next day was the tiny but long-necked chick, clothed in rust-colored down, seen. Appropriately named Rusty, the first whooping crane hatched in captivity, indeed the first whooper chick to be seen by modern man, rated headlines all across the nation and Canada. When the chick was three days old, Allen rushed to Rockport to give Connie the details. Rusty was six or seven inches tall and very active; the parents were taking good care of him. Everyone was guardedly elated—the hazards were many, too many. The next day little Rusty was missing, believed to have been taken by raccoons.

The J. Frank Dobies stopped by in early June to leave Edgar Kincaid while they attended the Southwest Writers Conference in Corpus Christi. Connie, too, was on the conference program, and Lockwood seized the chance to have Edgar all to himself. "Of all the crazy people I've met at Rockport, Edgar was my favorite," Bob would say, "because he is the craziest, you know."

The next week John Baker met several of his staff, including Allen and Charles Brookfield at the Cottages. They planned summer guided tours for the public, to be led by Brookfield, to various Audubon sanctuaries and other bird sites. Baker believed that "if people down here knew more about their treasures they would take better care of them." The tours, by boat circling the rookeries, were well attended by tourists and residents, the latter discovering previously unknown and ignored beauty around them.

Half the Cottages were filled in June by a group from Cleveland, Ohio, who focused on breeding birds. Again, nests of herons and egrets were crammed atop every prickly pear and Spanish dagger on Frandolig Island, where willets, Wilson's plovers, black skimmers, and laughing gulls also nested. Nighthawks, least terns, snowy plovers, killdeer, and horned larks occupied Copano Ridge and the shores of Salt Lake. Elsewhere they found nesting blue grosbeaks, scissortails, white-eyed vireos, lark sparrows, and the Bullock's race of northern orioles.

Bob Allen came to say good-bye in early July, unhappy to report that brown pelicans were at an all-time low on Second Chain sanctuaries, and after a disastrous flooding of their nests the spoonbills had failed to raise a single young. Sandwich and least terns, however, had done exceedingly well.

The Lockwoods were leaving, too, but would be nearer now, at McKinney, where he would be radiologist at the Veterans Hospital. His parting advice to Connie was to "keep up the beer," an admission that he finally agreed with Dr. Atkinson.

Though he fretted that she ate so little, he had doubted the efficacy of beer for her eyes. but nourishment she certainly needed, beer provided that, and her eyes were better.

The void her guests left was partially filled by a fledgling great-tailed grackle, blown from the nest in a storm and brought to Mrs. Hagar. Pet birds she did not want, ever again, but this creature had a broken leg, so she wanted to do what she could. With toothpicks and tape she made a splint and then made the mistake of hand-feeding the bird from Patch's bowl. Thereafter, the bratty orphan would eat only dog food from Connie's hand. The leg healed crooked, but the bird, a female, fattened and refused to leave. Squawk, named for her single vocalization, hung around, peering through windows, walking with Connie to the mailbox, the oaks, wherever, prancing in the prissy way of grackles despite the crooked leg. Oddly, she had white spots in her tail. Whenever Connie came home from birding Squawk greeted her boisterously.

"She is quite able to care for herself now," Connie said. "When we go to Corpus this afternoon, we'll leave her with the grackles at Moore's Pool." That they did, and upon their return late in the day, they were greeted by an overjoyed Squawk.

"Damn," Connie laughed, "but she is sweet."

"No," ruled Jack. He took her to a flock at Port Bay, and she was not seen again until the following spring when a flight of grackles flew over, and one dropped out to land on the Hagar porch, screeching a sort of "Look who's here!" in squawking noises. She went on with her friends but visited again the next spring. The tail had molted into proper black feathers, but the crooked leg and the glad greeting left no doubt that it was Squawk.

In the fall Jack traded for another blue Packard and proposed another trip, one tentatively planned for a long time: to Schenectady to visit Sonney and Alice May, and on to New England to see the fall colors and some of Jack's boyhood haunts. He arranged for a friend to manage the Cottages. Patch went, too; leaving him was never considered. It was a leisurely trip, up through the Old South, enjoying wooded scenery, stopping at historic places. One stop was at Port Gibson, Mississippi, to see

[186]

the Church with the Hand Pointing Heavenward, a small Presbyterian church, its clock tower surmounted by a spire and on it a large hand—twelve feet tall—closed except for the forefinger pointing straight up. It was built in 1859 on Church Street, the address of seven other houses of worship.

"Grandfather Yeater was pastor here before the Civil War," Connie said. "He left to go with Mississippi's poor, ragged soldiers as chaplain. He was captured and imprisoned for a year; I still have the letters he wrote Grandmother Yeater. When he came back he wanted to change his faith—and did. He was ordained and became rector of the Episcopal church here. On Sunday morning, Mama, who had been born just before the war, went with Grandmother Yeater, who would not change, to Presbyterian Sunday school where she sang in the children's choir, then went over to the Episcopal church to her father's service."

They spent a day in Williamsburg, bypassed Washington and New York City, and in Boston saw Jack's only living relative, a sister ninety-two years old living in their old home near the Harvard campus. They attended a service at the Mother Church of Christian Science, enjoying the music, on which Connie took notes for future use.

They then went to Schenectady and had a good visit with Sonney and Alice May. They toured General Electric—Robert Neblett's world—though Connie confessed that she wouldn't know a turbine from a nucleonic.

Among his colleagues were several members of the Audubon Society, who arranged a meeting with a special exhibit of bird art in honor of Neblett's sister. Assured that it would be a small, private gathering, Connie agreed to talk about birds. A packed hall awaited her, but it was a warm, responsive audience, and she "had a fine time," she declared.

Coming home they saw Niagara Falls, drove on through Ohio, Indiana, Missouri, and Arkansas, and stopped over in McKinney to see the Lockwoods and in Corsicana. "I saw lots of birds, no new ones, but I heard many bird songs I'd never heard at home," Connie reported. In her Nature Calendar she wrote, "Perfect three weeks."

The Conrad Richters engaged a cottage for three months.

The author of *Sea of Grass* and *The Trees* worked most of the time, but both he and his wife Harvey were interested in birds and had chosen this working vacation in Rockport because of them and Mrs. Hagar. Their own Pennsylvania songbirds they knew well; they wanted to become better acquainted with shorebirds and water birds. For starters they learned to separate gulls and terns, and they saw the dawn ballet of black skimmers. A single golden-plover came by so Connie could point out the few field marks distinguishing it from the abundant black-bellied plovers on the beaches. Many hours were spent watching the great rafts of ducks on the bays. Some land birds were new, too, the most admired being scissor-tailed and vermilion flycatchers.

Richter spent some hours of every day at his typewriter but never discussed work in progress. He read a great deal and discussed books he exchanged with the Hagars, but with Connie he mostly talked birds and shells, flowers and trees. With his host he discussed politics, Jack's favorite subject, and was regaled by Jack's stories of dumb Democrats. The Richters would return the following winter, he having won a Pulitzer Prize for *The Town*, and for the next decade Conrad and Connie kept up an intermittent correspondence.

As if to accent the dry season, another desert bird—a sage thrasher—appeared at Rattlesnake Point that Christmas week and remained to be listed on the Christmas Count taken by Connie, Georgie Belle Getzendaner, the Lockwoods, Dr. Tom Harrison, Mary Belle Keefer, and Kathleen Lafferty.

January, 1951, continued dry and very warm with very low tides, which suited birders from cold states, who got a bonus in the western species not expected in Rockport every year, including lark buntings, a green-tailed towhee found by Arly McKay, and the burrowing owl back at its station in the shipyard. Winter nests of verdins were now around Salt Lake; more brush had been cleared from the Cove to make way for more houses.

Albert Ganier of Nashville, Tennessee, arrived on January 26 and quickly added half a dozen species to his life list. Connie re-located the sage thrasher for him, and, to their mutual delight, a small flock of mountain bluebirds was found.

On the twenty-ninth the thermometer had climbed to eighty degrees; shirt-sleeved birders were all afield when at 4:00 P.M. a blue norther struck, dropping the temperature to thirty-five degrees. Great waves of pine siskins and white-crowned sparrows poured in behind it but ahead of still more severe weather—an ice storm that blanketed South Texas almost to the Valley. Schools closed, and sleet-covered roads were too dangerous for travel. On February 1 the mercury dropped to twenty degrees. From her window Connie saw an Inca dove motionless on the ground, perhaps frozen. Jack tramped across the treacherous ice to bring it in, still and lifeless, but she wrapped it and laid it near the fire and next day let it go, "good as new."

The storm abated as quickly as it had come. The days were warm, and birds were everywhere. Oldsquaws were among more goldeneyes and red-beasted mergansers than Connie had ever seen before; goldfinches, pine siskins, pine warblers, eastern and mountain bluebirds, sparrows—all had survived and were still present on February 15 when Brownie arrived. "How would you like mountain bluebirds for a starter?" Connie greeted him.

"It's a long way to the Hill Country," he said. "Were you planning to be back by lunchtime?" They were back by lunch; the bluebirds were at their usual place beside an oil rig. They counted six thousand pintails on Copano Bay. The bluebirds departed that night, but a winter wren claimed the oil rig next day.

Jack and Edith Stevens and Martin and Jane Paulsen came with another norther, which on March 13 brought in the first warbler wave. Hordes of migrants followed. Brownie's account of his first spring in Rockport had convinced James Leland ("Lee") Edwards, also a member of the Urner Club, to participate this year, and he also, usually with his wife Ruth, would become regulars. The Paulsens enticed Mary Donald and other Milwaukee friends to join them. These, with George Williams, his son, and the Houston birders kept Jack busy finding accommodations for them. Locke Mackenzie got there in time to see the mountain plovers, a new bird for him.

Frank Watson came again for what he called a "reunion of a

fragment of the Urner Club." He, Brownie, and Lee Edwards chose to spend a day at Port Aransas, returning in midafternoon to announce the presence of a surfbird and a glaucous gull at the jetty. Nobody believed them because it was April 1. But it was no April fool; others were finally persuaded, and all turned out the next day to see the birds.

Edwards and Brownie offered to take Connie to her two bird programs that month, provided they went early enough to bird along the way, which, she assured them, she always did. While she entertained the club in Beeville, the men were entertained by the courtship antics of a bronzed cowbird. Over and over, the male, with nape feathers inflated to a big ruff, fluttered vertically like a tiny helicopter to about three feet in the air then scaled down to face a female cowbird feeding in the grass, apparently indifferent to his performance. Unable to impress her, he finally gave up and searched the grass at her side.

In Victoria Connie spoke to the Brontë Club, a literary society organized in 1873 whose members had decided to dip into nature study at least once inasmuch as "such a famous naturalist as Mrs. Hagar was available nearby." Driving home on Highway 35, the birders found that cliff swallows were working on mud nests beneath the concrete bridges.

A migration wave brought down by a wet norther filled the oaks. Nobody left the grounds that morning, for in addition to the orioles, buntings, grosbeaks, tanagers, and others was a Swainson's warbler (very rare there), and five species of vireos—white-eyed, red-eyed, Philadelphia, warbling, and solitary. A swallow-tailed kite flew over, and an exhausted purple gallinule came down.

Roger Peterson and Edward Chalif arrived the day after the Lockwoods and Emerson. Thrushes, flycatchers, and catbirds were in the oaks, but the focus of the visitors was on wet prairies—for buff-breasted and many other sandpiper species, together with golden-plovers, Wilson's phalaropes, white-faced ibis, soras, and fulvous whistling-ducks. Cassin's sparrows were in full song.

From Maryland two weeks later came a book and a note from Peterson:

Dear Mrs. Hagar:

My brief visit to Texas and the several happy days with you and Guy Emerson at Rockport were just what the doctor ordered. I feel so much more like tackling my drawing than I did a few weeks ago.

Warblers have been pouring through the Washington area this past week and I cannot help wondering if they are the same ones that have been scanned by you at Rockport. In another year or two I plan to come down for a period of two or three weeks.

Thinking you might like to have a copy of the new *Field Guide to the Butterflies* by Alexander Klots, I am sending you a copy. My own part in its production was that of editor and adviser.

Sincerely,
Roger

While other birdwatchers came and went, Lee Edwards and Brownie stayed on. In a lull of activity at Rockport they decided to go see the Edwards Plateau specialties—golden-cheeked warbler and black-capped vireo, provided Connie would go along and enlist the help of her Austin friends. She would, and did so gladly. They made a one-day trip of it, also enjoying canyon and rock wrens, which never appeared in Rockport.

Edgar Kincaid was not long in returning the visit, to hear Cassin's and olive sparrows sing, but three hundred whimbrels that Connie had counted the day before had gone on. Dick Russell and Edgar reported unusual numbers of western kingbirds migrating with easterns, and on May 7 Connie and Brownie went to see them. They met the kingbirds, all eastern now, at the intersection of Farm Roads 881 and 1069. Flight after flight went over, more than had been seen all that spring, and above them were flights of Franklin's gulls. For nearly two hours the car was parked in that one spot as Connie and Brownie marveled at the streams of birds. Both kingbirds and gulls appeared to be coming straight from the south, but at this corner their paths diverged, the gulls pointing to the northwest while the kingbirds aimed northeast.

Early that evening a wet, stormy cold front moved in, forcing down another enormous migration. Telephone calls sent Connie and Brownie downtown to see hundreds of small birds swirling around the streetlights. Next morning the oaks were full, mostly warblers—many ovenbirds and many more bay-breasted. After counting 150 bay-breasts, Connie gave up.

Richard Pough, author of the Audubon field guide series, had arrived with the storm and gathered up the bodies of many birds that had been killed. The morning *Caller-Times* revealed that the storm had been worse on northern Padre Island. The birds were described as "an invasion of wild canaries." Residents rushed out with cages to capture canaries, the newspaper said.

But the storm was still far, far worse on South Padre Island. Dr. Pauline James of Pan American University at Edinburg heard of it on the radio and took a group of her students to the island. They found a scene of indescribable havoc. Drawn to tall bright streetlights in the county park, birds had struck poles, wires, and buildings by thousands. Some were rescued; most died. (Dr. James's full account of the devastation appeared in the *Wilson Bulletin* of September, 1956. She estimated 10,000 dead birds, 93 percent warblers. Her party counted 900 dead piled against one of the ten lampposts. Casualties were also on roadways and sand dunes. Dr. James collected 2,400 bodies in sufficiently good condition to make museum specimens.)

More migrants straggled through, including one hepatic tanager, and soon after their departure least sandpipers were returning in the fall migration.

On July 7 when the Charles Hamiltons of Houston and the Raymond Hills of Ohio were with Connie looking for olive sparrows, they flushed a rarity for Rockport—a Bachman's sparrow. A prairie falcon was certainly not expected in July, but on the twenty-seventh when she and the Lockwoods were watching pectoral sandpipers on the Rincon, a falcon with black axillars flew over. Then, only thirty feet in front of the car, the falcon hovered an instant, stooped so swiftly and was gone so swiftly, no one realized it had made a kill until Ann cried, "There's the bird!" Connie and Bob jumped out to follow the falcon's flight; Ann walked to the spot of the stoop and picked up a pectoral sandpiper. The sandpiper looked intact until they turned it over to find the entire breast missing, though scarcely a feather was out of place. In a flash the falcon had caught and dressed its kill and was gone. The remains made an excellent specimen for Connie to show at bird talks.

Now that buff-breasted sandpipers were being found every autumn, Connie realized that she probably had not searched the prairies early enough in years past. That August visitors reported 152 one day, and a week later she counted 350. Half that many were present for Labor Day when Bill and Agatha Anderson and the George Williams family came.

George and Steve Williams and Connie added another new species to the state list—gray kingbird, a Florida flycatcher, on the road to Lenoir's Landing. A hurricane had moved from the Caribbean into the Gulf, making landfall at Tampico ten days before; was it possible, they wondered, that the storm had swept this bird across the Gulf? It was not seen again.

In early September Connie went with the Andersons for a picnic supper on Rattlesnake Point. They were admiring the pretty pictures made by roseate spoonbills, wood storks, and white ibises wading in the setting sun at the edge of Copano Bay when a tiny black bird, a black rail, slipped silently through the marsh grass.

At midmonth a windy rainstorm knocked a hummingbird into the plate-glass front of the drugstore, and the bird was taken at once to Mrs. Hagar. A broad-tailed, she noted. Now she would have a specimen for those who doubted the presence of broad-tails there. But the bird was still warm; she held it between her palms until she felt a wiggle, and a head poked out between her fingers. This hummer chose not to become a specimen; it streaked away.

John W. Aldrich, Oberholser's successor at the U.S. Fish and Wildlife Service, came by at Thanksgiving and was amused to see an Inca dove on fresh eggs outside Connie's window. He had sad news about the Texas book; it would never be published, being entirely too voluminous—an impractical and costly undertaking. He, too, was sorry that so much valuable information would not become available to those who needed it.

Chapter 11

Dr. Harrison, the Lockwoods and Andersons, and Georgie Belle Getzendaner participated in the 1951 Christmas Count on a day the temperature hit 80 degrees. They listed 125 species, including a sage thrasher. On January 1, 1952, Connie wrote in the Nature Calendar, "25th year of notes." Sixteen of those years had been in Rockport.

The Cottages were booked for the spring months, the regulars in their favorites: Brownie in no. 7 from January to the end of May, the Edwardses in no. 5, the Stevenses in no. 9, Guy always in no. 2. Some used Rockport as their base for travels into Mexico and other parts of Texas.

Rockport was growing. There were many more motels, as well as a chamber of commerce and Lions Club in which Jack was active, promoting growth, as all active communities were expected to do.

A women's club had been organized with grand plans for a clubhouse for meetings, social events, exhibits, and other community functions. A war surplus building was bought at little cost, moved to the bayfront, renovated, and furnished with money raised by cake and pie sales, silver teas, and white elephant sales. Connie did not bake pies or cakes, but she presented a book review, *Giant*, which brought in $125 and was so well attended the club begged for another. She reviewed *The Mudlark*, drawing an even larger audience at the movie theater and raising even more money.

These accomplishments came about despite loose organization. Meetings of the Women's Club often deteriorated into gossip sessions when scheduled programs failed to materialize. Assignments were casual and committee reports informal. *Robert's Rules of Order* was an unopened book on the shelf. Alma Hunt, president, was a topflight bridge and poker player and money raiser but not a strict administrator; she never wanted to "hurt anyone's feelings," she said.

Alma understood the problem and had a solution—Connie Hagar. With a committee for support, she called upon her friend of many years. Would she take the presidency, just for a year, to put them on their feet again? "Nobody else can make us straighten up and fly right," the ladies insisted. Connie hesitated, but she remembered her father saying, "Do what your community asks of you."

"If I do," she told them, "you may be sorry. You'll have to go by the rules, take assignments, and whatever you start will be finished."

"We know," they agreed. "It will shock most of us, but that's what we need. We will stand behind you."

At her first meeting Madam President assumed the chair promptly, the secretary, whom she had collected en route, beside her. Exactly on the hour she rose and rapped the gavel; chattering ceased, minutes were read, the treasurer's report given, old business resolved, new business introduced. Women who straggled in late sensed a change and tiptoed to seats. No one was allowed to speak out of order, and if one who had the floor harangued too long, the president brought the subject into focus and reached a settlement. Instead of petering out, as most meetings had, this one was adjourned with another rap of the gavel.

Now, in the spring of 1952, Connie was finishing her term; programs had been excellent, projects successful, and the Women's Club was firmly on its feet and a viable asset to Rockport.

Birds had become vastly more appreciated in South Texas, but it was evident one afternoon that many more people needed to be educated, especially about raptors. Connie and some friends had driven to Beeville to hear Lincoln Borglum lecture. He had finished the Mount Rushmore sculpture begun by his

[195]

father, Gutzon Borglum, and Connie's party was invited to visit his studio after the lecture. On the way over they passed a ranch fence strung for miles with dead red-tailed hawks. Brownie was furious. "The stupid bastards," he raged. "They kill hawks and then complain because their land is overrun with rabbits and rats and gophers."

Other Texans had forgotten the message of the Dust Bowl. In February Aransas and neighboring counties were covered with fine dust blown down by fierce northwest winds from the high plains—dust that had been good topsoil up there. Hedgerows and shelter belts that could prevent wind erosion were considered too costly; they took space that could be planted in cotton. At that time, the conservation ethic had little popular support.

A golden eagle, Connie's second, was found on the Refugio road, where she also found rough-legged hawks. Brownie and Lee had held out against rough-legs at Rockport until they saw for themselves, whereupon Edwards opined, "It just means there is a breeding population somewhere that we know nothing about."

"I've had a tree full of them," Connie commented with an inelegant snort.

The anhingas (known to Connie as water turkeys) roosting one morning at the Tules were so numerous she thought they should be reported to *Audubon Field Notes*, so she counted—six hundred anhingas. Townfolk called about purple gallinules in their yards. They were so beautiful; could they keep them for pets? She explained that the birds were only exhausted and that they must not keep them.

Their predilection for D.O.R.s gave Brownie and Lee a rare opportunity to upstage the New Jersey birding fraternity. They picked up a sandpiper where it fell by the road one day after hitting a wire that broke its neck. It was a buffbreast, still warm, and it gave Brownie a ghoulish idea. With a wicked gleam in his eyes he vowed, "This bird we will eat. Just wait till we tell the Urners we have eaten buff-breasted sandpiper." The Urners envied him for this species more than any other. Connie removed the small breast and made a study skin of the bird. Ruth

[196]

Edwards cooked the breast, and the three of them, Ruth, Lee, and Brownie, each got a bite.

"You couldn't tell it from liver," was Ruth's judgment, but Brownie reported an ineffably fine flavor to the Urner Club.

It was the year of phalaropes. Several flights of Wilson's phalaropes had already passed through when, on April 26, Connie was at Salt Lake with Katherine Richmond, new to Rockport but not new to birdwatching. A single phalarope spun and dabbled on a pond nearby, and it was different, too small and too dark on the back to be a Wilson's. Wondering if it could be a red-necked, Connie wanted Brownie's opinion, so the women drove hurriedly back to the Cottages. He and the Edwardses were warbler-watching in the back.

"Anybody for northern phalarope?" Connie called.

"Can't be," the men proclaimed, all piling into the car. The bird still dabbled on the pond. Binoculars and telescope were fixed upon it, and nobody spoke. Then field marks were noted and called out, and evidence piled up. Ruth and Brownie were convinced—red-necked (northern) phalarope—but Lee, a structural engineer as meticulous about details on a bird as he was of steel bones for Radio City and other buildings he had framed, held out.

"Not until I see it fly. Everyone take a good last look and watch closely. I'm going to flush the bird." Broad white wing bands and a patterned back were revealed as the bird took off.

"We," announced Lee with a broad smile, "have a northern phalarope." All showered congratulations on Connie.

"Had it not been alone," she admitted, "I'm not sure I would have picked it out as being different."

Less than six months later, on October 5, she identified a red phalarope, also a lone bird, also at Salt Lake. All three species of the world's phalaropes had come to her at Rockport.

"There's something about a better mousetrap involved here," wrote George Lowery when he heard of it, "but I don't know how it applies to birds." He was hosting the AOU that fall at Baton Rouge and wanted her to come. She was tempted but decided against it.

The red-necked phalarope had arrived in time to be included in the *Checklist of Birds of the Central Coast of Texas* that Packard was completing, but the red was too late; the book had gone to press, but it was listed in a later edition. Griscom took notice of it in his seasonal *Field Notes* summary: "A first, also a sixth first for Mrs. Hagar in this area."

Meanwhile, between phalaropes, Milton Trautman had returned for the windup of the spring migration. A new couple, Ruth and Roger Ernst of Boston, had also come. He was on the board of the Massachusetts Audubon Society. A single field, blue with indigo buntings, and a mob of dickcissels chirping their onomatopoeic name from a thicket convinced the Ernsts that their stay was too short; they would come earlier and stay longer in future years.

They saw a roadrunner ignominiously routed by four angry mockingbirds, doubtless because paisano had been too nosy about a nest. Soon after, Connie saw a roadrunner snatch a baby quail from a covey but drop it when attacked by a parent bobwhite.

Don Bleitz and Henry Isham came to photograph nesting birds, having heard, Bleitz said, that Mrs. Hagar knew where every bird in her area nested.

"Not quite," she said with a smile, "but lots of birds are nesting."

"Scissor-tailed flycatcher?" he asked hopefully, especially wanting that bird. She stayed with him all morning at the scissortail nest. If he disturbed her birds unduly, she would hesitate to show him others, but Bleitz was infinitely patient and careful, so she showed him nests of Bell's vireo, northern (Bullock's) oriole, painted bunting, white ibis, and others.

But the prize was the sooty tern on Lydia Ann Island, discovered by Connie one day when she went with Don Gamble and Salty John, the warden. Her only sooty tern had been the dead bird sent long ago to Dr. Oberholser, but here was a beautiful adult, and with young. She visited the island twice, making sure the young fared well, and when Bleitz returned from the Valley, where he had been for a week, she arranged for the warden to take him to Lydia Ann. She could not go that day.

"This has been all too easy," Bleitz said in parting. "Your

knowing where to go has saved me many hours of searching." To prove his gratitude the photographer sent her copies of all his best shots from Rockport, and he continued to send others, including color prints processed in Europe.

The sooty tern picture, however, although exquisitely beautiful, puzzled her. It showed the tern, wings up, alighting on a nest with an egg in it. She had not seen an egg; the young had hatched when she discovered the nest. She wondered if there could have been another nest.

In July she indulged her fancy for shells, partly to help Winnie Rice, whose hobby they had become. On a day of low tide they drove down the beach of Padre Island, now accessible by a causeway from Corpus Christi, to Little Shell, a spot where Gulf currents deposited marine exoskeletons in abundance. Big Shell, farther south and much richer, was unsafe for driving except in four-wheel-drive vehicles. Little Shell was productive enough—thirty species, including olives, winged oysters, and scotch bonnets. Red knots, still in red-breasted breeding plumage, and black terns migrated along the shore.

Another day they took Winnie's cabin cruiser across Aransas Bay to St. Joseph's Island to gather purple snails. Owned and ranched by Sid Richardson of Fort Worth, St. Joe Island was closed to the public, but Connie and Winnie had the owner's permission to visit it any time. Wading ashore from the anchored boat, they saw a cowboy riding toward them, and Connie started to explain, but she never finished her sentence. The rider dismounted and stuck out his hand. "Now, Mrs. Hagar," he grinned, "I know you. You told us all about the birds in sixth grade."

Still another day she indulged her fancy for antique glass, which she shared with Mrs. Sellers, a local authority on the subject. They went to Corpus Christi to see a traveling exhibit of many fine pieces, and Connie realized that her own pieces were far more valuable than she had known.

Locke Mackenzie and his son Michael, who were going to Mexico, and Dr. Larasen of the University of Idaho, returning from Mexico, came by in August. Herb Clarke, "that sweet young man from Lake Charles" who had birded with her and his mother, also arrived. This time he brought his pretty bride

Olga to meet the Hagars and—incidentally, he pretended—to see birds.

There was nothing incidental about birds to Herb Clarke. They were a way of life to him. Just how deeply involved he was came as something of a shock to Olga. Her bridegroom was the first birdwatcher she had ever met; what she knew or cared about birds could have been written on a pinhead. She tagged along on field trips because no other entertainment was available.

She could appreciate roseate spoonbills—big and pink and beautiful—and painted buntings with all those colors. Storks paddling the muddy bottom of Little Bay were interesting and so were phalaropes spinning like dervishes, but what was special about lesser nighthawks? Or sparrows? And why was Dr. Mackenzie suddenly agog over those little prairie birds they called buffbreasts? They looked just like those called uplands, which excited nobody.

"Life bird," exclaimed Locke, "after all these years!" What, Olga wondered, was a life bird? The next day a party of New Yorkers exhibited similar enthusiasm.

Olga was troubled. She felt apart from something that evidently meant a great deal to Herb, and she wanted very much to please her husband. She sought a private talk with Mrs. Hagar and confided her feelings. Connie was understanding and reassuring. "Herb loves you more than anything in the world," she declared. "He will always love you. But I do believe that since he is so fond of birds you would be wise to take an interest in his hobby. Learn something about birds, enough to go with him and not be bored. You may have to pretend at first, but nature study teaches us many things. You may find you enjoy it as much as he does."

Olga doubted that, but she would at least try. Connie had no doubt that anyone "with as good a mind as Olga's would make a good birder," and she was right—again. On each of several visits the Clarkes made thereafter, the young woman had made astonishing progress, and Connie would call her one of her prize pupils. They corresponded intermittently through the years, and after the Clarkes had moved to California, Olga wrote her a long letter describing her birding activities, saying:

You would be proud of me, Mrs. Hagar. I've taken to this birding like a duck to water, and I feel I owe it all to *you*. I'll never forget your words of wisdom and I've never regretted taking up the hobby. We have made such marvelous friends from all walks of life. It still amazes me sometimes. I think birdwatchers as a whole are the most congenial people I've ever known, and birdwatching certainly must have therapeutic value, I'm convinced.

Connie saved and treasured that letter, which always reminded her of the joy of sharing.

In mid-December a glaucous gull spent an afternoon at a trailer park only a block from the Cottages, and a week later a sharp norther brought sparrows earlier than usual. White-crowned and white-throated sparrows sang by the frog farm, and among them were several handsome Harris' sparrows and a green-tailed towhee.

Jack could boast that people from nearly every state in the Union had come to see birds at Rockport, but Connie's pride was in the growing number of Texans awakening to their state's natural heritage. The big cities had bird clubs; Corpus Christi would organize one that year. The time was ripe for a state organization, and it was in the making.

On a warm day in early January, 1953, on his way home from Mexico, Edgar Kincaid stopped by to apprise Connie of plans for the society. As they sat on her front steps, he was interrupted by a hummingbird that buzzed a red hibiscus blossom and then flew almost into his face. "That's no ruby-throat!" he exclaimed. Connie secretly smiled; Edgar, she knew quite well, suspected that some of her hummingbird accounts were "unsanitary."

"No, Edgar," she said sweetly. "That is a broad-tail. But go on with your story." He did—after pursuing the bird and satisfying himself that it was indeed a broad-tail.

Announcement of the new organization brought in fifty-four members, half of whom attended the charter meeting in Austin on February 14, at which Charles H. McNeese and Carrie Holcomb, both of Houston, were elected president and secretary, respectively, of the Texas Ornithological Society (TOS). An early order of business was to make Dr. Oberholser, who was present, and Mrs. Jack Hagar honorary members. A major goal was to achieve publication of Oberholser's book on Texas birds.

Connie would agree with Jack, who alleged that the best "birds" of that winter were the Teales, Edwin Way and Nellie, who spent a week in late January with them, the first of six visits, all longer than their first one. It was another case of instant rapport among them, Patch included. The Hagars felt they already knew the author of *Dune Boy* and *North with the Spring*. Nellie was an extra delight.

From his early fascination for insects Teale had developed a concern for all wild flora and fauna; nature was his religion. They had come to Connie to learn more birds and more about birds. He was extremely modest about his fame and dreaded publicity. When Jack wished to notify the newspapers of their visit, Teale consented to please Jack, but so reluctantly that Jack saw it would embarrass him, and he held off until they departed. Nellie, on the other hand, was as friendly as a muddy puppy and able to thaw her husband in small gatherings of individuals who would ignore his celebrity status. He was never comfortable in crowds. He dressed conservatively and, except for the camera always at hand, "looked like a stockbroker, even in the woods," Connie said. He didn't smoke, drink, swear, or criticize those who did. "But I guess he didn't mind my cussin'," Connie would add. "He kept coming back."

To go with her newly published checklist, Connie had small maps of birding areas printed. With these and pertinent directions she could help many whom she could not accompany in the field. Most members of the new TOS had gone birding in Rockport; those who had not hastened there to make a birding trip. Most were advanced students, especially in their home areas, but were eager to learn the birds of other areas as well. Among these TOS members were Fred and Marie Webster of Austin, strong on land birds, weak on shorebirds, which they found utterly confusing, but not for long. They were "willing to dig," Connie learned, and never had to be told anything twice. Fred, a government statistician, was to become the longtime

South Texas regional correspondent for *Audubon Field Notes* (now *American Birds*).

Among rank beginners were Mary Gene Kelly and Kay Bynum, reporters on the *Corpus Christi Times*, who arrived in March with their copies of the *Audubon Field Guide* they had given one another at Christmas. They had pinned down a good many birds in the interim, relying almost entirely on Eckelberry's picture pages; if a bird looked like a picture—that was it. They had all but ignored the texts, including the introduction on "How to," and were oblivious to seasonal changes in populations, to ranges, and to behavior.

With infinite patience Connie explained that the fifty or more ruby-crowned kinglets haunting Redbug Corner were winter birds. "Don't look for them in summer," she advised. The solitary sandpiper, so like the lesser yellowlegs, had an eye-ring and was not always so solitary. "I've seen nine in a bunch," she said.

The showpiece of the month was a black phoebe, discovered by Brownie and the Edwardses with a push of golden-crowned kinglets in a marsh by Copano Bay. It was a western bird, she told them, far from home, the first she had seen at Rockport. That point was wasted on the beginners; they blithely expected black phoebes anytime (and did not see another for seven years), but another point their teacher made, while watching the phoebe, did sink in. "Girls, when you see a bird leave its perch like that, to sally out and snatch an insect and return to its perch—you have a flycatcher." It dawned on them that behavior was a clue. They were on their way.

Mary Gene had learned some birds as a Girl Scout, but Kay had recognized exactly two before she opened her field guide that Christmas—the scissortail, from childhood in West Texas, and the brown pelican, from Mrs. Hagar herself. That was during World War II when, for six months, Kay had been editor of the *Rockport Pilot* and had needed the information for a story.

She and Connie had been great friends. They drove identical blue Packards, but birds were never among their mutual interests except when a story was involved. Now Kay drove a cherry-red Chevrolet convertible with black trim, dubbed the

Scarlet Tanager by Connie. The gaudy vehicle was to be seen often in the Hagar driveway.

Winter weather had not been unusual enough to explain the presence of unusual birds, though the black-throated gray warbler was not so unusual as it was simply rare. Harris' sparrows remained at the frog farm until Dr. Tom Harrison could see them. There were many of the Audubon race among the usual myrtle race of yellow-rumped warblers, slate-colored juncos, and a red-throated loon one day. The glaucous gull left, returned, left again, and returned for months, prompting John Baker to wonder, "What's that crazy glaucous doing in Rockport, Texas?"

Brownie's interest in D.O.R.s suggested another revelation. On a trip to the Valley he picked up twelve dead barn-owls by the roadside. "This," Connie said, "looks like a migration to me, but I've been told that barn-owls do not migrate."

March was a month of owls and of birding in pajamas and nightgowns. Often, an hour after lights were out at the Cottages, a great horned owl would call from the oaks. A back door would open and someone would slip out to listen. The horned howl was answered by a barred owl, sometimes two barred owls. Other doors opened, and soon the Paulsens, the Ernsts, Karen and Whitney Eastman, and others stood in the dark hearing the nocturnal choir. One night when Guy, the Gillens, and Helen and Harry Stiles were there, the tremolo of screech-owls was heard. Counting the short-eared owl seen by day, four species of owls were listed that month.

April 20 Mary Donald and Katherine Richmond added another species to the Rockport list—a blue-throated hummingbird.

Brownie organized the Big Day Count held April 25. He put Connie, Katherine, and Patch in one car; himself, Mary, Neil Dickerson, and Bob Fox in another. They covered Live Oak Peninsula and up Highway 35 to Aransas Refuge, starting at 4:00 A.M. and going until dark. At times the paths of the parties crossed, and quick consultations were held for possible changes of strategy in the "Big Day" game of listing as many species as possible in a single day.

The high temperature that day set a record for April, and by midafternoon the game was more work than play, but nobody thought of calling it quits. Fred and Marie Webster joined them in late afternoon, adding four species. After supper they met in the Hagar living room to tally—204 species. They listed four owls, seven vireos, twenty-five warblers, twelve sparrows, four wrens, and two towhees, among others, but inexplicably missing were birds seen the day before and which would be seen again tomorrow. However, they were content. It had been a great day.

On the afternoon of May 18, Connie and Brownie were eagerly watching and waiting for sight of the station wagon driven by Roger Peterson with his British counterpart, James Fisher of London. The two were on a hundred-day marathon sweep around the perimeter of North America, designed to be the Big Year of all Big Years.

They arrived in midafternoon, late because they had driven through a near-hurricane-strength rainstorm up the coast, and though they had been on the road for five fast-moving, intense weeks, both were still in a high key of excitement. Fisher, on his first look at America, found everything wonderful; he wore a perpetual smile.

Everybody talked at once. Brownie had staked out birds of special interest—all present and accounted for on a circular tour of the peninsula, including Cassin's sparrows caroling over nests in catclaw thickets. But mostly they talked—nonstop. Birds were secondary on this visit; the men had come mainly to see Connie Hagar, described by Fisher as "the best bird in Texas."

At dark they bade farewell and went on to Port Aransas where Dr. Gordon Gunter would put them up at the Marine Science Institute and next morning take them to Lydia Ann Island for nesting birds.

Though running late and due in the Valley that afternoon, Peterson, as a favor to Connie in behalf of her friend Kay Bynum, consented to stop by the *Caller-Times* for a brief interview. It was held on the parking lot outside the newspaper offices under a sizzling sun that had already wrecked Fisher's fair skin. Clicking her camera, Kay pointed out a hooded oriole in a tall palm. "Tallyho!" cried Fisher, as he did each time he listed a new bird.

Peterson and Fisher would continue their marathon into

Alaska; they had seen more kinds of birds than had ever been listed for the continent by a single party in a single year. Roger's personal list of species seen north of the Rio Grande in a year eclipsed the thirteen-year-old record held by Guy Emerson. Their experiences, with drawings by Peterson, filled the book, *Wild America*, published two years later.

The Nature Calendar had only one entry for June 14: "67 today. Too old." But not too old to thrill at the sight of her second sooty shearwater a month later on the Harbor Island causeway. Her sister Bert and Blake White were visiting. The trip was made for them, and such a treat was unexpected.

Late August rains turned the few uncleared lots at the Cove into a garden of wild flowers—wild snapdragon and morning glory climbing over thorny shrubs, gaillardia, polypteris, silverleaf sunflowers, and wild turk's cap—a red mallow that Ellen Schulz and Connie called Mexican apple. The red mallow was a hummingbird favorite and seemed to be designed for them; the tubular corolla curled inward and never opened fully, making it difficult for any but a long-tongued nectar sipper to reach inside. Sunflowers were the second choice of the hummers, which occasionally sipped at milkweed.

Hummingbirds swarmed at the flowers. Noisy and belligerent, they scuffled over choice blossoms and perches, chittering and dashing here and there; they seemed to fight more than they sipped. Some days there would be only a dozen or so, other days up to a hundred, mostly ruby-throats and black-chins, a few broad-tails. On August 31 a bright male rufous arrived and promptly took possession of the choicest flowers.

Rain fell in torrents one day—Jack emptied his six-inch gauge twice—and continued intermittently for a week but failed to discourage the hummingbirds or those who came to see them. Dr. Harrison counted 175 at the Cove one day, but there were hummingbirds all over town, too. Wherever the birders went they saw hummingbirds—scattered, perhaps, because the clearing of land for buildings at the Cove had diminished the food supply.

A male rufous was seen at intervals throughout the migration; whether they saw the same or a different bird was uncertain. It was present one day for Stan Quickmire and Bob Fox, when broad-tails were predominant.

Texas Ornithological Society members converged on Rockport at Thanksgiving for a fall field trip. Twenty vehicles were crammed with birdwatchers, who saw one hundred species the first morning, among them five hundred long-billed curlews in one pasture, three sage thrashers, and fortuitously, two very late scissor-tailed flycatchers, the adopted symbol of TOS.

In the quiet weeks that followed, Connie had one great surprise: chickadees on the Market Loop, far out of place, with no unusual weather conditions. Marsh wrens and bluebirds were at Salt Lake, and a burrowing owl had taken a post by the old tin barn on the road to Bayside.

A Christmas Eve norther sent the mercury down to thirty degrees, a great horned owl called through the night, and there was ice on the ground on Christmas. It quickly melted under a bright sun. On the last day of the year Connie found Harris' sparrows again at the frog farm and lesser goldfinches with the usual American goldfinches.

The Christmas Count made New Year's Day, 1954, included a masked booby for the Lockwoods, a new bird for them. Among the 128 species counted was an unexpected Tennessee warbler with the pines, a palm, yellowthroats, and both races of yellow-rumped warblers.

Next day Connie took Hal H. Harrison and his wife around to see Rockport birds. He had come to photograph whooping cranes but could not pass up a day in the field with Mrs. Hagar, he said.

She was at choir practice an evening in mid-January when Jack settled Dr. and Mrs. A. A. Allen in no. 8, but the distinguished Cornell University ornithologist with white hair and white mustache was at her steps when she started her rounds the next day.

"Good morning," he said. "I am Arthur Allen. May I go birding with you?"

With an unladylike snort she exclaimed, "Now I have seen everything, when Dr. Arthur Allen wants to bird with me!"

The day was his, for shorebirds mainly, and seeing them in

abundance, so close by, just sitting in a car, was an exceptional experience for him. Next day he retraced their route in order to tape voices of the birds. Late that afternoon a caller from the fish house reported a stowaway on one of the shrimp boats, a booby. Connie went for it, and the guests were gathered in front when she returned and got out of the car with the big bird wrapped in a towel.

"What on earth is it?" one asked when she opened the towel.

"It's an immature masked booby," she said, then, suddenly embarrassed, handed the bird to Dr. Allen, saying, "Here I go showing off when we could have an expert opinion. Dr. Allen, will you identify this bird for us?"

"It's an immature masked booby," he said, stroking the bird and adding in a low voice as if speaking to himself, "Imagine having a masked booby alive in my hands."

The bird was released. It lingered a while, then took off. The Allens went on to the Valley but were back ten days later. Having retired from his post at Cornell University, he was on an uncrowded lecture tour that allowed him time to record voices and photograph birds as he traveled. The Allens returned several times, always in winter. "It's the place to be in winter," he said.

During their stay in the Valley Connie had found and then lost a strange buteo. It had everything the field guide said it needed to be a short-tailed hawk, but that species was a nonmigratory Florida bird. Brownie found it again the day after his arrival in February; he was alone that day because Connie was out with Velma Geiselbrecht and a group from Beeville. He too thought it was a short-tailed hawk, dark phase, but its being a bird of such limited range, and that range so far away, Brownie doubted his own eyes. Would Connie mind if he called Frank Watson? She didn't; all available brains were needed for this case.

Watson could not get away immediately. "Just hold the hawk," he urged, and when he did come nine days later Connie had a program in Corpus Christi. Brownie had located the hawk again, and when she got home that afternoon Frank's greeting

[208]

was, "Miss Connie, you do have a short-tailed hawk. Heaven only knows how it got here."

The bird hung around in the vicinity of Port Bay Club for three weeks; many people saw it, and more than one of scientific bent wanted it collected. Connie adamantly refused to let a bird be killed just for a record, even for a Texas record.

On a program trip to Laredo she enjoyed seeing many Chihuahuan ravens, as well as caracaras and Harris' hawks on nests, and she especially enjoyed dining across the Rio Grande in Nuevo Laredo—she never passed up Mexican food. Driving home she noted again, as she had the previous spring on the King Ranch, that many pyrrhuloxias had bright red beaks, mostly males she suspected, but could not be sure.

She mentioned it to the Edwardses, and Lee promptly challenged. Possibly orange, but *not* red. "The bills look like cherries stuck on their faces," Connie insisted tartly. "I think it is a transient color phenomenon like the translucent blue on Louisiana heron bills at the peak of mating excitement." Brownie was also skeptical.

"I'll show you," she said, stressing the verb, and that week she led them on a tour of the King Ranch pasture loop. Many pyrrhuloxias had fiery probosces.

"Amazing," said Lee, and when Brownie refused to concede, Lee added, "It's there Brownie. Give up."

Still smoldering a bit, Connie had the last word. "I'll be glad if you boys ever learn that I do not make up these stories."

Peace was restored by black-throated sparrows galore and mountain plovers, and near home, on the Bayside road, chestnut-collared longspurs foraged in short grass.

In mid-April all birders rushed to Goose Island to see the swallow-tailed kite discovered by Ruth and Roger Ernst. It remained through Easter for Guy to see. A Couch's kingbird was a bonus.

Dr. J. L. Baillie of the Royal Ontario Museum led a group from Toronto that came in May, the first of many Canadians who would come in future years.

The busiest nurseries that June were around Salt Lake and on Copano Ridge: common and lesser nighthawks, black-necked stilts, gull-billed and least terns, black skimmers, snowy and Wilson's plovers. At Moore's Pool yellow-billed cuckoos delivered slender green worms to a stubby-tailed offspring so freshly feathered, its pristine white shirtfront was thickly ruffled on both sides. Bell's vireos tended a nest in the Hagar oaks.

One day a common merganser rested on a shell reef off South Beach; it had to be a bird in trouble, Connie had learned, otherwise it would not be there, or at that time. And she wondered what a gnatcatcher was doing in June at Redbug Corner. She focused on it, waiting until the bird finally cocked its tail so she could see the underside—black, a black-tailed gnatcatcher. It stayed two days.

Jack was involved in the big fish fry the Lions Club gave on the Fourth of July. The day before, Connie drove as far as Little Bay, saw clapper rails lead seven silky black chicks into the reeds, and turned home. She was not well; things were out of focus. At home she pretended to read. The book floated before her eyes, but she would not trouble her husband; the Lions Club meant so much to him.

Through the Fourth the uncomfortable sensations came and went. Between spells she felt all right, but on the fifth she could not lift her head without everything swimming to the left. Jack's Lions Club brother, Dr. Elliot, found her blood pressure alarmingly high. He put her to bed, prescribed medications and regular rest, as well as less activity, fewer visitors, fewer speeches, and no long distance driving to make them. Jack nodded agreement; she had made forty speeches in the past year.

He hovered like a mother hen, turning away callers, not always tactfully, during her rest periods. He was a worried man. To her, the worst part was that she could neither think nor remember. But the worst lasted only a week, and then she began to venture out with others on short excursions. By the end of the month she was making daily but shorter rounds. Many of her August notes were of birds seen by others, but in September a black-tailed gnatcatcher popped up in her own yard. Could it be another? Or had the same one been around all summer unseen?

Connie was sick again in October, the same symptoms, and

Jack had been ill, too. Though he was well now, it depressed her; they were getting old. She resumed her bed rest and by the end of the month was again much better.

In November she went out with the Paulsens for an hour every day but was not along when Jane heard the unmistakable nasal call of a red-breasted nuthatch. Knowing it would be new for Connie in Rockport, they rushed back to get her and found it again, working its way down a tree trunk. They saw it the next day, too.

The Texas Ornithological Society came again at Thanksgiving, and though she could not participate, Connie appreciated and thoroughly enjoyed the short visits of her friends—short because Jack forewarned them and stood watchfully in the background to make sure his wife did not tire.

Her family came at Christmas, much concerned about her health, but she felt well then. It was a lovely Christmas Day, beautiful weather, wild flowers blooming all over—to the amazement and delight of another party from Toronto.

The new year, 1955, meant a wonderful new toy for Jack—television. The Corpus Christi station was not high-powered, and the signal was too weak for really good reception in Rockport, but Jack had added all the supplements available to get a signal at all and was enchanted with the programs he received, erratic though they were. Next to politics, prizefights were his favorite entertainment.

Bay tides were extremely low in late February, shorebirds and waders fed far out on mudflats, and one clear afternoon Connie and Guy, standing on the shore of Lamar Peninsula, looked across St. Charles Bay to the southern tip of Blackjack Peninsula and saw three whooping cranes stalking the shallow water. Only twenty-one cranes returned to Aransas Refuge that winter, and for the first time in several years they had failed to bring back even one young one.

March came in like a lamb, and soon the migration was in full swing, the Cottages full. All the regulars came: the Stevenses, Edwardses, the Stileses, the Ernsts.

They made up parties to charter boats and cruise up the Intracoastal Canal to see the whooping cranes; it was the best way because the big birds were not as shy of boats as they were of land vehicles. The guests gathered each evening on cottage steps to talk about the day's lists.

One evening Roger Ernst left a group saying, "See you later. I'm going up to see Connie for a few minutes." Halfway there he dropped to the ground and was dead when the others reached him. The tragedy stunned them all. The Hagars were deeply shaken; nothing like this had ever happened before. But Ruth Ernst stood the shock bravely. If it had to happen, she said, she was thankful that it happened when they were among friends and when Roger was doing what he most liked to do. The friends arranged for her sad trip home.

Katherine Richmond added another new species to the area list, albeit a dead one, found on Mustang Island while she was with Dallas friends. It was in good condition, and she took it to Connie for identification. Connie was out, and Brownie took it, a strange one to him, too, as it was to Connie when she came home. "It is a shearwater," she said, "but not a sooty. Let's get the books and key it out." The bird proved to be an Audubon's shearwater. She prepared the skin and sent it to Lowery for his museum collection.

The shearwater was Brownie's last life bird. He left at the end of May and would not return. He fell ill in the fall, and surgery followed. Ruth and Lee Edwards saw to his needs and kept Connie informed. Brownie improved for a while, but a sudden reverse was fatal. Connie grieved for him as she had for few people. Through the years whenever his name came up, as it often did, she would go misty-eyed and say, "My but he was a good birder. We had some wonderful times together."

Leonard Hall, author of a syndicated column about wildlife on his Possum Trot Farm in the Missouri Ozarks, and his wife came at the end of their long Audubon Screen Tour travels to rest up and to meet Mrs. Hagar. He wrote a column about her and sent her a copy from the Saint Louis newspaper.

Another spell of high blood pressure put her to bed for several days in August, but she could help others by marking places on her little maps.

Even fewer hummingbirds came to the Cove; more lots had

been cleared, more houses built, and only the tip of the shell reef was left in a wild tangle. Connie felt deprived, but she found another formerly impenetrable wild area at the north end of Live Oak Point, the peninsula abutting Copano Bay. A shell-covered roadway had been laid to accommodate an oil rig, which upon producing, was converted to an inconspicuous and inoffensive Christmas tree installation.

The road circled by but left intact a grove of grand old oaks, and ran through a broad spread of granjeno, brasil, briars, and abundant wild turk's cap, or Mexican apple, so attractive to hummingbirds. The tract was nearly a mile long and half a mile wide between Highway 35 and the fishermen's mecca, Oystercatcher Point, and the bay. In its center it sloped into a swale that often held fresh water all year.

On Live Oak Point in late August, when the red mallow bloomed, Connie discovered her missing hummingbirds. Early one morning with Patch beside her, she turned her car into the bumpy road and saw hummers darting across it. She drove on. More hummers. Leaving the car, she stood on the bumper guard to look over the shoulder-high wild shrubs; there were hummingbirds as far as she could see in all directions—darting, chittering, fighting, and sipping at the turk's cap.

Every day, morning or afternoon or both, she visited the Point, often bringing others who were interested, and never was there a day without hummingbirds. Numbers varied as migrants moved on and others arrived. Some days there were fifty, other days up to a thousand. Females and young she did not attempt to identify, and they were most abundant, but many male ruby-throats and black-chins were present, fewer broad-tails and rufous. One morning as she walked slowly around, she came face to face with a big hummingbird with a bright red throat and crown—an Anna's hummingbird. It darted after an invading enemy but came back to perch on a dead coral bean branch. It defended that territory for half an hour as she watched. This Anna's did not remain for her to show to others, but in September after Hurricane Hilda sideswiped the coast and went into Mexico, a very aggressive male Anna's stayed on for several days, hissing and twittering at lesser hummers, and was seen by many.

[213]

For several days a female Anna's was seen defending a red hibiscus at Palm Village.

So many hummingbirds came that they spilled across the highway as far as the Jolly Roger Camp. One day Connie estimated three thousand hummingbirds within a square mile.

Connie wondered where these birds came from and where they went when they departed. That year, and in succeeding years as the phenomenon was repeated, she alerted Valley birders and others to be on the lookout for similar congregations. She mentioned it in a radio interview and again in an article about her in *Texas Game and Fish* magazine.

Response was limited. Dr. Pauline James wrote that on a field trip to South Padre Island, she and her students were dazzled by so many hummers; a party breakfasting on the north end of the island reported hummers streaming south behind the dunes during their entire stay. Occasionally, they said, one paused to sip at a goat's-foot morning glory but quickly pushed on—in a rush. A Del Rio woman wrote that she had seen a big fall flight there, and one day when Connie was talking about birds to a gathering of nurses at the Corpus Christi Naval Hospital, she mentioned the hummingbird migration and immediately saw excitement in their faces. The nurses said that in the previous fall they had dodged hundreds of hummingbirds flying through the breezeway of their quarters.

Black terns and red knots migrated along the shore on a hot September afternoon when Dr. Clarence Cottam and Caleb Glazener of the new Rob and Bessie Welder Wildlife Foundation and Refuge near Sinton called to meet the "famous bird lady of Texas," as the ever-gallant Cottam called her. She was familiar with his long career in the U.S. Fish and Wildlife Service, the last eight years as an assistant director, and with his research so frequently cited in Bent's *Life Histories*. Glazener had been with the Texas Game and Fish Commission nearly as long.

They told of their plans for the foundation and refuge and urged her to come soon for an introductory tour. She accepted within the week. Creation of the foundation under the will of Rob Welder, of a pioneer ranching family, was virtually unique in

South Texas, where wildlife was still more exploited than appreciated. With other naturalists, Connie had high hopes for the project; it could change attitudes and perhaps start a trend.

In his car, equipped with a steel shield on the bottom so it would ride freely over low brush, Cottam took her over the seven thousand acres still wild and undisturbed except by grazing cattle and a few oil wells, included in the bequest. It was a wild ride; the steel plate beneath them was indeed requisite because Cottam all but ignored the few roads. He was euphoric about the possibilities. The refuge had everything typical of brushlands: oak mottes, hackberry mottes, pecan mottes, low hills, a small lake, several ponds, grasslands, and the Aransas River on one long border. All this was inhabited by deer, javelinas, coyotes, and other mammals, as well as reptiles and amphibians; myriad insects, including mosquitoes; and a vast variety of birds. There would be research assisted by visiting graduate students and protection of wildlife. Connie sang in her heart and aloud on her way home; something very fine was in store for Texas.

Following a cold front in October thousands of Canada geese honked their way south, and at a lower level, monarch butterflies by the thousands also were bearing south, tilting and fluttering from plant to plant. There were other butterflies in numbers—queens, angelwings, sulphurs—but monarchs dominated the scene.

Connie had read of the monarch studies of Dr. F. A. Urquhart of the University of Toronto and had learned more from the Stileses of Grand Rapids and from Dr. and Mrs. Jaquith of Toronto during their stay the previous January. Both Harry Stiles and Mrs. Jaquith were cooperators in the Urquhart program and had been extremely interested in the monarchs they saw in Rockport at that season. This fall migration seemed exceptional to Connie; she decided to keep notes on it and report it to Dr. Urquhart.

Another tundra swan was shot by a hunter that fall.

Carrie Holcomb and the Charles Hamiltons came to share Thanksgiving with the Hagars and to remain for the weekend TOS gathering. The Friday evening session was held on the

Hagars' back lawn with Julian Howard of Aransas Refuge talking about whooping cranes and Cottam about plans for Welder Refuge.

The Hamiltons and William Harrisons of Dallas had birded Mustang Island that day and were late for the evening session but had news that almost broke up the party. They had found a bird they were not going to call a cattle egret until Mrs. Hagar said they could. There was a stampede to Mustang Island next morning, and Connie agreed, as did all, that it was indeed a cattle egret. This species, native to Asia and Africa, was presumed to have made its way under its own power in recent years to South America, later into the Caribbean, and recently into Florida. Finally it had reached Texas. This individual, however, remained only three days—to be seen, that is.

Early in December Connie found a large caterpillar, handsomely banded in yellow, green, and black, which she recognized as the larva of the monarch butterfly. It was chewing on a milkweed. Here, perhaps, was a chance to observe at least a part of the life cycle of the creature. She cut the milkweed stem with the worm attached and placed it in a large open jar, which she set near the north window of her bedroom.

In a few days the caterpillar quit eating; it was ready for the next dramatic phase, and she watched as it shed its skin and became a beautiful pale green chrysalis with gold spots, "like a glass house with gold nails." There the chrysalis clung, inert, for two weeks. On the day after Christmas the glass house began to crack, the form inside struggling feebly, and slowly it emerged, a limp thing with wrinkled, drooping, damp brown-and-black wings. Clinging to its shell, it rested. Then, in a series of violent convulsions, it pumped fluid into the black veins of the wings and they spread wide. Again it rested, for nearly two hours, as the wings dried and became stiff. At midafternoon Connie released a perfect monarch butterfly to fly free and wild.

Chapter 12

Life magazine called one December evening in 1955 during the quiescent period of the butterfly chrysalis. On twin chaise lounges squeezed into Jack's small office, the Hagars were watching the boxing matches on television. The telephone rang as the program ended. Jack took the receiver. "New York calling Mrs. Haaaggaaah," he sang out. The caller was an editor of *Life*, who said they were planning a picture spread on famous amateur naturalists and since she was among those included, would she consent to a photograph?

Politely asking for a moment to consider, Connie turned to Jack with a giggle. "Now I'm famous," she said and then explained. He beamed, giving his enthusiastic consent to a dozen photographs if they so wished. She thanked the editor and accepted. She would be advised well in advance of the photographer's arrival, the editor promised.

Jack was ready the next day and every day thereafter for weeks until his impatience became despair and disgust at the fickleness of magazine editors. Had they changed their minds?

Connie was flattered by the request but not overwhelmed; few Hollywood starlets had been photographed more than she, by amateurs and professionals alike. She almost forgot the offer. A brown creeper during the visit of Dallas birders was more exciting and so was having Norma and Jerry Stillwell there to record bird songs, and Dr. F. O. Novy of Michigan to band birds, and the Whitney Eastmans to show their color slides of birds and scenes encountered on their travels abroad.

Certainly more exciting was a friend who came with Dr. Arthur Allen—Dr. Robert Cushman Murphy, who was rather surprised but plainly pleased that Connie knew who he was. He was most amused by a territorial scuffle between two vermilion flycatchers.

February, 1956, was nearly gone before *Life* called again; the photographer would be there at half past eight Tuesday morning, the twenty-eighth.

His plane landed at the Corpus Christi airport before daylight. James Rowe, *Caller-Times* reporter and *Life* stringer, met him with the rented car he had requested. The photographer sniffed the warm February air. "Clear," he observed with satisfaction. "New York is bogged down in snow." Driving into the city he asked, "Will I get good pictures? Lots of birds?" Rowe warned him that the subject was a birdwatcher, not a birdcatcher.

Twelve hours later when Rowe returned him to the airport, the photographer, dean of the picture staff, with seventeen years' experience on the magazine, growled unhappily: "Editors sit around a table in New York and think up pictures, expecting them to turn out exactly as planned without any idea of how they may be gotten or whether they fit the subject. And if your pictures don't conform to their preconceived plans, they don't like them, even when they are better pictures."

Rowe laughed. He knew Mrs. Hagar well and could imagine the contrast she must have been to a preconceived notion of a Texas bird woman, leather-skinned and in baggy pants.

Punctuality being almost a disease with Connie, she was dressed well ahead of the appointed hour in a full skirted, snug-waisted lilac frock freshly washed and ironed, and a matching lilac sweater. Her white hair was immaculately waved beneath an invisible hair net; her white slippers were sturdy and low-heeled.

Precisely at 8:30 A.M. the bell rang, and Connie opened the door for a broad-shouldered, impatient-looking man with dark wavy hair retreating from his forehead. She noticed his large, sensitive hands.

"Good morning. I am Alfred Eisenstaedt, sent by *Life* magazine to take three study portraits of Mrs. Jack Hagar: one in her living room, one with her dog, and one with the birds."

His name made an impact. Few literate or illiterate people could be unaware of the work of Alfred Eisenstaedt. Connie had an impish impulse to apologize for lack of a red carpet but instead spoke in her sweetest, candle-lit, receiving-line manner.

"Come in, Mr. Eisenstaedt. I am Mrs. Hagar." He did a doubletake, scanned the dainty figure from head to foot and then back to head again, apparently adjusting to a surprise.

"When can we start?"

"Right now. I am ready."

It was too much. "My God," he said, "does your hair look like that all the time?"

"Yes, sir."

"My God, do you dress like that all the time?"

"Yes, sir."

He clamped a large hand in her hair, gently turning her head one way and another. "I can't take you like this outdoors; for the living room it will do." They went into the living room; Jack helped transport enough photographic equipment, he estimated, to shoot up the town. Eisenstaedt paced the room, considering angles, adjusting tripods and lenses; he examined the shell collection on the bookcase, the antique glass. The string holders intrigued him. All this was apparently to put her at ease, an unnecessary effort. She was quite comfortable, except that it was difficult to resist laughing.

Riffling through a stack of sheet music, he elicited the history of her piano, then of the carmine-and-blue oriental rug on the floor. He asked questions but was less intent on the answers than on snapping shutters, exploding flashbulbs. His impatience vanished when he was at work; his concentration was unfaltering.

He posed her at the piano. "Play," he commanded. "Don't pretend, and don't pay any attention to me." She sat with a book. "Read. Don't just look at the book." There was a session with the aging Patch, the dog obliging but unimpressed; snapping shutters and flashbulbs were not new to him either.

Plainly unhappy with his shots, Eisenstaedt decided to go on to the beach; it was such a beautiful day. He began loading equipment in the car but paused in the doorway to blurt, "Haven't you something to wear that it more suitable for the outdoors?"

Connie beckoned him into the next room and pointed to double folding doors on the wall, saying, "You are standing in my bedroom, Mr. Eisenstaedt. There is my clothes closet with my entire wardrobe in it. You select something."

Unembarrassed, the photographer pawed the row of dresses from one end to the other then, hopelessly, pawed back to the first end. No slacks, no shorts, no pants of any kind. It must be true; she did look like this all the time! Finally, he handed her a bell-skirted charcoal cotton with a broad white starched collar, and Connie disappeared into the bathroom to change—and to laugh out loud. This was funnier by the hour.

"My God," he barked when she reappeared. "You're as dressed up as you were before!"

"I can't help it, Mr. Eisenstaedt. This is the way I dress."

"Nobody will believe it," he declared flatly. "Let's go." But he delayed again for one final effort to salvage something of the preconceived notion of a Texas bird woman; he had her remove the modest makeup she wore, and the hair net.

Jack Baughman, photographer and editor of the *Rockport Pilot*, joined them at the beach. Connie had relayed his request to be allowed to look on for a story and, for him, a golden opportunity to watch a *Life* man in action, particularly this *Life* man. Eisenstaedt had consented readily and was unfailingly gracious to the country editor—as gracious as he could be in the state of gloom that had settled on him, though the bright sun lifted his spirits some.

Yards of film were exposed, all unsatisfactory to the perfectionist behind the shutter. Baughman happily followed them around, taking pictures of Eisenstaedt taking pictures. At half past eleven Connie announced that it was time for her to go home and put Jack's lunch on the table.

"My God," cried the *Life* man wildly, "eat when the sun is shining?" Connie assured him that the sun would also shine that afternoon. He still resisted.

"My husband is a Yankee," she explained. "We eat three times a day—at six and twelve and six. I will take you to a restaurant if you wish, but we will be pleased to have you eat with us."

He accepted her invitation, sitting between the Hagars at the kitchen table and gazing out the window at the sunshine flooding the grounds. He ate fruit salad and melba toast and drank grapefruit juice, served with a paper napkin and the century-old Conger silver. But he was oblivious to everything but the sunshine. He had come to do a job and had not yet achieved his goal.

Connie did not mention her prescribed afternoon nap; she saw her guest as a craftsman of great skill and admired his unswerving devotion to his task. Soon they were at the Tules for more pictures. Patch was called in for some scenes, but nothing was right. At one point Eisenstaedt burst out woefully, "My God, can't you look rough?"

Back to the beach. The sand, the sea, and the shorebirds were what he really wanted. Willets and marbled godwits waded the edges, laughing gulls in fresh sooty snoods yakked raucously about matters that mattered to laughing gulls in springtime. Eisenstaedt fumed, and Connie serenely performed as directed, even sitting in a canvas chair to look at birds—which she never did on the beach. Baughman maneuvered the gulls into the air about the seated subject's head. Her binoculars were at the desired angle, her hair was blowing, she was smiling, and her eyes were "right." The shutter clicked and the photographer shouted gleefully: "That's it! That's what I want. It will make a beautiful spread." For the first time that day he smiled broadly, even laughed. Content, he packed his gear.

Again he sat with the Hagars, this time on the shaded back lawn, drinking more grapefruit juice and placing his chair to gaze into the setting sun. "I hadn't seen the sun for six weeks," he told them. Connie drank her delayed three o'clock beer, which rather startled him but also was somehow a comfort; it made her more human. At five o'clock he bade them a pleasant farewell and drove away to the airport and a plane bound for snowbound New York.

Connie was thankful that his appointment had been on Tuesday. On Wednesday the Nature Calendar noted, "Warm. Big dust storm from the Panhandle. Brown dust everywhere. No birds out." Brown dust blew for two days, during which Connie regaled her guests with accounts of the day with a *Life* photographer.

The result did not appear until September 10, 1956, another great strain on Jack's patience, but he had been consoled by the magazine's gift of a fat portfolio of the day's pictures.

In the six months between the photo session and the published result Connie recorded "the best migration in eight years." It was witnessed by birders from coast to coast; the Hagars welcomed the return of Ruth Ernst, who brought her cousins Jack and Rosalie Fiske, their first of many visits. They were early enough to be entertained by the frantic preparations for the mating season made by a male cactus wren on Frandolig Island. Within the week he completed his third nest in a thorny thicket, singing incessantly.

Verdins built nests nearby, Cassin's sparrows sang on the Rincon, and lark sparrows caroled in oak motts. Cattle egrets reappeared on Mustang Island, a highlight for a succession of Canadians. By month's end snowy plovers were on eggs.

Mid-April rains grounded songbirds in spectacular numbers. "More ceruleans than I ever saw," Connie wrote in her Calendar for April 23—a rather late date for them. And there were other warblers never common on the peninsula—blackpolls, Cape May, worm-eating—also a bit late. Wet pastures appeared to be undulating as masses of shorebirds foraged them.

One who benefited splendidly from the good migration was a young man from England, Stuart Keith. Upon finishing at Oxford he had come to America the previous fall to botanize a year before starting a career in finance in London. A great variety of birds in the Florida Keys, however, had diverted his purpose. He knew British birds and many Asian species learned during military duty in Korea, and on impulse he decided not only to see as many American birds as possible but also to do it in one year. Now on his own birding marathon, he was challenging the Peterson-Fisher record and knew from their account that he should be in Rockport in April, with Mrs. Hagar. She took him to the oaks behind the Cottages, introduced him to others, and left him "seeing many life birds all in one view," he said later. After an hour he rushed back to her door.

"Mrs. Hagar, please help with this bird. It's a hummingbird but so big and so gray." Female blue-throated hummingbird, she told him, having seen it the day before with Barbara Bodman of Baton Rouge.

"Of course! Of course! Thank you," he said, dashing back to the trees.

He scoured the area and stalked the oaks every day, his list growing to nearly three hundred by the time he left. More were added on his return in July with his brother Anthony, and the Harris' sparrow, among others, was added in November when he stopped by again, meeting Herbert Mills of the National Audubon board and birding with him for the first of many times.

"One of the side benefits of birding with Connie," Keith said often, "was meeting other birders."

He ended his year in Canada, setting a new year record with 594 species, a feat detailed in the September, 1961, issue of *Audubon*. By then he had abandoned his intended career in finance and was to become an associate of the American Museum of Natural History, and a founder and the first president of the American Birding Association.

On June 14, 1956, the Nature Calendar again had only one entry: "70 years old today. Quite too long."

In the tallest tree in the Rincon pasture was that month's prize exhibit—a downy white-tailed hawk chick in a nest. Through a telescope set up beside the road, Connie showed it to many visitors and watched it grow into a hulking youngster lurching around the platform and squealing hungrily when mice and rats were delivered too slowly.

Doris McGuire was with Connie often that summer. She had come several times with the Dallas birders but now came alone, for the single purpose of learning shorebirds. Her purpose and her dogged determination struck a chord of sympathy in Connie; shorebirds had brought her to the coast to live and would in time bring Doris to live next door.

Another bout with high blood pressure restricted Connie's activities in early August, but by the twentieth she was well enough to drive to Rattlesnake Point where the young white-tailed hawk soared high and a migration of three hundred nighthawks moved southward across the prairie. At Live Oak Point hummingbirds, dominated by black-chins, were massing to sip nectar in red mallow.

Their telephone began ringing before the Hagars themselves saw the September 10 issue of *Life*, and in the following weeks more calls, telegrams, and letters poured in from virtually every person who had ever visited Rockport. In time, everyone who wrote received an appreciative reply from Connie.

Under the title "An Eminent Company of Amateur Naturalists" was a nine-page spread of photographs and text. The introduction stressed that the "eminent company" all considered themselves amateurs, their avocations no part of their primary careers, which ranged from power-line troubleshooting to direction of a famous publishing house, but each had won the respect and admiration of professional scientists.

Four other women were cited: Margaret Morse Nice of Chicago for research on the song sparrow; Len Howard of Sussex County, England, also a bird student; the Honorable Miriam Rothschild of the famous banking family and Britain's foremost authority on fleas; and Nancy Rogers of Washington, D.C., speleologist and authority on bats.

Pictured were twelve Americans, six Britons, and one Swiss. Their interests covered birds, butterflies, fleas, bats, timber wolves, ants, ferns, reptiles, oology, abalones, conchology, and leopard sharks.

Eisenstaedt was right; the last picture he took that day was chosen for a full page in the magazine with the caption: "Probably the world's champion bird watcher is Mrs. Jack Hagar, 70, who lives on the Gulf Coast at Rockport, Texas. Watching migrant birds, which pass over her home in millions, she has added significantly to scientific knowledge of bird migration routes and has succeeded in correcting some scientific misconceptions about them. Here she sits on the beach with binoculars ready while overhead wheels a flight of terns, laughing gulls, and godwits."

The *Rockport Pilot, Corsicana Sun, Corpus Christi Caller* and *Times*, and other Texas newspapers made much of this recognition of a distinguished citizen. Several publications, including the *Christian Science Monitor*, followed up with stories of their own about her. Within the family Jack was euphoric, sister Bert chilly, Sonney and Alice May delighted. Soon thereafter, her brother had occasion to express his pleasure to the photographer when Eisenstaedt came to Schenectady for a *Life* story on General Electric's latest turbine.

[224]

"He told me," Sonney wrote, "that my sister was a fine subject, the most cooperative model he ever had. He was so nice I had the nerve to tell him that all the camera bugs in the plant yearned to meet him and watch him work, to which he agreed, and the shutterbugs had a field day, everybody shooting photos and talking cameras and lenses with the expert—all thanks to you."

Though unanimously pleased by the citation, not all her friends were pleased with the photograph itself. Opinions varied from "perfect," to complaints that it made her look old and that she was prettier than the picture. One from Kansas City wrote the *Life* editors:

> Sirs: In your amateur naturalists story was a full page picture of my friend Connie Hagar of Rockport, Texas. This lady of 70 is out each morning at 7 and can spot a Bullock's oriole on a wire at 50 yards against the sun. She is no chair birdwatcher and she knows each egg on Rattlesnake Point. Yours, Archibald J. Brier, M.D.

Connie enjoyed it all immensely, but her attention was focused on the monarch butterfly migration, so prolonged and abundant that she undertook tagging some for Dr. Urquhart. Also, the hummingbird scene on Live Oak Point was fantastic; an Allen's had appeared with a wave of ruby-throats and black-chins, and a rufous was present for comparison with the Allen's. An Anna's soon followed. Many birders were coming to see them, some skeptical until they saw for themselves.

One afternoon a young man in the uniform of a Navy lieutenant came calling, introducing himself as Burt Monroe, Jr., a name familiar to Connie and any reader of the *Auk*. He was on a short assignment to the Kingsville Naval Air Station. Many years later in College Station, Texas, for a meeting of the AOU, of which he was then an officer, Dr. Monroe spoke of his several visits to Rockport.

> I had, of course, heard of Mrs. Hagar and was delighted that this assignment gave me a chance to meet her, so I presented myself at the earliest opportunity.

We sat and chatted a long time, about mutual friends and birds, then drove around a bit, seeing roseate spoonbills, wood storks, the small plovers. I was most impressed by her knowledge, but I had one reservation—Anna's hummingbirds. Just too, too unlikely, but I didn't mention hummingbirds then.

On my next visit I felt that we were good enough friends to challenge her and I said I just could not accept that Anna's hummingbirds would show up at Rockport, Texas. Could she be mistaken? I asked.

She answered with a question, did I have enough time to go look? I said I had all the time in the world. We got in her car and drove to the Point. As I got out of the car a male Anna's hummingbird buzzed me right in the face!

Dr. Cottam telephoned; Anna's, Allen's, and rufous hummers had also been seen on Welder Refuge though there was no evidence of a mass migration in his area.

The vast numbers amazed Phil Lenna, who was visiting from California, where the suspect species belonged. Never, he said, had he seen so many hummers at one time in one place. He wondered, as did others, what circumstances made it possible.

Lenna had no car; Connie dropped him off at the Point every morning, and he birded back afoot. He had missed the Allen's, but on the second day of his visit, Lenna discovered a Costa's hummingbird, adding still another unexpected species to the incredible Rockport list. The Costa's lingered for several days. (A year later, on a late September visit, Lenna and Dr. Harrison found at the Cove a Lucifer hummingbird, which also lingered for several days.)

Another Costa's, or the same, was seen again with a fresh wave of birds that came after a weak cold front on September 29. In this push an albinistic hummingbird, believed to be a broadtail, arrived for a two-week stay at Dobkins Cottages on Fulton Beach. A pretty creature, it was white except for faint gray on wings and tail; eyes and feet were black. The bird followed a set menu—sips at yellow esperanza, a dip into red hibiscus, then to a lavender vine, and back to the esperanza again.

Other birds were not ignored, and again, as Connie often remarked, "the kindness of other people" opened her eyes to new phenomena. Shirley Rozelle, a shrimper, brought a bird strange to him but not to her, a chuck-will's-widow, but it was found in a strange situation. It was one of a flock of about twenty-five like it, he said, that followed his boat from about twenty-five miles out in the Gulf. This one fell dead on the deck, but the others had moved on. Goatsuckers migrating across the Gulf was new to her.

On October 2 Jane and Martin Paulsen, pretending to be unaware of any special significance of the date, so insisted on taking the Hagars out to dinner that Jack broke a long-standing habit and accepted. It was his eightieth birthday.

Dr. Lawrence Walkinshaw, who had shared honors with Connie in the *Life* story, his wife, the Houston bunch, and Burt Monroe were visiting when a downy woodpecker, far from home, visited the oaks. A Connecticut warbler also came.

A busload of Oklahoma ornithology students and their professors were too many for Jack to house at Thanksgiving, but Connie told them where to go for birds they most wanted to see. On their last evening, the wife of one professor came to show Connie two wonderfully constructed nests she had collected and was most proud of—verdin nests. Connie was shocked and spoke angrily without thinking: "You should never have taken those nests. They are the birds' winter roosts. Where will they sleep tonight?"

The woman was so contrite she almost wept. Her ashamed husband knew about verdins and cactus wrens but had simply forgotten. They wanted to replace the nests, but the damage was done. After they left and Connie cooled down, she too was ashamed. The professor was a gentle man who would not knowingly harm birds. "I should not have been so rough on them," she apologized to Jack. "But, damn. They are ornithologists and should have known better."

A December flock of white-throated sparrows contained a melanistic member, black all over. A small flock of pink-sided juncos foraged leaves beneath the oaks, which were inhabited by a black-throated gray warbler.

New Year's Day, 1957, was foggy, but Connie looked like spring when she stepped out in festive attire that afternoon, noting that the orange-crowned warbler sipped again at the red mallow, a peculiarity this individual had shown since its arrival. Because Mrs. Jackson was such a longtime friend, and Annie Ruth's mother, she had consented to pour tea at the Jacksons' open house.

She wore navy blue silk sprinkled with bright flowers, chosen by Cleo Townsend, who had opened a dress shop in Rockport and bought Connie's entire seasonal wardrobe when she went to market twice a year. It was a great boon to Connie because women's clothes in her small size were hard to find; besides, she disliked shopping. For shoes she simply telephoned a favorite clerk at Lichtenstein's in Corpus Christi who knew her size and preferences.

She wore the flowered dress again at midmonth when she was guest speaker for the Women's Club luncheon at Kensloe House in Corsicana. Winnie Rice went along to drive, in the face of a blizzard that pushed the mercury down to twenty-two degrees. They stayed with Bert, Connie occupying her old room in the Neblett home, which Bert had maintained just as it had looked in the period in which it was built.

There were many new faces in the audience but many old friends, too, and Connie felt a warm glow to be among them again. Typically, Bert interrupted her sister's talk with comments that were not always helpful, and on the way home next day, through a frozen landscape half the way, Winnie declared that Bert had been entirely too caustic.

"Somebody has to keep me in my place," Connie answered cheerfully.

While visiting Lonnie Ring at Alamo in February, her worst spell of high blood pressure befell her; she was too ill to be moved for several days, and after Lonnie brought her home, she remained bedridden for two weeks. Until the end of March she was able to go out only for short rides with guests, who faithfully kept lists for her. Into the month of April she felt insecure among more than three or four people; too many voices confused her, her head swam, and she could not hear well.

Another spectacular spring migration, as good as the previous year's, was "the best" to Judge Allen Simpson of Racine, who was staying a month, longer if the birds cooperated he said. On previous visits with the Wisconsin birders he had stayed only a week, fishing and playing golf. Now retired after twenty-seven years on the bench and long widowed, he proposed to travel as much as he had always wished to do—and the emphasis would be on birds, "in self-defense," he said. "Ninety percent of my friends are birders. Besides, birds add so much meaning to travel." He took no. 7 and for many years thereafter called it his second home.

Judge Simpson enjoyed people as much as he did birds, and it was mutual. Several guests would arrange their stays to coincide with his. Women appreciated his courtly manners, men his affable disposition and entertaining yarns.

Whenever Connie was indisposed, the judge, with pride, efficiency, and elegance, took charge of guests who needed guidance. He was available when Connie needed an escort, and many of her morning and evening rounds were made with him in his Cadillac. Patch, relegated to the back seat, did not complain.

He organized a chartered boat trip on Easter to see the whooping cranes, spotting fifteen of America's tallest birds. Connie did not make the trip. She went to the Easter sunrise service with Doris McGuire and Jack.

Her thousands of indigo buntings reported over so many years had aroused the curiosity of Aaron Bagg, editor of *Audubon Field Notes*; he had asked the previous year for actual numbers, explaining that he was making a study of the species and wondered about so many being at Rockport. "Nobody dreamed that such numbers traveled around the Gulf," he wrote. "It has been thought that most come north through Florida." Connie had counted up to forty thousand and quit, insisting that counting individuals in such masses deprived one of seeing other species.

However, Bagg had asked for numbers again, and she agreed to help. Henry Wiggins and Bennett Keenan of Boston were counting also: 600 on their first round, 274 in another field, 65 on the Hagars' front lawn their first day and on through other days when the migration picked up. Connie wondered about the coincidence—or was it? These men were friends of Bagg; why were they especially interested in indigo buntings? Were her reports still disbelieved until verified by the Eastern elite? When she sent in her report, she suggested that Bagg consult these two men, and the editor replied: "The day your letter arrived Keenan was with me relating all the wonderful things he saw at Rockport."

May Day saw the entire peninsula swarming with eastern wood-pewees, surely at least a thousand pewees it was agreed; five hundred Franklin's gulls beat against a northwest wind over a field of yellow-headed blackbirds, scissor-tailed flycatchers, and many grasshopper sparrows. A south wind on May 3 brought a swallow-tailed kite and a long migration of broad-winged hawks that Connie and Mary Donald followed on Farm Roads 1781 and 2165 for an hour, and still the hawks were coming when they turned home at lunchtime.

Next day the wind came from the north, hard and cold, with a storm in the Gulf that wrought havoc among migrating birds. The afternoon *Times* had a front-page photograph of Chaparral Street in the business district of Corpus Christi, littered with hundreds of dead birds that had been hurled against the building by the winds.

The storm kill was widespread—huge kills in other places in the city, plus many birds confused and swirling around. On Padre Island Pug Mullinax and Fred Stark saw thousands of birds seeking refuge through an open door in a building under construction. "The room was stacked with birds, many alive, but more dead," Pug said.

Perhaps because of the storm, a great kiskadee appeared on Farm Road 881, but soon left. Friends filled sacks with storm victims for Connie—warblers, vireos, grosbeaks, buntings, thrushes, orioles; almost every migrant family was represented.

But the lives of the unfortunate avian travelers were not entirely wasted; next day Connie displayed the colorful victims to a class of fifth-graders, their teacher, and some parents from Corpus Christi who came for a bird talk in her backyard. The children handled the birds tenderly, marveling at the bright colors and awed by Mrs. Hagar's explanation of their travels and how they had died. None of these children, she believed, would ever take a bird's life lightly.

Concerned about the diminishing colony of wood storks in Florida, National Audubon had assigned Bob Allen to do a comprehensive survey and a study of possible causes. He wrote for Connie's records and asked her if she would keep exact counts that summer. For him Connie would cheerfully have counted peep tracks in the sand.

"Your flintheads," he speculated, "may come up from Mexico. Try a little Spanish on them." In closing he said, "Everything is fine here except both youngsters are grown and away from home, so Evelyn and I are back where we started."

Dr. Cottam shared Connie's concern about the brown pelicans and was making a survey of them; in recent years fewer and fewer were breeding on the Texas coast. On Corpus Christi's bayfront, where pelican antics had so long entertained tourists, there were still tourists but no brown pelicans. No longer did misguided fishermen destroy nests and young on the breeding islands; that atrocity had been stopped, so they were not to blame. Scientists suspected that the residue of pesticides and herbicides so lavishly poured on farmlands was washing into the bays and being ingested by fish that the pelicans ate, but nothing had been proved.

Between long gaps in the Nature Calendar during August, 1957, were occasional notations, "Out with my head." Connie spent much of the month in bed; propped up with pillows she could read a short time, write a letter or two, or chat for a while with a caller.

Patch occupied the foot of her bed, methodically fringing the pink towel on which he was supposed to stay. From time to time he paused, kinky pink threads dangling from his teeth, to gaze adoringly at the head on the pillows.

A big migration of common nighthawks, followed by small flights of lesser nighthawks, passed over the Cottages September 2, but larger flights passed over Corpus Christi two days later. Kay called from the newspaper to say that people all over the city noticed it and wanted an explanation. Many asked if they were dangerous.

Connie was much better when the Edwin Way Teales arrived the evening of October 2, and early the next morning she rushed them to the Cove to see the Lucifer hummingbird lest it leave and they miss a new species for both. They would indeed have missed it for the bird, found by Phil Lenna and Dr. Harrison earlier in the week, left that day.

On Pike's Peak the Teales had finished nineteen thousand miles of the coast-to-coast travel for his next book, *Journey into Summer*, and, taking the long way home to Connecticut, they would have two weeks in Rockport, strictly for pleasure, Teale said, though he never neglected his notebook, camera, and typewriter for even a day.

He exposed yards of film on Patch, intrigued by the dog's perfect birding manners. One like him, Teale said, was worth a magazine story and he would write it. The story was published in *Nature* magazine, October, 1958.

They spent a day on Welder Refuge with Dr. Cottam, an afternoon with Winnie and Rob Roy Rice on the *Rusty* cruising to Lydia Ann Island to see 150 white ibises and many spoonbills. Monarch butterflies crossed the water all afternoon. The guests made the morning trips with her but prowled on their own each afternoon, lingering with the hummingbirds still passing on Live Oak Point.

Connie drove slowly along South Beach one morning, Teale beside her, Nellie, Doris McGuire, and Patch in the backseat, when Teale glimpsed a shining object awash at the edge of the water.

"Connie, back up. I think there's a bird in trouble."

"It's a fish," she said, not stopping.

"Feathers," Teale insisted.

"Fish," she reiterated, but shifting into reverse anyway. A large dead drum floated in the shallows.

"Edwin Way Teale, if you can't tell feathers from scales," she said scathingly, "I'm never going out with you again." He grinned sheepishly.

A few days later there was a bird in trouble. The town's one taxi driver came to tell her indignantly that some boys were leading a white pelican around on a leash; it was now tied up behind the shell shop.

"I'll go after that bird," Connie blazed. "I'll take Patch." A small torch of fury, she went for scissors while Jack backed out the car, glad to be on this end of her mission rather than the other.

Tied to a post, the pelican panted in the scorching sun. She cut the cord, wrapped the big bird in a towel, and marched angrily back to the car. If anyone saw her they dared not interfere—certainly not the culprits. Headed for the beach, she remembered that the Teales might like to see the bird and turned home. Guests gathered around, some astonished that so small a woman could handle such a big bird and even more astonished that she would dare to confront naughty boys.

"When I'm that mad, I feel big as the courthouse," she said, "and would be if it took that to get the bird, but when I cool off, I'm weak as a sponge."

At the beach Teale photographed her, ankle-deep in the water, setting the pelican down and giving it a shove. It settled quietly, head and pouch resting in its breast. Then he wanted both women in the scene.

"Step out to the end of the spit, and Nellie, you get behind Connie." His amply upholstered wife, barely taller than Connie but considerably wider, guffawed.

"That will be the day, when I hide behind Connie!"

The printed picture showed both women shading their eyes from the sun, squinting speculatively at the pelican. "You look as if you were praying," the photographer commented.

Rockport did not figure in Teale's next book but did in the one following, *Wandering through Winter*, which would earn him a Pulitzer Prize. It was this visit in 1957, however, and others to follow that furnished material for the longest chapter in the book—on Connie and the hummingbirds. Also on this visit, the Teales met Sibyl and Earl Means—and their seventy-nine cats.

The Meanses had made it in oil and had retired early enough to enjoy their wealth. They bought twenty-seven acres facing Fulton Beach near Live Oak Point, and in a grove of magnificent oaks they built a ten-room, one-story house around a large circular patio, designed so that each main room had a view of the bay. In a large greenhouse Sibyl grew orchids and other exotic plants. The garage wing housed four vehicles, servants' quarters, and a complete kitchen for preparing meals for the cats.

Wishing to learn birds, Sibyl had sought the fountain of knowledge, and because she, like Connie, always had a hearty laugh ready, they became fast friends. In her enthusiasm Sibyl had acquired an almost complete set of Dorothy Doughty's porcelain birds, including the scissor-tailed flycatcher, the only wall piece, with which Connie had assisted the Englishwoman through correspondence.

All this intrigued the Teales, but the cats were paramount, as they were to Earl and Sibyl. One pedigreed, long-haired tabby had come with the couple to Rockport, and Sibyl had purchased two others of impeccable lineage—all others were strays. Most of them had been dropped off in front of the Means place by the kind of people who would thus discard an animal. Many had arrived as helpless kittens. Each one was examined by a veterinarian, neutered, and welcomed into the fold. In the book Teale would devote six pages and photographs to the story of the good life inherited by these unwanted felines.

The year ended with still another new species for the watcher on the flyways, a Barrow's goldeneye discovered by Col. R. E. Montgomery. Ducks were his forte; at his home in the Valley he studied black-bellied whistling-ducks and enticed them to his place by providing nest boxes in trees. The ducks favored old carbide cans.

Chapter 13

Christmas week, 1957, had been bright with sunshine and the usual wintering birds swarming the peninsula; robins, eastern bluebirds, pine warblers with the hundreds of yellow-rumps on Goose Island; pine siskins with American goldfinches at Redbug Corner; ruby-crowned kinglets and blue-gray gnatcatchers; a solitary vireo.

The weather changed abruptly with a cold front and welcome rain on New Year's Eve. The Cottages were full for a clear but cold New Year's Day. Guests incuded the Deans of Chicago, who always came at a different time of year in order to see the variety of birds that would pass through Rockport, they said. The Hagars were vaguely aware that Dean was involved with government bonds, but two women among the guests knew his involvement precisely. When Jack casually introduced Howard Thayer Dean, the women were visibly awed; they worked in the bond department of Alamo National Bank in San Antonio. "You are the Howard Thayer Dean whose signature is on the bonds we handle?" He was, and affably inscribed that signature in their bird books. "Just wait 'til we show these at the bank!" they beamed. The signature outranked Sprague's pipits and the rufous hummingbird that so excited other guests.

An orange-crowned warbler shared the red mallow at the Hagar doorstep with the rufous hummingbird, but not always amiably. It had to be the same warbler that had fed there the previous winter, Connie thought; no other orange-crown had ever been interested in nectar.

[235]

High winds, high tides, and more rain marked the week; on January 5 Jack measured eight inches of rain and rejoiced. All through the fifties Texas rainfall had been below normal; crops, if any, were poor; dust storms and heat oppressive. Hopes were high that the seven-year drought would end, especially high when more rain fell on the tenth and a "gully-washer" on the twenty-third. Still the earth soaked up the water hungrily.

Mountain plovers remained on the Bayside prairie until mid-February; it was a tightly knit flock of thirty-one, numbering the same for two months. Hermit thrushes were numerous, and a yellow-breasted chat, overeager for spring, appeared at Lenoir's Landing.

Guests from the North chided natives who complained of cold; the weather was "bracing," said Lee Edwards. "Makes for good birding." Good fishing, too, thought Judge Simpson, who with a friend caught eighty-two trout, which he shared generously, and in the tiny kitchen of no. 7 cooked a fine fish dinner for himself and the Hagars.

Early-morning trips up Highway 35 to see the prairie-chickens dancing were enhanced for a short time by a large flock of lark buntings on the prairie, the males nearing perfection in their black nuptial plumage. In the other direction, three hundred avocets on Harbor Island and four hundred red knots on Mustang Island Beach were attractions.

The Hagars were saddened by the death of Dr. Atkinson. For forty-three years he had treated Connie's eyes, and she was desolated, also a bit frightened, but she would keep up the beer, as he had advised.

With Jack and Edith Stevens one day they found both species of bitterns, soras, and solitary and pectoral sandpipers in one swale, Baird's in another. Anhingas accompanied a flight of broad-winged hawks, followed next day by Mississippi kites. Golden-plovers in wet fields were too many to count, "at least a thousand," they agreed.

Burt Monroe with Francis Weston from Pensacola found an arctic loon near the Mustang Island causeway. Judge Simpson and Connie went at once to see it—it was new for both. It was late March, and the loon was in breeding plumage, as was a

Bonaparte's gull, a treat to Connie who knew them best in winter dress.

For once, birds that spring were of secondary interest to Connie; she was enthralled, as were many others, by the renascence of wild flowers. The long drought was over at last; roadsides and fields were blanketed with glorious colors. Seeds that had lain dormant for seven years responded to the winter rains, sprouted, and bore blossoms that had been almost forgotten. The phenomenon was statewide; newspapers commented in editorials and ran feature stories with color pictures. The flowers rejuvenated the spirits of drought-weary Texans.

Connie and Guy gave an entire late April day to the flowers. Though many of her favorite sites had been taken over by developments, her "secret garden" she had explored with Ellen Schulz and the Rockport cemetery were still safe and producing abundantly. Bluebonnets, paintbrush, winecups, larkspur, and many others all but covered the headstones in the cemetery. Next day they estimated five thousand dickcissels on Lamar Peninsula.

Roger Peterson joined them. He had come to Texas with Guy Emerson but had gone first to Austin for a few days with Edgar Kincaid. They had momentous news for Connie, but Guy had kept it quiet; it was Roger's right to tell her that the Texas Game and Fish Commission had engaged Peterson to write a field guide to the birds of Texas! She was overwhelmed; Texas alone among the states would have its own Peterson field guide. Connie felt no compunction whatever about her chauvinism; nothing was too good for Texas. She wanted to hug the world, to dance all over the front lawn. Peterson's asking her for help was a superfluous question.

They talked far into the night, examining her records, discussing problem birds, migrations, all aspects of the book. Sunday morning while Connie played for the church in Aransas Pass, the men went to see the buff-breasted sandpipers, gull-billed terns, and others. Then back to the records that afternoon and again far into the night.

He wondered about her limpkin records for Texas, a place where limpkins did not belong. Connie had indeed seen one

[237]

years before in East Texas; Bessie Reid had had it in her bathtub, probably the third record for the state. And as for two other Florida birds, the short-tailed hawk and gray kingbird, the former had been verified by Brownie and Frank Watson, the latter after a hurricane in 1951, when George and Steve Williams were with her.

Other birds were discussed then and in animated correspondence that kept Connie in the clouds all summer. The bill color of Caspian terns disturbed Peterson. Connie had mentioned orange-red, as had Griscom, but Peterson had never seen it among the thousands of Caspians he had looked at. Connie wrote back that the orange-red was distinctly different from the yellow-orange of royal tern bills, but she did not rely on bills to separate them; better field marks were the Caspian's darker wing tips, stockier build, and in winter, the notable difference in crowns. The Caspian's forehead was always a bit streaked, while the royal always had a white crown and a shaggier black crest.

As for meadowlarks, her checklist indicated that westerns were as common as easterns, which Edgar doubted, at Rockport, anyway. True, she answered, the checklist applied to the western part of the seven-county area covered in the checklist—though it should have shown them to be much scarcer in summers.

Peterson hoped to return to Rockport in the fall for the hummingbirds, "about as exciting as anything I have heard of lately," he wrote from Old Lyme, Connecticut, where he had moved. "I for one am not a doubting Thomas; it all seems quite logical."

He sent proof sheets from time to time for Connie to check, and he wrote, "We will have a good book because of all the fine help from you and others in Texas." He was corresponding with twenty-seven cooperators at the time.

Carl Buchheister and John Baker brought several Audubon board members to inspect the sanctuaries in May. They were elated by so many birds on eggs and many fledglings but sad that too many cardinals were rearing young bronzed cowbirds instead of their own progeny.

In July Bob Allen thanked Connie for her wood stork reports. He enclosed stamped cards for future news and wrote, "Although we have learned quite a lot about these birds there is still much to learn. Wish we could learn where the Texas birds come from! No colonies in Mexico to our knowledge, only small concentrations. Sandy Sprunt made a survey."

August was a blur to the Hagars. Patch was sick, soon so sick they took him to the animal hospital in Corpus Christi. They telephoned daily, only to hear that he was progressively worse. On August 18 the Nature Calendar noted, "Little Patch put to sleep. He was 13 years old."

Jack and Connie could not talk about it; to talk was to weep, so they sorrowed silently. Doris McGuire quietly removed the dog's little four-poster bed, piled half-full with his toys and a collection of well-gnawed bones of miscellaneous shapes. Bones had never been thrown away; Patch liked to work on various ones at various times.

A September hurricane bypassed Rockport but brought rain and a migration of black terns that stretched for a mile over the peninsula. Nighthawks, flycatchers, swallows, and swifts also passed. Huge marsh mosquitoes swarmed, especially at Live Oak Point with the hummingbirds. Birders earned their hummers that month and had bloody battle scars from the clouds of insects to prove it.

Groove-billed anis pushed well north of their Valley range that fall; Velma Geiselbrecht reported one in Beeville, another was in Indianola. A small colony had taken up at Flour Bluff in Corpus Christi, and a small flock found off Farm Road 881 remained for the winter.

High blood pressure troubled Connie in November. Jack drove her around when she was able to ride, but when the TOS came again at Thanksgiving, she was well enough to enjoy seeing old friends for short calls. The birders were most excited about the anis.

In early December she shopped happily for a wedding present for two of her favorites on the *Caller-Times*. Bob Mc-Cracken, managing editor who wrote the daily column "The Crow's Nest," which the Hagars as well as many South Texans always read first, and Kay Bynum were married. She was also well enough to attend the big Christmas open house held by Sibyl and Earl Means. Connie really loved a party now and then, just not too many close together.

The Lockwoods came for Christmas of 1958 and met the Hagars' new pup, a registered terrier given by a friend who "couldn't imagine the Hagars without a dog." Cheko was a nice puppy, but there would never be another Fuzzy or Patch. Rain poured all Christmas Day, but Bob and Ann went out after dinner anyway; Connie and Jack watched television and reread the hundreds of greeting cards and letters they had received.

When a hard January freeze threatened the turk's cap by the steps, Connie threw a blanket over it at nights lest the rufous hummingbird starve without it. The bird disappeared anyway, but after ten days it was back sipping nectar. Another hummingbird was not so hardy. Gertrude Cowie sent a dead Lucifer she had found frozen on her doorstep in Beeville.

"Such a pity," Connie said. "But if it had to die I am glad to have it. Those people who do not believe sight records will have to believe this."

Locke Mackenzie brought his wife for a long-promised visit, and the Hagars agreed she was indeed as beautiful as he had said. The doctor most enjoyed the seaside sparrows and golden-crowned kinglets and was surprised that tree swallows were migrating so early. They had first shown up January 6, Connie told him.

Benign February weather gratified guests from the cold states, as did a mockingbird singing all through moonlit nights. Connie and Judge Simpson, birding the oil field roads near Bayside and Bonnie View, discovered sedge wrens, counting fifteen in the tall cordgrass growing in a ditch. A prairie warbler was among the early March migrants, but Connie was again confined to her bed, as she would be more often that spring.

Against Jack's wishes, she had consented to a dozen bird talks for 1959, but fortunately the promised dates occurred between her spells of illness. They deprived her, however, of much of the gaiety attending the stay of two newcomers to the birding circle, both Scotsmen. Sir Robert Erskine-Hill had written from Edinburgh saying he wished to extend a Houston business trip in order to bird in Texas, and New York birders had recommended the Hagars.

"A baronet, a hyphenated baronet at that," commented Jack, eyeing the stationery. "How the devil do you address a baronet?"

"I don't know. I never met one," his wife replied, "but I will ask him," and she did.

"Just call me Erskine-Hill," replied the guest pleasantly. She was unable to do more than welcome him and retreat to her bed, but by then the other Scotsman, Ivan Sanderson, had arrived, and he and Judge Simpson, himself Scottish, did the honors for a day on Aransas Refuge, where they found whooping cranes, top species on Erskine-Hill's want list.

Sanderson, a popular science writer and mammalogist trained mainly in Britain but keenly interested in other sciences, was re-exploring the continent to gather material for his fifteenth book, which Random House would be publishing. The emphasis would be on ecology, a rather esoteric science at that time. He was also writing a related series for the magazine *Sports Afield*. His purpose, Sanderson said, was "to see what's left of our country before all of it is knee-deep in beer cans, Coke bottles, used-car lots, and atomic energy plants."

Traveling with him in a Plymouth station wagon specially equipped for their trade was Roy Pinney, a photographer. After meeting him, another guest found that covers of nine magazines on the drugstore newsstand were by Pinney; there was a rush for autographed copies; he signed Connie's *Better Homes and Gardens* for April, 1959.

In Sanderson, Jack Hagar met his match at one-upmanship and buffoonery. Their screwball antics and ceaseless exchange of gratuitous insults brought on a siege of levity lubricated by frequent cocktail parties featuring tequila and rum acquired on side trips to the Valley and Mexico.

In seeking Connie's advice on subjects treated in the book, Sanderson warned her that he was deemed a renegade by the "scientific boys" because he wrote for a wide audience and made lots of money from his books and from radio and television shows in America and in Britain. "Even being thanked by me for assistance is the kiss of death in the tight little scientific circle," he said, "so I am warning you in advance." She laughed and gave what help she could.

His book, *The World We Live In*, came out in 1962. Rockport was treated generously, and the *Pilot* boasted at length under the headline, "Rockport Makes the Book Again."

Erskine-Hill wrote his thanks from New York and again from Scotland, regretting that Mrs. Hagar's health had forbade his having more time with her. To Judge Simpson he had expressed amazement at the breadth of her knowledge and appreciation for her always immaculate appearance. The judge had agreed. "When I am with her I feel I have an encyclopedia at hand, and she always looks dainty and ladylike."

Roland Clement of the Audubon staff came with Baker's party in June, and Connie was able to go with them to see nesting fulvous whistling-ducks, least bitterns, and others at Moore's Pool. Ruth Ernst spend a long vacation with her; they had remained close since the death of Ruth's husband at Rockport. Sandy Sprunt, also of the Audubon staff, came later to determine the nesting success of several species.

Doris McGuire, who was the widow of a Dallas orthopedic surgeon, came to see birds and discuss her great plan: she wanted to move to Rockport to be near shorebirds and Connie. She said she had never liked cities anyway. The Hagars agreed to sell her two of their acres on which she would build her home, back from the street, behind their own cottage. The prospect of having her for a neighbor delighted Connie and Jack.

Edgar Kincaid came several times for the hummingbirds, often bringing his aunt, Mrs. Dobie, so she could see the wild flowers, which were having another good year. Edgar and Connie had a joint mission—to prove to Roger Peterson that reddish egrets did not always have a two-toned bill, as he had stated in his eastern field guide. They studied every reddish egret they could find, keeping counts on bill types. Those with dark bills lacking the pink base were young-of-the-year, they believed.

Texas Game and Fish magazine asked for another story from Connie, this time on the hummingbirds; five species appeared in that fall migration. Her story, "Whither the Whirly

Birds?" appeared in the October issue. It was an enthusiastic account, and informative, stressing the mystery of whence and why came the western birds, but it contained a few lapses of the pen. Connie wrote spontaneously, in longhand, and without a plan; she neither rewrote nor edited herself, nor was she edited—who would question her? Thus, "Nine species are regular in September and October" should have read "Nine species have occurred." Only two species were regular at any time, some others very rare. Another sentence reversed the status of ruby-throats and rufous. All this she realized too late; it was printed. Her spells of high blood pressure could have been responsible for the errata.

Her second black phoebe visited the same swale her first had visited six years before; the groove-billed anis returned, and a roadrunner took up residence at the Cottages, defying Cheko to oust him.

On Christmas Day Connie was called to Corsicana. Her sister had suffered a heart attack, and the outlook was grim. She was soon on her way, as were Sonney and Alice May, but none arrived in time to see Bert alive. They buried her beside their parents in Oakwood Cemetery where, so long ago, they had learned so many birds.

Grief was ever a private matter with the Hagars; January guests, all new people, were unaware of the sadness their hosts felt. Indeed, her sense of obligation to them helped alleviate Connie's heartache. Allegra Collister, a Colorado birdbander, strung a net behind her cottage and caught a northern shrike, a winter visitor Connie had suspected but never verified. Two days later, January 25, a prothonotary warbler was trapped and banded.

The bird of the month was a tundra swan—this one alive! A hunter saw it come in, and he rushed to telephone Mrs. Hagar. "I saw this big white bird sailing down toward Oystercatcher Point," the excited man said, "and though it has been many, many years since I've seen a swan, I knew what it was before it settled on the bay."

Connie rushed to the Point. The swan swam gracefully and apparently contentedly in a shallow cove bounded by a shell-topped road to an oil rig. It was a subadult, dusky white with a pinkish bill. She telephoned the happy news around the state, and many others rushed to see the bird. They need not have hurried; it moved to the little pond on Live Oak Point and remained through most of February. Birders from eastern parts were also pleased to see the black phoebe, still hawking bugs at the Girl Scout Camp.

Two weeks of wretched February weather turned warm and full of sunshine on the twenty-second, as if by special dispensation for a long-planned and eagerly anticipated event in Corpus Christi—Connie Hagar Recognition Day. The Hagars had consented to the event with the assurance that it would be a simple and short affair. Arranged by the Audubon Outdoor Club and the birdwatchers she had helped for a decade, the occasion at Del Mar College Auditorium was tied to an Audubon wildlife film, *An Ozark Anthology*, by a speaker-photographer the Hagars already knew, Leonard Hall. Sonney and Alice May came from Schenectady to take the Hagars to the program and to the small dinner for special guests at the Student Center. All sponsors of the Audubon films participated—the club, the college, the *Caller-Times*, and Corpus Christi Museum.

Invitations had been sent to many of Connie's friends near and far, the distant ones not really expected to attend but instead to send messages for the honoree. The invitation was accepted, however, by the one person most wanted by all—Roger Tory Peterson, who thereby endeared himself to all who loved Connie Hagar.

He flew in for an afternoon of birding on Padre Island with his hosts and could hardly be torn away from the enormous rafts of redheads on the Laguna Madre. "Must be half the world's population of redheads here," he commented. Leonard Hall and his wife Virginia also arrived early.

Peterson's attendance had been kept secret as a surprise for Connie. She was overwhelmed; the occasion was a success before it started. At the dinner, informal and without speeches, she sat between him and Hall, and other guests simply listened to their conversation. When she and her party walked to their seats on the auditorium stage, the audience cheered. Rockport appeared to have turned out en masse, and other towns were well represented.

Connie was a picture of dainty perfection in crimson cotton lace, her silver hair like a crown, her cheeks pink. Seated beside her were Peterson and Hall; Dean Grady St. Clair of the college; Edward H. Harte, publisher of the *Caller-Times*; and Fred B. Jones, president of the Audubon Outdoor Club and a farmer whose avocation was botany. She had often consulted him for information on wild flowers.

Leonard Hall did the honors, keeping the tone light, recalling amusing incidents from his visits to Rockport, and reading from the stack of letters and telegrams in his hand. The praises sung that night included some for Jack, which pleased Connie, and he received his own round of applause. One message saluted her as the "first lady of ornithology in Texas, and of that neighboring country, the United States." There were too many to read then, but Connie would read and reread them at home.

Peterson was asked to say a few words and promptly stole the show. He preened the feathers of his chauvinistic listeners by first praising Texas birds and Texas as a bird state, and then he launched into an informal, jocular reminiscing of birding with Connie, concluding each anecdote with a "Didn't we, Connie?" She giggled a "Yes, Roger," to each, and he soon had her laughing out loud with the audience.

Climaxing the ceremony, Fred Jones called her to center stage and presented to her a silver bowl inscribed with words of appreciation for her leadership in wildlife conservation. She stood smiling, her spirits so high she felt no fatigue, and when Jones had lowered the microphone fourteen inches, she spoke her thanks in a clear, firm voice. Her words were brief; she could not have said more, she confided later, without breaking down. But one man was disappointed; he wrote to the newspaper to complain that "Mrs. Hagar should have had more time to talk."

She waved to the crowd, which stood and cheered as Jones led her offstage. The Nebletts took her home; it was long past the Hagar bedtime, and Hall went on with his show. When it was over the speakers, sponsors, and others gathered in Kay's apartment for refreshments and mutual congratulations and then to talk far into the night about birds, Peterson and Hall being encouraged to do most of the talking. Locals rarely heard such interesting conversation.

Peterson's *Field Guide to the Birds of Texas* was off the press that week but not yet in the bookstores, otherwise he would have been held up autographing copies.

The silver bowl took a prominent and permanent place on the antique table in the Hagar living room, and Jack made sure no caller overlooked it. The newspaper stories, photographs, and an interview with Peterson were pasted in Connie's scrapbook.

She had a day of rest to read the messages and bask in the glow of the evening, grateful for so many friends. The next day she went with Sonney and Alice May to Corsicana to undertake a sad task that had been postponed until after her Recognition Day. They had to liquidate the Neblett estate, the home that Bert had kept so full of memories, so little changed since their childhood. Blake White, Blanche Bush, and others helped her through the ordeal, and when it was over the Bushes took her home. With Bert gone, Connie said, "There's nobody left to put me in my place when I get out of hand."

More recognition came Connie's way when she and Jack were named guests of honor at the annual Rockport Chamber of Commerce banquet. Jack received a full share of the accolades, much to his wife's satisfaction. Then the Women's Club staged an afternoon gala with a program patterned after a popular television show, "This Is Your Life," in which members acted out scenes from her past, which were also depicted in an elaborate scrapbook prepared by Mrs. Jackson.

An invitation to be a panelist on a real television show, the long-running "$64,000 Question," she didn't even consider, though it would have included a trip to New York for her and Jack.

When Jack Stevens and his wife Edith arrived on April 1, he announced his intention to concentrate on the "pesky" little peeps. A few days later Connie noted a gathering of varied small shorebirds in a marsh on Highway 35 opposite the Tules; she

[246]

thought it a good place for study and made a date with Stevens for the afternoon.

Stevens slowed the car to a silent stop off the highway, overlooking shallow water flowing from under the culvert, around a bare sandspit, into grass, and on toward Little Bay. Several species probed and pecked, but one stood out. It fed differently, it looked different, yet in many ways it looked like the others. Neither spoke as they focused on the bird, Connie mentally sorting field marks. This bird matched no species she could recall. Stevens could stand the silence no longer.

"Call it, Connie," he demanded.

"I can't. It is either a bird I never saw before or one in plumage new to me."

"Not a pectoral?" Jack suggested.

"No. Too many things are wrong for a pectoral. And notice that every other bird out there has flown off and come back a time or two while this one had gone on feeding right where it is. It is the most deliberate feeder I ever saw."

They discussed other birds, their field marks and actions, but kept coming back to the stranger. Perhaps there were white spots on the sides of the tail, but Connie would not let it be flushed for fear they would never see it again. She called it quits, impatient to get home and to the books. They pored over the literature. It was not any American bird described. Everything pointed to its being a ruff, an Old World bird and rare vagrant on the East Coast. Jack and Edith had to leave to attend a dinner engagement in Corpus Christi. Connie kept searching and found one record for Texas—a ruff on Padre Island in 1902!

She was ready to call it a ruff, but decided to have another look, taking along Judge Simpson and the O'Hearns, Lila and Joe, who made motion pictures. They pushed aside a spaghetti dinner and took off. But the marsh was empty of shorebirds.

Everybody was back there early next morning, and the judge, recently returned from a trip around the world, including stops at the haunts of the ruff, spotted the bird first. "There's the ruff," he said, "looking just like it did in Scotland."

Connie called around the state; Edgar Kincaid arrived first,

[247]

others followed. O'Hearn exposed a reel of film, Fred Webster took data for *Field Notes*, and newspapers covered it, mostly with photographs of crowds of people staring through telescopes and binoculars at an obscure little creature out on the sandbar. Guests arriving at the Cottages were directed to the little stranger before they unpacked.

The ruff remained eleven days, and on the eighth day of his bachelorhood on this alien coast he was joined by a female of his species—a reeve. It was a superlative inexplicable to birders. Also, the ruff's plumage became noticeably richer with a hint of the gaudy neck feathers to come with nuptial dress, and there were episodes suggesting courtship; the birds crawled to one another, breasts to the sand; met bill to bill; then settled down to feed indifferently, side by side.

One day a low-slung roadster stopped, and a young man got out to ask what the attraction was. When he was told, he took a casual look and remarked, "It's a long way from home." So was he, a birder from Holland who had no need to come to Texas for a ruff.

A few days after they left, the ruff and reeve were reported on Padre Island, but Connie saw them no more. In late April she and Jack Stevens added another species to the Rockport list— western tanager.

Chapter 14

Guy Emerson's weeklong visit in May was a heart-wrenching experience for the Hagars; their favorite of so many years was a victim of Parkinson's disease and almost feeble, yet he insisted on pursuing his hobby and his work. Long a trustee of the Samuel H. Kress Foundation, he had, upon retiring from the bank several years earlier, become the foundation's director, dedicated to the acquisition and distribution of art, mainly of the Italian Renaissance. This, too, involved travel and, of course, birding.

On his travels he was now accompanied by his young and very able secretary, Mary Davis (who would succeed him as director). Mary was also something of a mother hen, unobtrusively easing the way for him at every step. She had to be unobtrusive because he stubbornly refused to admit his infirmity, even to acknowledge the disease. He resented gestures others made to help him. One day he would have fallen had Connie not caught him, and it made him angry.

The birds, however, soothed his spirits. Drives around the area were peaceful and rewarding. Mary enjoyed the birds, too, and that pleased him.

On his annual inspection of coastal sanctuaries Carl Buchheister, now Audubon president, was accompanied by John Baker, Charles Callison of the staff, and six directors.

They found most wading birds faring well, but there were distressingly few brown pelicans. Equally distressing were conditions on Lydia Ann Island, long one of the most productive

[249]

sanctuaries. It was virtually empty of birds, and there were signs that oily bilge from Intracoastal Canal traffic was the cause.

June 14, 1960, the Nature Calendar noted, "Seventy-four today. Still don't know all about birds, but keep trying. Club sang Happy Birthday for me. Kay and I worked two hours."

Kay McCracken, on a sabbatical summer at her Fulton Beach cottage, had begun a series of interviews about those seventy-four years for a book. As a latter-day Dr. Johnson of the birds, Connie joyously accepted Kay as her Boswell. Thus, after her morning tour, Connie had Jack drop her off at the beach cottage, where they talked until noon and Kay delivered her home in time for Jack's lunch.

June 20: Connie had been home only a short time when Jack appeared with a note for Kay—having no telephone was half the joy of the sabbatical to her. The note read: "Dear Boswell: Just had a call from Doris Barnett saying she saw two noddy terns on the breakwater at Port Aransas. Think we should make a run and see what we can see. Dr. Johnson."

Kay would be there when Connie finished her afternoon rest. The Barnetts, of Dallas, had a summer place on South Beach, and since she had learned the regular birds so well, she could spot strange newcomers in an instant. She saw the birds while fishing with her husband off the south jetty, and she had done her homework before calling Connie. The noddies seemed to be attached to a particular granite boulder marked with their lime droppings, and they were not shy, she told Connie. They allowed her to stand quite close.

Connie and Cheko were waiting; they drove straight for the objective, pausing only to see the colony of black skimmers and least terns nesting on Harbor Island. Connie whistled softly, a sign of contentment, as the ferry took them across to Mustang Island; bottle-nosed dolphins romped around the vessel.

The wind had risen, white thunderheads rose high in the blue sky, and sudden rain began pelting the car the moment they parked on the sand near the jetty, lined on both sides by anglers, who ignored the shower. For their convenience the state had laid a concrete cover down the middle of the nearly mile-long jetty of huge chunks of red Texas granite.

Scanning the scene through the wet windshield, Connie and Kay could find no strange birds. Then the rain ceased, the sun beamed, and they climbed onto the jetty and started seaward. At the same moment they saw a brown bird beyond a group of fishermen, but one man moved and the bird flew out over the waves. They walked on, Cheko on a leash but managing to sniff the piles of fishing gear and other splendidly odoriferous things along the way. Kay was for walking to the end but Connie demurred. "I think we should go back to that one rock and wait. Birds often return to where you saw them, and Doris mentioned that they seemed attached to that location."

They strolled back slowly, watching both sides of the jetty and across the ship channel. They were near the lime-stained boulder when Kay whispered, "Look, a bird." With its bill pointed into the wind, the bird swayed gently but held firmly to the rock, only a few feet away. It was cocoa brown, big but smaller than nearby royal terns. Its silvery cap, like a spoonful of thin sugar icing, extended from the bill almost to the nape. After a long, silent inspection the women started jabbering in low voices, citing all aspects of the bird. The tail was a bit ragged but certainly wedged. At times the noddy shifted with the breeze, and the cap seemed to disappear; it spread its wings, showing darker primaries.

On the eastern horizon the sky had turned dark blue; the wind gusted, threatening another shower. They should leave, but Kay was greedy. Mrs. Barnett had seen two noddies; where was the other? It arrived at that instant, alighting on the same rock, facing the wind. The birds were twins except one seemed a bit smaller.

Back in the car, barely ahead of another downpour, Connie remarked that this was probably a second record for a noddy in Texas. Attwater had found one dead on nearby St. Joseph's Island in 1890. Nearing Rockport she said, "I feel light as a feather, without a care in the world. We must go by and thank Doris Barnett."

The bay off South Beach was still and smooth. She saw Kay staring at something in the water and turned to look; a large bird swam parallel to them only about fifteen feet out.

A loon in Rockport, and in June, was strange enough, but when Connie studied the bird, she decided it wasn't even a common loon. It did not appear to be injured, but something had to be amiss for any loon to be in Aransas Bay in the summer. Then she called it. "It's an arctic loon," said Connie, who had seen one only once before. Then they told Doris Barnett about the arctic loon. It was a new bird for her, so Connie felt she had partly repaid Doris for finding the noddies.

Edgar Kincaid was detained a day, and both the noddies and the loon were gone when he arrived, though he scoured the jetty all one day and half another. But he had enjoyed the other birds. "No frigatebirds, though," he said to Connie. Frigatebirds were among his great favorites. It was "frigatebird weather," so Connie suggested a drive to the Cove before he left. As they turned on to the beach, they saw six long-tailed, long-winged birds hanging high in the sky out over the water. She hummed happily as Edgar stood out in the wind taking long looks at the birds. She had not seen these individuals before but "just knew" some would be there.

On through the summer, Kay in her role as Boswell filled a stack of notebooks, constantly amazed at Connie's memory. They studied wild flowers together, as well as birds; the secret garden was a small wonderland.

The Lockwoods visited again, bringing their baby daughter, who promptly took possession of the Hagars' hearts. They found Connie happily helping the housemaid learn birds, sometimes taking her along on the afternoon rounds. The maid, a Mexican-American, was a quick learner, Connie told them. This was a surprise to Ann and Bob, who recalled that early in their acquaintance Connie's unabashed attitude was that Mexicans and blacks "were all right—in their place." They had dared challenge her once, disbelieving that a person of her talent, education, and generosity could be so narrow-minded in that one way. Tears had come to Connie's eyes as she admitted, "I know it's probably wrong, but it's the way I was brought up and now it's too late to change."

But she had changed, obviously without realizing it, for when they teased her about it she seemed surprised. Laughing, she admitted it, saying this was the second Mexican-American housemaid she had taught, the first also having been a good student. Then she told of the class of black children she had entertained in her backyard. In writing for permission to bring her pupils, the Robstown teacher had identified herself as the only black in a group of teachers that had previously visited for a bird talk.

"Those children were the most attentive and sweetest audience I ever had," she said.

In early November Connie drove alone out Farm Road 881 past Port Bay looking for longspurs, but suddenly she felt very weak and had trouble making her way home and to her bed. She lay there a month, weak, frail—and very sad. She had lost the vision in her left eye. It was the most severe illness she had ever had, and though she rallied a bit in early December, she was confined to bed again until the Christmas holidays.

Magazines and books were always within reach, and during her confinement Connie learned to read with one eye. A lesser person would have been bitter, but not Connie Hagar. "I have been threatened with blindness for fifty years," she said. "I am grateful to still have one good eye." The damage did not change her appearance.

Doris McGuire, now living in one of the cottages while her home was being built, took charge of birding guests, whom Connie could see one at a time and hear their reports.

Rains beginning in November continued into the spring, but Christmas Day was bright and warm, and Connie was able to attend church for the first time in two months. She recovered rapidly, regaining the weight she had lost—down to eighty-eight pounds from her usual ninety-seven—largely because Doris made her eat and made sure she ate the things she needed, many of which Doris, an excellent cook, provided. Connie's spirits rose with her weight. Daily drives were resumed when weather permitted, she kept promised dates for bird talks, and she spent a little of every day at her piano; though she knew her technique was poor, she could at least strike the right keys.

The peninsula was flooded when Dr. Arthur Allen brought a group for three days in February, but undaunted, he declared that the standing water only made birds more visible. Connie took the group early one morning to see the black skimmers perform their mass flight with elegant precision. Three brown pelicans among their white cousins in Little Bay were a welcome sight to her, and Dr. Allen was dismayed to learn that brown pelicans were disappearing.

Jack, still vigorous at eighty-four and never happier than when very busy, was overseeing another renovation of the Cottages, repairing and refurbishing them one by one as vacancies occurred. However, they remained air-conditioned by nature only, and the simple furnishings stayed that way.

The many rain pools still standing in late March had probably looked like an attractive habitat to the masked duck discovered by a visitor off Highway 35 just twelve miles north of Rockport. Connie and Judge Simpson saw it one morning on their return from the daybreak dance of the prairie-chickens. A dozen other birders were already at the pool, spread out along the roadside with glasses focused on the odd one among the ruddy ducks. The little stiff-tail was not much to look at in drab female plumage, but it was something to see—in Texas, at least. The state had very few records of the species. Whitney Eastman turned to his wife Karen and said wryly, "Here we have been searching Mexico for this bird and find it in Rockport."

The masked duck floated for long periods in one spot; sometimes it swam slowly among the emergent vegetation, sometimes it dived, but it always appeared content. It remained two weeks and was seen by birders from all over. Though accustomed to the sometimes odd behavior of birders, Rockport people thought the man who flew down from Dallas, took one look, and flew back again was rather extraordinary.

Newspapers gave the masked duck due notice. The articles were circulated among the guests, and one, upon reading the San Antonio account, was inspired to comment: "Don't quote me, but I do believe Texans are beginning to learn that birdwatching is a respectable avocation and that not all birders are lunatics." Then she added gaily, "But most of us are, aren't we? And ain't we got fun."

Moore's Pool, filled to the brim and picture perfect with saucer-size lotus blossoms tall above platter-size floating pads, was Connie's showpiece for Carl Buchheister and his party in June. The group included bird artist John Henry Dick and Helen and Allan Cruickshank. As ever, with Cruickshank along there was never a dull moment. They saw purple gallinules and moorhens stroll on the lily pads, least and pied-billed grebes with grebelets, ruddy ducks with ducklings, and a least bittern lurking in the grassy edge where fulvous whistling-ducks and white-faced ibises sunned and preened.

The Hagars had entertained birders from Europe, even one from Iraq, but none had traveled so far as the twelve thousand miles claimed by a couple who came in June, Mr. and Mrs. F. G. H. Allen from First Port, Malaya. He ran a general store there, he said, that handled everything from needles to tractors. They had read about Mrs. Hagar in the Peterson-Fisher account in *Wild America* and determined to meet her themselves. After crossing the Pacific to British Columbia, they had driven down the West Coat and then to Rockport for three days before turning back. "Nowhere," the couple told the *Pilot*, "have we seen anything like the birdlife in this area."

That summer a Corpus Christi ophthalmologist, Dr. Gordon Bryson, began treating Connie's right eye for incipient glaucoma; she would see him every three months thereafter and that eye would be saved. She had adjusted very well to birding with one eye, through a monocular, an instrument she did not know existed until it was given to her by Swede Sorenson, who was not a birder but a friend from their first days in Rockport.

Terry and Maurine Gill came September 1 to celebrate the twenty-fifth anniversary of their first visit to Rockport. As they departed, a tropical disturbance was forming off the coast of Yucatan, soon to increase in size and intensity; its direction was uncertain but the entire Gulf Coast was alerted. It grew into a tropical storm, then into a hurricane—Carla. On Saturday, the ninth, the Weather Bureau warned that landfall might be anywhere between Brownsville and Galveston, most likely on the Central Coast, and that Hurricane Carla was an enormous storm, a killer.

Although they always asked guests to leave when storms threatened, the Hagars had never run from a hurricane and had not intended to run from this one despite warnings that it was more dangerous than any they had experienced. However, when Dr. Cottam drove over early Sunday morning with an invitation that was virtually a command, they consented to ride out this one with him and Margery on Welder Wildlife Refuge. The leading edge of the storm was already being felt.

The first of their three days there was the worst. Rain poured without cessation, winds howled, big trees shook, and limbs blew off. Inside the sturdy mission-style home Dr. Cottam played symphonies from his large collection of recordings, and at Margery's urging Connie recited a score of her favorite poems. From time to time they heard radio and television reports. Hurricane Carla swept the coast from Corpus Christi to Galveston, devastating the area between Port Lavaca and Freeport, where she went inland and continued far into the state.

Utility lines were down and highway travel was severely restricted for two days. Wednesday the Hagars were able to go home. On the way Connie noticed that shorebirds were making the most of the bounty of food on the flooded prairies. The Cottages escaped serious damage. The grounds were littered, the sign down, and the TV antenna blown away. Cleanup crews had worked apace, piles of fallen trees and debris awaited pickup on the streets all over town, but Connie found no dead birds. Farther afield she found the Cove, Live Oak Point, and Rattlesnake Point flattened; there would be no food for the hummingbirds.

Ruby-throats came through before the week was out, but none lingered; the western hummers were very scarce all that fall. A week after the storm the Hagar oaks were full of warblers—mourning, black-and-white, Wilson's, chats, and redstarts—as well as cuckoos, chuck-will's-widows, and a vermilion flycatcher. Thereafter the migration went on as usual.

A week before the hurricane Dr. Andrew W. O'Neil, physician and surgeon from Falfurrias, had called on Connie for help with birds, to which he had taken a fancy in the spring, but the storm threat had curtailed his stay. He checked in again for an October weekend and was out early Saturday morning with Connie and Doris.

Dr. O'Neil proved to be the kind of pupil Connie most enjoyed—a quick learner with a good memory, and one who did his "homework," in addition to being good company. His promise to return on every free weekend and on his Thursdays off elated her. A new student of his caliber was a tonic, especially one several generations younger than herself—and male. She was patently partial to the opposite sex.

He kept his promise. His visits stimulated her more than any medicine could, and in one respect he exceeded his mentor; he learned and remembered voices of birds—songs, calls, chip notes—mostly from recordings he played repeatedly. He enjoyed hearing birds as much or more than seeing them. Dr. O'Neil was the first to be called when Connie and Doris found two red-necked grebes in the ski basin.

Few but the Hagars grieved when Cheko died in early December. A handsome but pesky brat, he was still undisciplined after three years. He stuck his nose into everything and one day stuck it into a storm-wrecked house and rat poison; an autopsy revealed thallium, an element that was commonly used in rat poison.

The year ended happily with the Cottages full of longtime friends. The good times were not to last, however. Spells of high blood pressure recurred, and in January, 1962, Connie was twice confined to bed for a week or more at a time. Furthermore, she was without a doctor. None then in Rockport felt qualified to take her case, but from long experience she treated herself.

Lee Edwards kept her list going: Harris' sparrows and sedge wrens on the Bayside road, Harlan's hawk on Highway 35. Mountain bluebirds and mountain plovers were at Bonnie View. Bald eagles nested again; an ash-throated flycatcher in January was much too early.

When Dr. O'Neil came at the end of that month he found Connie in bed; her illness was new to him. She asked him to take her blood pressure, saying, "I'm in a pickle. No doctor."

"You have me," he answered firmly, proceeding with a thorough examination, taking a history of her troubles and outlining a program of treatment and medication. Medicines would be supplied at no cost to her by Dr. O'Neil's close friend Marshall Franklin, a pharmaceutical detail man who had visited the Hagars with him. Doris McGuire would see that his instructions were followed.

Connie was well enough to see the western grebe that

[257]

graced Little Bay in February and to share most of the spring migration with guests and especially with Little Doc, her pet name for O'Neil. Both had looked forward to it eagerly for it was the previous spring migration that had inspired him to become acquainted with all those colored feathers flitting in the trees in his own yard in Falfurrias. With Connie he learned many species, regretting only that the songbirds were not very vocal in their rush through South Texas. Future travels would have to satisfy his wish for songs.

Mr. M. Owen Davies of Cleveland, a friend of Dr. Oberholser's, spent several days at the Cottages along with his mother and an aunt and had left one April morning on their way to Mexico, but from Sinton he telephoned Connie to say that he had seen two redshanks on the mudflats of Copano Bay by the Farm Road 881 bridge. He knew the birds from Europe and was certain of their identity. The word was passed around, and in half an hour Connie was on her way with Judge Simpson and Miss Ruth Emery of Boston, the "Voice of Audubon" for the Massachusetts Audubon Society. She took a book to study on the way about the species from the Old World. The birds were far out on the mudflat, but the judge set up a telescope and was satisfied, as were others, except Connie. She made out the white rump but realized sadly that she would have to accept the judgment of others. With her one good eye she could never have identified those birds alone and to her own satisfaction.

To Connie the snakes in her grass were mostly friends: the hognose, amusing for its ridiculous play-dead antics, and green snakes and checkered garter snakes, which ate insects. However, they ceased to be friends when they preyed upon her birds. When she found a garter snake curled up in a cardinal's empty nest, where there had been nestlings the day before, she dispatched it without remorse. She was sorry when the lawn mower decapitated a hognose snake, but it had an interesting bulge in its midriff. She asked Jack to lend her his pocket knife.

"Oh, no," he said in mock panic. "I don't want snake steak for lunch."

"I'm not thinking of your lunch," his wife laughed. "I'm thinking of what this snake had for breakfast, and if you don't want me to use your knife, I'll get the butcher knife from the kitchen."

Jack opened the largest blade in his knife and with one stroke opened the snake's belly. Connie bent down and removed a full-grown house sparrow—feet, feathers, and head intact.

A Checklist of the Birds of the Central Coast of Texas was now ten years old, so Fred Packard and Connie arranged for some revisions in the third printing. The graphs on seasonal abundance were unchanged, but Packard wrote a new introduction and she supplied a list of species, with dates, seen in the vicinity since the first printing. There were twenty-two new species for the decade.

Dr. Cottam had gladly responded to her request for criticism since he was compiling a checklist for Welder Refuge, and comparison would be interesting. "In the six years I have been a native Texan," he wrote, "I have listed a number of races that you do not simply because I have done some collecting. Conversely, there are still more species and subspecies that you have which I have not run into over here."

A taxonomist of the Oberholser persuasion, Cottam found races as important as species. He noted that she lumped all Canada geese whereas he had specimens of six races that wintered on Welder. Her one record of Treganza blue heron he could verify with a skin of one that died on the refuge; her one record of aplomado falcon he could top with three sight records, including one shared by Colonel Wolfe of Kerrville, an authority on raptors.

He had several good records of greater scaup, one of black rail, and two of white-throated swift. He had seen Henslow's sparrows but had not collected one. He had not seen a buff-bellied hummingbird and knew of only one record so far north— a specimen from Corpus Christi in October, 1891, now in the National Museum. He was surprised that her checklist recorded purple gallinules for every month of the year—and so was Connie. It was a gross error that should have been corrected.

When the Audubon group came in June, the talk was all about the Society's annual meeting to be held at Corpus Christi in November. It would be the third in Audubon history outside

[259]

New York City, the first in the South or West. Carl Buchheister told Connie that she was their reason for coming to Corpus Christi. "You never come to the annual meetings, so we are bringing the meeting to you," he said.

She thanked him for the pretty compliment, not really believing it was quite true or that she deserved it. She was mistaken. As president, Buchheister had determined to take National Audubon to the membership all over the country; future meetings would be held in other centers, but Corpus Christi had been chosen for the first because of the prime birdlife to be seen, the hospitality offered by the King Ranch, and, above all, because of the great affection Audubon officers held for Connie Hagar. Roland Clement, biologist and Audubon vice-president, had come a month earlier to make local arrangements and to engage the Robert Driscoll Hotel for the event.

As always, the Fourth of July was a big day in Rockport, and, as always, Jack was at the bayfront helping with the Lions Club barbecue. Fortunately, he was at home the next day and, just as fortunately, it was a Thursday and Dr. O'Neil was expected. A kind Providence had a way of coming to Connie's aid in times of stress. They had finished lunch, Jack had gone into his office, and she was clearing the table. As she lifted a dish and turned to the refrigerator, she heard a sharp crack, and a searing pain shot through her left leg, centered at the knee. Jack heard her cry and rushed in. Tears streamed down her white face as she clung to the table, unable to move her leg.

Half carried, half hopping on one foot, she made it to her bed. Jack had to straighten her leg; never had she felt such pain. He brought water, the only thing he could think of to do. They hoped fervently that Little Doc would arrive soon. It seemed an eternity, but it was only half an hour before he and Marshall Franklin were at the door. "They were the most beautiful men I ever saw in my life," Connie declared later.

Diverting her with bird talk and teasing, the doctor examined the leg; there was a blood clot on the knee, already turning black and swelling. He bound it snugly and, packing up his instruments, announced: "Three weeks in bed, my dear. Immobilized, with this leg elevated on the pillow like this. You must not set foot on the floor."

Feeling better, she considered the outlook and was appalled. "Can't I even go to the bathroom?"

"You cannot. Jack will bring whatever you need."

She was not tempted to disobey; the memory of that pain was enough to subdue potential insubordination. Her progress was good, and the prescribed daily hot packs would be no problem. And Doris, the new neighbor who had come for help with birds years ago, was a trained physical therapist, able and willing to assume daily care of the knee and to see that the doctor's orders were followed. (Doris had treated Franklin Delano Roosevelt at Warm Springs, Georgia.) The hot pack routine would go on for many weeks after the patient was up and about.

"Bread upon the waters," Connie mused as she lay with pillows under her head and knee. "The birds brought me a doctor, and the birds brought me a wonderful therapist."

The summer was hot and very dry but remarkable for flocks of white ibises at Rattlesnake Point and on Goose Island. From mid-July until mid-August hundreds of Wilson's phalaropes were spinning madly on Copano Bay at the Farm Road 881 bridge. Connie could not drive but could go with others to see them. In August she was ready to resume her place at the Christian Science church in Aransas Pass, and she began to practice at her piano, reading the music with one eye, working the pedals with one foot. Ready for Sunday services in her blue, lace-trimmed dress and starfish jewelry, she was a picture of well-being.

Chapter 15

The tranquility of the old daily routine was short-lived. Before the month was out, Connie's world was shattered, and for the first time in her life she refused to face reality; the prospect of life without Jack, the prop she had leaned on for thirty-six years, was intolerable.

Again a benevolent Providence provided support. Blanche and Bob Bush, as much family to her as any blood relative, were with the Hagars for a long visit. That Saturday afternoon, August 18, 1962, they were to come to Jack's office to watch a television program, and as the time neared, he decided to go for them. They were leaving their cottage, and he called out, "Bob, how have you managed to live with that old bat this long?"

They were his last words, typically bantering Jack Hagar. He gasped, reeled, and fell before Bob could reach him; he lay unconscious, hemorrhaging at the mouth. Blanche ran to Connie and to telephone Jack's doctor; she would not let Connie go to him, not wanting her to see what she had seen. The doctor arrived quickly, and soon the ambulance from Aransas Pass took him to a hospital in Corpus Christi. Connie saw him later, Dr. O'Neil at her side. The stroke had paralyzed Jack's right side, and he remained unconscious, breathing under oxygen, until the end, Monday morning at two o'clock. He was eighty-five.

Connie lay on her bed, dry-eyed most of the time, gazing out the window, waiting for this nightmare to go away. She thanked friends who came but said little else, except that she was grateful he went quickly, without long suffering. "The way I want to go," she affirmed.

She would not discuss a funeral, but when pressed, specified only "something simple." Doris McGuire and Bob Bush made the arrangements. Mrs. Jack Baughman took charge of notifying distant friends, but few telegrams were sent. Connie did not want anyone to think they must come; letters would do. Mrs. Baughman wrote dozens.

Robert and Alice May arrived Tuesday, and the next day Jack was buried in Rockport Cemetery with a simple graveside service. Mr. Harry Carter, elderly lay reader for Doris's own Episcopal church, read the Ninety-first Psalm, gave a short eulogy, and closed with a prayer. The Lions Club handled details.

Back at home, in the privacy of her bedroom, Connie leaned on her brother and for the first time wept uncontrollably. Little Doc let her cry it out, then put her to bed and to rest.

Edgar Kincaid and others from Austin, and some from San Antonio and nearby towns had come, but missing were Dr. Cottam, Irby and Anna May Davis, and Kay—all in Salt Lake City at the annual AOU meeting. Margery Cottam telephoned her husband, and he found Kay, the Davises, and others. George Lowery, then president of AOU, made the sad announcement at the meeting, and as it broke up, Roger Peterson, the Cruickshanks, the Eastmans, and many others gathered in little groups to commiserate.

"All is over for me," Connie wrote in her Nature Calendar the day Jack died, but a week later another notation appeared: "Upland plovers moving." There were still birds, and they could not be ignored, not by Connie Hagar.

The Nebletts stayed on, Robert to settle his sister's affairs, but in a few weeks he realized it would be a long, tedious business and decided to return later when he could devote more time. Friends from Corsicana alternated visits with the Bushes so Connie would not be alone. The Cottages had been closed, reservations canceled; they had been Jack's business.

Connie went out with Doris, Little Doc, and other close friends, but strangers were turned away with gentle explanations by whoever was with Connie. She was not up to seeing strangers though they kept coming, not knowing the situation.

Early one morning in late September when Connie was sitting alone on her little porch and Blake White had stepped inside, a car turned into the driveway and stopped. She was trapped. They had seen her, and it would be impolite not to speak to the two middle-aged men who approached, binoculars in hand, one carrying Peterson's guide to Texas. Their faces shone with anticipation.

"Mrs. Hagar," they said, recognizing her from photographs, "we are from Virginia, seeing Texas birds for the first time. So many of our friends have talked about you. Will you tell us where to go, please?"

They had spoken an irresistible phrase—"Texas birds." She smiled warmly. What did they especially want to see? Both spoke at once—roadrunner, reddish egret, roseate spoonbill, and others. "I have a little map," she said, going inside and returning with copies and a pencil. "Here for the spoonbills, here the roadrunner . . ." and on down the list. The men were profusely grateful. She hummed softly as they left. Another car stopped. Strangers again, two young men, the same plea. They also got maps, after being nearly stunned at seeing their first broad-tailed hummingbird dart from one hibiscus to another.

Blake had remained inside, listening and thankful, knowing the men were the best medicine her lifelong friend could have. The Virginians returned after dark, having been in the field until light failed; they simply had to report all they had seen, "right where you said they would be!"

Connie slept well that night. She would go on, as Jack would have wanted her to, and though it would never be the same, there would still be people wanting to see Texas birds. Next morning she began answering the hundreds of letters that had poured in. One opined that Jack had given Saint Peter a full account of his wonderful wife, the silver bowl, and other honors. Another was sure that Patch and Fuzzy had met him at the Pearly Gates. All had love and admiration for Jack, and she was pleased that so many recognized his role in her achievements.

[264]

Texas Game and Fish magazine asked for another story on Texas birds for the November issue, to coincide with the National Audubon meeting in Corpus Christi. She felt unequal to that task and would have declined, but Kay offered to put it together if she would dictate, and it was done—"Bounty of the Birds," by Connie Hagar, with a photograph of the author.

Getting her to the Audubon meeting was a prime concern. Carl Buchheister was to surprise her with a special award at the convention dinner. It had been planned from the beginning, and it was one reason Corpus Christi had been selected for the meeting. Connie had meant to go, of course, but since Jack's death she demurred; the effort was too much. The president enlisted the support of the Nebletts, Guy Emerson, and others, including Dr. O'Neil, who offered to take her to the dinner, but only to the dinner and then get her home. That suited everyone, and Little Doc persuaded her by saying he would not go without her. She promised.

Buchheister's plan for taking Audubon to the members succeeded beyond his wildest expectations. Nearly nine hundred, tripling any previous attendance at annual meetings, had registered in advance, and reservations were still sought when he and his staff arrived in Corpus Christi several days early.

Local facilities were strained to the limit. Extra buses from San Antonio were engaged for field trips, the local Audubon Outdoor Club volunteered themselves and vehicles for the overflow, and regional Audubon officers came in to provide additional assistance.

For the dinner the Corpus Christi Shell Club supplied a huge variety of seashells as table decorations, all to be claimed as souvenirs by guests who wanted them. Assisting Mrs. Buchheister, local birders scoured the city for native and tropical flowers to be strewn among the shells. Three ballrooms on the mezzanine of the Robert Driscoll Hotel were opened into one. By dinnertime the mezzanine was so crowded that moving about was nearly impossible.

Buchheister, John Baker, and other board members lingered near the elevator. Up to now the meeting had been all they hoped for, but the climax would be the dinner—with the guest of honor present. She had promised, but they were anxious and wondering if she would be physically up to it.

A relieved and proprietary smile spread over the president's face as the elevator door opened and a petite figure on the arm of Dr. O'Neil stepped out. She wore pink taffeta with a bouffant skirt and a stole of starched pink chiffon. Beneath softly waved white hair beamed a heart-shaped face, fair and furrowed by seventy-six years of laughter, study, and intense living.

"Well, boys," she said with a contralto chuckle, "I made it."

Baker took possession saying, "I saw her first." He referred not to the evening but to his prior friendship of two decades. Buchheister took her other arm, and together they escorted her directly to the ballroom; smiling guests made a path for them through the crowd. She returned the smiles and some greetings but was not allowed to stop. The tables filled as she was seated next to the president on a platform. Dr. Cottam was on her left. From a nearby table O'Neil kept an eye on her. She nibbled at the food. Eight o'clock was far past her dinnertime; she had eaten at home at six. She did eat the dessert but regretted the big steak on her plate. Had there been a dog at home, he would have dined elegantly on it.

The customary courtesies were observed: introductions, announcements, compliments, thanks to all who had assisted with the meeting. Then Buchheister came to that part of the program which, he told the audience, meant a great deal to him. They believed him, he spoke so proudly and sincerely.

Shifting the big centerpiece of flowers so that his subject could be seen, he drew Connie to his side—her head barely reached the boutonniere in his lapel—and displayed a beautifully hand-lettered plaque, bright with gold leaf and color, and read the inscription:

NATIONAL AUDUBON SOCIETY
awards this citation to

CONGER NEBLETT HAGAR

Ornithologist and conservationist

Good citizen of the Rockport she helped make famous

Friend and mentor to three generations of field students of birds

You opened our eyes to that great miracle of the natural world, the migration of birds

You enriched our knowledge by patient, open-minded, and courageous observation and reporting of the facts—so many of them at first unbelievable

In your selfless devotion to the truths of Nature

You have literally discovered the link between heaven and earth

You stood so straight among the wind-bent trees of your coast that you saw what others before failed to see.

November 12, 1962   Carl W. Buchheister
                                     President

Misty-eyed, the honoree tilted her head far back to smile at the president. Then, hugging the plaque, she turned to the sea of faces, and though she had spoken before countless gatherings, she could muster only two words.

"Thank you."

She sat down, a bit shaky. The applause went on and on, and she rose to whisper "Thank you" again. Buchheister nodded for silence and proceeded with his program.

As soon as attention was diverted from her, Dr. O'Neil signaled, Dr. Cottam led her to him, and they quietly slipped away. Hands caught and pressed hers as she passed, not daring to pause for fear she would give way to her emotions, and public display of emotion was not her style. She had realized, of course, that she would be introduced and that something nice would be said about her, but the citation was a complete surprise, far more than she expected. In the car, gliding home through a clear night, she was buoyed by euphoria. Stroking the plaque tenderly, she spoke lovingly of all who had brought about the occasion. "You knew about this," she accused Little Doc. Sure, everyone did except her, he said, and everyone was scared stiff that she would not be able to come. "Well, even if I am sick tomorrow, I'm glad I came. I only wish Jack could have been with us."

She went to bed at once but did not turn out her light until she had read again, and yet again, the words on the plaque.

Robert and Alice May came at Thanksgiving, to stay the winter if it took that long to settle his sister as happily as possible. She would live in Rockport; any other arrangement was unthinkable to her, and she preferred to live alone. There was little left in the estate except the Cottages, and Robert, the methodical engineer, was appalled by the state of the accounts; in his later years the happy-go-lucky Jack had ignored tedious details—it would take time to untangle, indeed. Connie was no help; she had never taken part in the business. Many old-time guests were urging her to keep the Cottages open somehow, but it seemed impossible.

Dr. O'Neil had a solution. He and a colleague in Corpus Christi, Dr. Paul Goodman, would buy the place and employ a couple to run it. He, like others, could not imagine Rockport without the spring migration of birds and birdwatchers to see it. Besides, Connie needed to continue her routine as much as possible. The arrangement included building a separate home next door for Connie. Neblett converted proceeds from the sale into an annuity for his sister, and Weldon Cabaniss, attorney, though retired, was a longtime friend and would advise her on financial matters.

Neblett designed and supervised construction of her new home, much like the one she was in but with a larger living room, more efficient kitchen, and second bedroom and bath for the companion Connie would certainly need. She protested that, insisting she could do with a daily maid, but she was overruled in one of several spirited arguments—typical Neblett stubbornness.

Before leaving for Schenectady in March, Robert and Alice May saw her comfortably settled in the new place. The move was traumatic for Connie; she pouted, not wanting to give up the old place. She turned her back and would not help, so Alice May, Sibyl Means, and Doris McGuire saw to arranging the furniture. When it was done, however, Connie was grateful and happy.

The Rockport Cottages, with some refurbishing, were re-opened with new managers. Jack and Edith Stevens were the first to occupy their familiar quarters.

Connie did manage very well with a daily maid, but on doctor's orders a small sign was posted on her door limiting visiting hours. Sibyl completed Connie's contentment with Sudie, a small black dachshund. The animal was sweet-tempered, clean, and loving, with legs too short to climb into Patch's old bed, so the bed's wooden legs were shortened and the bed placed by Connie's own so that she could drop her hand over the side and stroke the small black head.

The birders came as before, and she went out with someone almost daily. Little Doc was there often, and again the Audubon group with Buchheister in June, very gratified to see her doing so well. Much of the time someone was in the house with her— the Bushes, old friends from Corsicana—and when Doris took off for a summer of birding in Europe with Annette Koon, Carrie Holcomb, now retired, came to live in Doris's home and to see Connie daily.

There were recurrent spells of high blood pressure, but most of the time she was well. She would drive her car around Rockport but no farther. Then she began having trouble with her good eye. Hypertension and generalized arteriosclerosis had very gradually progressed over the past decade, Dr. Bryson explained. There were infrequent but disturbing minute hemorrhages in the eye and brain that the doctor called transient ischemic accidents or TIAs. He would treat her with medications and see her every three months, without fail. These appointments Kay assumed as her own, occasions they both enjoyed, and thereafter for the rest of Connie's active life, Kay drove to Rockport for her early, took her to the doctor, and brought her home. They always had lunch at La Fonda and invariably ordered the same Mexican favorites—chalupas compuestas (thick with guacamole), and green enchiladas with sour cream sauce, and Connie drank Carta Blanca, the light Mexican beer she preferred. Pecan pralines were dessert. In the early years of these expeditions they would stop briefly at Lichtenstein's, the big department store, or at a bookstore, and finally at the Six Points Bakery for divinity candy or pastries for Connie to take home. Later the shopping was abandoned, then the bakery; Connie was too tired and had to get home to bed.

The way she ate at La Fonda was in striking contrast to her eating habits at home. The maid complained that Mrs. Hagar didn't eat enough to stay alive, though she did drink her beer. Sibyl, Winnie, Mrs. Jackson, and others brought special things, usually carbohydrates, and these she ate. Doris, however, who often cooked for Connie as well as herself, prepared the nourishing dishes Connie needed and sometimes sat by to see that the food was consumed.

Despite occasional setbacks, 1964 was another good year. The old friends came as always, new ones checked in, and Judge Simpson stayed for the entire spring migration, escorting Connie wherever she wished to go and helping with other guests when needed.

Late in that year, what threatened to be another tragedy became instead an abiding joy to Connie in that she could return favor for favor; her Little Doc became the patient and she the comforter. In late November Dr. O'Neil suffered a coronary occlusion, and after three weeks in Spohn Hospital he chose to convalesce at the Cottages.

In early January a slight relapse sent him back to the hospital for a month, then another month with Connie before resuming his practice. Twice daily she walked the short distance to his cottage to sit by his bed and talk birds. Soon she was able to take him on short drives.

Dr. O'Neil realized that Connie could not possibly see the diagnostic details on many of the smaller birds she called, but she called them correctly without fail. She had come to know the attitudes, behavior, and habits of the birds so well that lesser details were unnecessary; she knew them by "jizz," as British birders called it.

By taking occasional meals with Connie, O'Neil saw for himself how little she ate. He was aware of her anemia, but this was shocking; she was so undernourished, he marveled at the strength she had. Again he took her in hand, prescribing iron supplements and more protein, and persuaded her of the importance of proper diet. She obeyed, though it was distasteful, but Little Doc demanded it, and she did improve.

Still another severe blow was dealt Connie that spring. In May her brother, her last surviving blood relative, died in Schenectady. He was fifteen years younger than his sister, who had vainly hoped he would outlive her. Yet his death was in the family tradition; except for Grandmother Neblett, the men and women on both sides of the house had, for at least three generations, died before reaching seventy.

What had made her the exception? Several years earlier when observing a birthday in her mid-seventies with Corsicana friends who knew the family tradition, one had asked, half jesting, "What keeps you, Connie?"

In the same vein she had replied, "It must be the birds. I live for the birds, and they won't let me go."

Alice May spent much of the summer with her, for mutual consolation and to assume responsibility for Connie's welfare. It would be by long distance, but Weldon Cabaniss would continue to help, as would many friends.

From out of the distant past, Dick Russell, now stationed at Bryce Canyon National Park, came by on his way to Washington, D.C., to spend several days with Connie, seeing the fall migration and the hummingbirds. Such visits were tonics to her.

Before the year was out another young man—at fifty he was young to Connie—knocked at her door for the first of what would be hundreds of times. Dr. Leonard Goldman, a dentist, native of New Orleans, and veteran of World War II, had been advised for medical reasons to seek a small-town practice and take up a hobby not physically strenuous. He had chosen Rockport a year or so earlier and, upon hearing so much about Mrs. Hagar, had chosen birdwatching for the avocation. With binoculars and a field guide he had studied some on his own before approaching the noted authority, albeit somewhat apologetically and apprehensively.

He was the stimulant she needed; a new and eager pupil, especially a male, gave her a transfusion of spirit and energy. And he was a godsend to her women friends, who could not always meet her needs for diversion and inspiration. Soon Leonard was calling nearly every afternoon, as soon as he closed his office, to take Connie and Sudie for an hour or more around the peninsula.

A Reformed Jew, he was also a better than amateur Hebrew scholar, and Connie, familiar with the tenets of so many faiths and always interested in learning, encouraged him to discuss those of Judaism, most of which were unknown to her. They became such good friends that she felt she could tell him about the Baums, the only Jews she had known in Corsicana, or indeed the only ones she had known until she was middle-aged. The Baums were the only Jews accepted in the Neblett social circle, and just why they were exceptions Connie never fully understood. Perhaps it was because Mrs. Baum, their Mrs. Malaprop, made it clear to all that they did not "percolate with Jews" and therefore were allowed to "percolate" in Gentile society. When she and Jack, who had no ethnic reservations, opened Rockport Cottages, it had not occurred to them to discriminate. Anyone interested in birds was welcome.

"I was never conscious of being racist, as they call it now," she told Leonard. "It was just the way things were in those days, and I never knew when things changed. It just happened. The birds didn't care who looked at them, so why should I?"

She missed a month of the 1967 spring migration when an intestinal obstruction led to discovery of cancer of the colon and surgery in Spohn Hospital. Dr. O'Neil assisted and remained a day or two in a nearby motel to make sure of her recovery. She came through the surgery very well but had lost much of her strength, and it was clear now that Connie could no longer live alone. Arrangements were made for a live-in companion to care for her, and there would be a succession of such women over the years. Connie resented their presence but had to accept it. Not cheerfully, however; she had spells of peevishness that made it unpleasant for whoever was with her.

An era in birding ended for many with the end of that spring migration. The Rockport Cottages were closed permanently. It was too difficult for the doctor-owners to keep good managers, and the cottages themselves, having served for more than forty years, were now too outmoded to provide the comfort travelers expected. Without the charm of the Hagars as hosts, even old friends elected to stay elsewhere. Rather than leave the row of little white houses as reminders of times gone by, the doctors had them removed and the land cleared.

It was both trauma and relief to Connie. She had wanted, and had tried, to be her old self with the guests, but the effort was exhausting, and those who knew her best sometimes saw her more as an imitation of her old self. She tried that hard. The drives with Dr. Goldman and old friends she still enjoyed; no pretense was needed.

The summer of 1967 was exceptionally wet and notable for the lack of storms, as if nature were saving her fury for the massive late hurricane that was born off the Lesser Antilles on September 9 and grew in size and strength as it milled around in the Gulf, threatening one coastline then another, for ten days. On September 19 the weather forecasters told a tense population all around the Gulf that Hurricane Beulah would make landfall that night somewhere on the lower Texas coast but warned that gale winds would be felt for more than a hundred miles from the eye in the northeast quadrant. Rockport was in that quadrant.

More concerned about Connie than herself, Doris packed overnight bags for both, and some food just in case, and after a hasty lunch put Connie and Sudie in her car and started inland. She had no destination in mind, perhaps San Antonio, but at Beeville she turned north on U.S. 181. Perhaps Austin would be better. By then they were wondering if Hurricane Beulah was a myth; stiff winds blew, intermittent rain fell, but otherwise it was a warm and sunny day. Topping a hill out of Kenedy, they saw ahead the Mockingbird Motel, and Doris slowed down. Why not? It looked attractive and safe, all brick around a big courtyard, a restaurant nearby; the name was a good omen. Would they admit Sudie? They did.

Connie thoroughly enjoyed the outing, the rolling landscape reminded her of the Hill Country, the restaurant food was good; it was all rather like a picnic. They had connecting rooms, and while Connie slept most of the time, Doris read, walked Sudie, and listened to the radio.

In the night Hurricane Beulah went ashore near Brownsville, turned up the coast to Corpus Christi, then inland toward Alice and southward into Mexico, brushing Monterrey, then turned again to the coast and died near the Gulf five days later.

Connie and Doris found their homes undamaged but much of the town awash.

Beulah set a record for tornadoes, spawning ninety-five of record, others suspected. A lingering nine-foot storm tide was also a record, and the rains exceeded anything experienced in South Texas for many decades. Thousands of acres were flooded, and in many low-lying places water would stand for three and four years.

Thus, a year later in 1968, Hurricane Beulah produced a bonus to birders and another bird record for Texas and North America, established by two of Connie's most treasured protégés, Doris and Little Doc. More rain, supplementing the floodwaters, had created the habitat preferred by masked ducks—shallow ponds and lakes with an abundance of emergent and floating vegetation. The several records of masked ducks in Texas included one on the upper coast of adults with young, suggesting breeding, but no nest had ever been found in the United States.

Aware of the possibility and with his home range, Brooks County, extensively inundated, Dr. O'Neil was alert for this species, and late in the day on September 1, 1968, he saw what he was hoping for—a pair of masked ducks swimming on Mesquite Lake among willows and huisaches that were belly-deep in water, among water lilies and rattlepod and other emergent plants. The drake's blue bill shone like a sapphire.

He visited the birds nearly every afternoon, often taking others to see them. Sometimes the pair was on the other side of the road, also flooded; sometimes they were not seen at all, and they swam under the water as much as on it.

On September 15 Doris and Kay were with him, but the ducks were out of sight on their first survey; they searched another area but returned to Mesquite Lake, where O'Neil spied the female bathing in a small open area.

He kept his glasses focused on her through a prolonged bath, a careful preening, and her leisurely swim toward his car.

He lost her a time or two in the vegetation or as she swam underwater but managed to locate her again as she entered a chimneylike clump of rattlepod, spatterdock, pickerelweed, and reeds, where she stayed. Peering more intently, he made out a brown mass of weeds about twelve inches above the water level, and on it nestled the duck.

Masked ducks nesting in Texas—a first for the American list!

The observers hardly breathed. The nest was less than thirty feet away, on the other side of a barbed-wire fence. After sitting tightly for about twenty minutes, the duck swam away. Impelled by her own interest but more by knowing what Connie would expect of her, Doris slipped off her shoes and into the water lapping at the roadside. Through the fence, the barbs snagging her blouse, she waded ahead to the clump of weeds. The water was only a few inches above her knees. Parting the plants carefully, she counted six creamy white eggs, noted there was very little down among them, and waded back to the car, acquiring more rents in her blouse. The torn shirt was a willing sacrifice. She had seen eggs in an active masked duck nest, another first for Texas and North America. They waited to see the little hen resume incubation of her treasures, and then they floated away on a cloud of contentment. Connie was avid for details, and as proud as if the achievement had been her own.

Five eggs hatched, and through the winter into April, 1969, the ducklings were seen following one or both parents around the lake. The drake was not seen after February, or perhaps was not recognized since he could have molted into female-like plumage. In April there were only four ducklings, trailing a parent in a broken line, replicas of the mother but not quite so big.

Chapter 16

The Texas Ornithological Society met in Brownsville that Thanksgiving, and another record was set for Dr. O'Neil, then president. It was the wettest TOS meeting ever. Some field trips were rained out, but the Brownsville Chamber of Commerce consoled birders with a reception featuring Border Buttermilk, a tequila concoction so potent that birds were easily forgotten.

Many members stopped off on their way to the meeting to visit Connie, and she welcomed them; it was much like old times. She had gained strength, her several ailments were fairly well under control, and she was back at the piano in the Aransas Pass church. Also, she was writing a monthly column, "Nature Trails," for the *Rockport Pilot*. They were short pieces, rarely more than three hundred words, but they were enthusiastic, stressing the beauties of nature—butterflies, wild flowers, seashells, birds—and often including the phrase, "never a dull moment on the central coast for the nature watcher."

In March, 1969, she was back in Spohn Hospital with a urinary infection, a stay she rather enjoyed; she was allowed visitors and the beer Kay stashed in a cooler in her room. Alice May came to take her home, where Judge Simpson was waiting to take her birding.

The birding fraternity continued to come, to see the birds and always to see Connie. The Teales had been with her in 1968, and again in 1970, not on working trips for the writer but just to be with her and Doris, also a cherished friend, who now answered most of their letters to Connie. On this, their last visit, they could see more clearly than those who were with her every day that Connie was losing ground distressingly.

One Sunday in late November of 1970 she lay on her bed for her prescribed afternoon rest but could not sleep. A norther had entered the Texas Panhandle in the night and was due on the coast before the next morning. At 2 P.M., with warm sunshine flooding Live Oak Peninsula, the prediction was hard to believe. She longed to be outdoors, and tomorrow it might be impossible. Leonard was to come for her later, but on an impulse she telephoned and asked him to come earlier.

Going up Highway 35, they stopped at the little park on the north side of the Tules. The great oaks on the south side, where herons, egrets, spoonbills, and others had once roosted, had been thinned out to make spaces for campsites and recreation vehicles. Like hermit crabs, people now traveled with their homes wrapped around them, moving into larger and larger shells as their affluence grew. Some of the motor homes parked among the oaks that had been spared looked as big as transcontinental buses, complete with living, eating, and sleeping facilities; television; and all the other comforts of the homes the owners were escaping.

But thick shrubs still surrounded the small park on the north side where a brown thrasher hopped and flew an undulating course from treetop to bush and up again, pausing to utter the warning "Chack-chack-chackss." A dozen or so yellow-rumped warblers flitted about. "I've seen a thousand myrtle warblers here, in migration and all through the winter," Connie said, adding rather wistfully, "but we never see so many at once any more."

Turning on Farm Road 1781 toward Copano Village, they found gaillardias still in abundant bloom; open pods of coral bean revealed rows of scarlet seeds; matrimony vines held a feast of small red berries for winter birds; and cow-itch vines drooped, heavy with clusters of the purple berries loved by mockingbirds and golden-fronted woodpeckers.

Lured by standing water, herons, egrets, and ibises fed in low pastures; pairs of mottled ducks swam in roadside borrow

[277]

ditches; cormorants perched on piers spread their wings wide to dry. "Mostly double-crested cormorants now," Connie said. "But a few olivaceous are still around."

October rains had also spawned a festival of frogs; thousands that were tadpoles the previous week freckled the sand and pavement; a belted kingfisher hovered, plunged, and rose again with lunch kicking in its bill. Swarms of dragonflies—electric blue, pale green, deep purple—darted over a swale; a loggerhead shrike chose one with a bright magenta body. False willows were turning brown, their month of glory past, but frost-weed was in its prime.

"Oh, goldenrod!" Connie exclaimed. "It was never abundant here but now has almost disappeared. Ours is the sweet goldenrod, with the anise-like scent." Leonard got out and crushed a cluster; it smelled like anise.

They turned toward Copano Ridge, a reef of sand and shell between Copano Bay and Salt Lake so narrow one could stand on its low backbone and toss a rock into water on either side. At its outer end, the light greens of wild lime, brasil, and agarita contrasted with the very dark green of a mott of taller ebony trees among them.

"This is the last stand of native ebony on this peninsula that I know of," Connie said. "They grew in several places when I first came to Rockport, but like the blackjack oaks they are nearly all gone—so many developments. And look at this."

Another development was all around them—the paved road they had driven on, which replaced a rough, shell-topped path among Spanish dagger, prickly pear, chaparral, and a myriad of wild flowers. The ridge had been a haven for birds and small earth creatures, creeping, crawling, and hopping in a little world of balanced ecology where wild things preyed and were preyed upon but somehow managed to breed and die in the orderly scheme by which nature ensured perpetuation of species.

The ridge had been discovered by man—larger animals that also preyed but were not preyed upon except by others of their kind. Native vegetation had been scraped away, and stakes and strings marked off lots for sale. On a few the skeletons of houses were going up and on another few stood shiny mobile homes. The owners had set out nursery-grown, balled and bur-lapped shrubs to offset the nakedness. Slits in the bayshore had been dredged for future boat slips.

"Horned larks used to nest here," Connie recalled, "and snowy plovers and least terns and nighthawks. And look, there are two horned larks on that vacant lot." One pair had not entirely surrendered their ancestral home. Leonard looked toward a new row of utility poles.

"Can that be an osprey?" he asked. The big bird flew across Salt Lake, clutching in its talons a foot-long fish. It swept past them, and Connie was elated. Ospreys had become rare in recent years.

"That's a hardhead catfish he's planning to eat," she said, adding, "All this building has happened so fast, I was wishing we had not come here, but we would have missed the osprey, so now I'm glad."

On the main road again Leonard stopped to examine a low plant with glossy green fruit partly wrapped in papery brown covering. "Ground cherry," said Connie." It never grows high, but I have seen one really big bush in my secret garden. We will stop there on the way home."

A long migration of snout butterflies had passed over Rattlesnake Point two days earlier, but today there were no snouts. It was a day for queens and also for cloudless sulphurs and cabbage butterflies. A Gulf fritillary alighted and folded its wings to display the silvery spots.

"My mother got me started on butterflies," Connie reminisced. "She also taught me the stars and constellations." Chuckling at the old memory, continued reminiscing. "She didn't give a damn whether I learned anything about astronomy. I had to know the constellations so I would understand Greek mythology and literary allusions. She considered that essential to a proper education."

Other roadsides were dominated by the yellows of broom-weed and yellow aster, but mixed in were lavender wayside asters, portulaca, and cottonweed. A kestrel hovered, dropped, but flew away with empty talons. They stopped to pick a few stems of many-flowered buckwheat, so effective in dried ar-

[279]

rangements, and she had a friend who would appreciate them. Fulvous whistling-ducks preened on the edge of a pool. Nearing town she told Leonard to turn left at the next corner. She was whistling softly to herself.

They turned. She was surprised and apprehensive to see the street paved; she had been expecting a dirt road that ended in a swale and a grove at the edge of a grassy field. Instead there was a swimming pool and beyond it, a sprawling brick house. Connie surveyed the scene silently for a while before speaking quietly: "This was my secret garden, a long way from town then. Ellen Schulz and I used to come here to study the flowers, so many varieties, and many that grew nowhere else on the peninsula. It was a classroom for botany and the cycle of the seasons. I learned so much. Our last stand of Eve's necklace was here. Take me home now, Leonard, please."

The way home was by Little Bay and what had once been Frandolig Island, now a development standing high above the waterline behind a concrete bulkhead; on it were imposing homes, a clubhouse, swimming pool, restaurant, and small shops. Like a fringe around the bulkhead was a fleet of yachts, cabin cruisers, sailboats and motorized craft. Beside the short, arched bridge over the narrow inlet separating the subdivision from the mainland was a large free-standing sign, artistically lettered, proclaiming KEY ALLEGRO, A Birdwatcher's Paradise. The irony was obvious to the most insensitive observer.

"But it was a birdwatcher's paradise when it was Frandolig Island," Connie said. "It was low and sandy and covered with grass and brush, a few small trees. It was paradise at nesting time to herons and egrets, and to ibises and least bitterns and willets. Even cactus wrens and verdins nested here. I learned so much on that island. And in winter it was heaven for thousands of shorebirds and waders. We had seaside sparrows the year round." Then she added, "It's still a paradise for house sparrows. They love it."

They were passing Little Bay, where coots, redheads, scaups, pintails, and other ducks swam around the Connie Hagar Wildlife Sanctuary sign standing out in the water. "You may see several hundred ducks out there now," she told Leonard,

[280]

"but I've seen thousands of redheads and pintails alone and all the other ducks here at one time. The speedboats scatter them these days."

She did not speak bitterly; long ago she had accepted the inevitable. Jack had subscribed to the chamber of commerce creed that "Big is better, growth is good at any price." He had been proud of Rockport's growth, and Connie never quarreled with her beloved Jack.

The changes saddened her, of course, but she could be thankful, and indeed was, for having lived in Rockport before the changes. It occurred to Leonard that she was not really living in Rockport today but rather in the past, dwelling on the years when Live Oak Peninsula had been a birdwatcher's paradise.

That was their last long outing together. The arteriosclerosis worsened, as did the hypertension; the little strokes, TIAs, were more frequent and lasted longer. There were periods of disorientation, though brief, and also episodes of momentary paralysis of her limbs.

In January, 1971, Connie suffered hallucinations; she imagined disasters of global proportions and personal dangers. For the first time in her life she was afraid to be alone. She had good days all along, but at her best the delusions persisted and she rambled in conversation about them.

It did not help that in March the Aransas County Navigation District approved a developer's application to dredge a marina for still another subdivision in Little Bay, a part of the Connie Hagar Wildlife Sanctuary. It would wipe out the small bay on the land side of the beach road where wood storks always gathered in summer, where rails spent the winters along with countless other shorebirds. The application aroused a bitter confrontation between environmentalists and the proponents of "progress." Letters of protest sent to the Navigation Board and to the newspapers came not only from the immediate area but also from afar. At a public hearing on the issue, popular opinion against the project predominated—but lost.

Connie took no part in the battle, but her name, her activities, and her contribution to Rockport's fame were cited in most letters against it. Bravely, she tried to thank all who participated, and the loss hurt her deeply. Most of the time now she lay on her bed gazing out the window, often with the little dog Sudie in her arms.

She grew weaker by the day through April but resisted hospitalization until the twenty-seventh, when it became mandatory. She rallied enough to order the ambulance herself, and Leonard saw her off, but she was almost unconscious on arrival at the hospital.

Strangely, even as he bade her good-bye, Leonard was flushed with a sudden fever and was himself admitted to the same hospital late that afternoon, where he died the next day.

Connie was not told; she was so weak she had to be fed. Doris, Annie Ruth, Kay, and others took turns at her bedside until Alice May arrived and arranged for nursing. She improved gradually but after ten weeks in the hospital, where she passed her eighty-fifth birthday, she was transferred in July to a nearby nursing home. The quick passing that she had always hoped for was not to be; she lived thirty long months in the nursing home.

For a considerable time, the nurses, aware of Mrs. Hagar's background, made a pet of her, and she reacted to the special attention with pleasure, on good days telling funny stories about birds and birders, and reciting poetry. But as the months dragged on and on, she became just another helpless creature, usually indifferent to efforts to brighten her days.

They were miserable months, as dreadful for her friends as for the patient, perhaps more so. Doris kept her supplied with her favorite sugar cookies, Kay supplied beer, and Annie Ruth brought photographs of her growing children and talked of good times past. They and other friends also reported on birds; she smiled feebly to hear that scissortails were coming through, there was a good hawk migration, buff-breasted sandpipers were back on the Rincon.

She was never forgotten. On holidays and often in between there were letters and cards and fresh flowers in her room, ordered from cities and towns across the nation. For Christmas Day, 1972, her room was a bower of blossoms. Kay spent the afternoon with her, reading the letters and greeting cards and holding them up for her to see. There were more than a hundred, and Connie managed a weak chuckle when Kay told her, truthfully, "Believe me, I do not have this many friends."

Many names meant little or nothing to her, people she could not recall, mostly known in the more recent past, but all the names from the distant past, the heyday of Rockport Cottages, brought signs of recognition to her face, perhaps a word or two of comment on shared experiences. A few days later she asked for the messages to be read again and lay listening with closed eyes, but fell asleep before the list was finished.

The sad months dragged on, but Connie would not see another Christmas.

The Texas Ornithological Society met in El Paso that year at Thanksgiving, and many of Connie's friends were there, including her Little Doc, Doris, and Kay. On Saturday morning, November 24, 1973, they had left the motel early on all-day field trips and not until late afternoon did O'Neil get word to call his partner in Falfurrias. Dr. Davis had heard on radio that Mrs. Hagar passed away at half past two that morning. O'Neil made the sad announcement at the convention dinner, but the teary eyes were not because she was gone but in thanks that the long, punishing illness was over, and in relief that she was released at last.

O'Neil caught an early plane Sunday morning, but Doris and Kay were driving; it was 625 miles as the crow flies, much longer for earthbound creatures, but they were on the road early.

It had been many years since Kay had been a regular reporter on the *Corpus Christi Caller-Times*, but before leaving the staff she had written a lengthy obituary on Connie, complete with all but the final date, and had gone back over the years to take it from the library files and update it. She wanted to be sure that when Connie's time came she would depart with a bang and not a whimper.

On hearing the news Saturday she telephoned the editor, John B. Anderson, her longtime friend, to remind him of the story in the files. Anderson assured her that the obituary had been found and would run in the Sunday paper and on the wire services. The funeral would be Monday, he told her. Annie Ruth and her husband Maynard Abrahams were making the arrangements, but the hour was uncertain, depending on when Alice May would arrive.

Taking turns at the wheel, Doris and Kay drove all day, stopping at every open station for gasoline; the country was in an energy crisis and many stations were closed on Sundays. In Uvalde at 5 P.M. another telephone call to the newspaper told them the funeral would be at four o'clock Monday. They would be in time, but they drove on another forty-two miles to Pearsall for the night and were in Corpus Christi by noon next day.

The Sunday paper was still on Kay's doorstep. Newspaper styles had changed; lengthy obituaries now were granted only to prominent figures, but Connie got the celebrity treatment. The lead headline and a two-column photograph dominated the front page.

As Connie would have wished, the services at the funeral home were short and simple; the Episcopal minister read Bible verses and one of her favorite poems. The mourners were bird-watchers from across Texas, and the eulogies were spoken by them, one to another, how they loved her, how much she had meant to all.

Then they all followed her along the beach road to the Rockport Cemetery overlooking the Connie Hagar Wildlife Sanctuary, where she was laid beside Jack, who, she so often had said, made her wonderful life possible.

APPENDIX

Bird names mentioned in the text but which are no longer used are listed on the left, with the corresponding current names opposite.

Former Name	*Current Name*
arctic loon	Pacific loon
Mexican grebe	least grebe
Mexican cormorant	neotropic cormorant
great white heron	a morph of great blue heron
Treganza's heron	a morph of great blue heron
Wurdeman's heron	a morph of great blue heron
American egret, common egret	great egret
Louisiana heron	tricolored heron
white-faced glossy ibis	white-faced ibis
fulvous tree duck	fulvous whistling-duck
black-bellied tree duck	black-bellied whistling-duck
whistling swan	tundra swan
blue goose	a morph of snow goose
baldpate	American wigeon

Former Name	Current Name
marsh hawk	northern harrier
Harlan's hawk	a subspecies of red-tailed hawk
caracara	crested caracara
sparrowhawk	American kestrel
duck hawk	peregrine falcon
prairie chicken	greater prairie-chicken
common gallinule	common moorhen
golden plover	American golden-plover
upland plover	upland sandpiper
Hudsonian curlew	whimbrel
knot	red knot
northern phalarope	red-necked phalarope
noddy tern	brown noddy
ground dove	common ground-dove
red-shafted flicker	northern flicker
yellow-shafted flicker	northern flicker
pewee	eastern wood-pewee
Wied's crested flycatcher	brown-crested flycatcher
tropical kingbird	Couch's kingbird
Derby flycatcher	great kiskadee
chickadee	Carolina chickadee
short-billed marsh wren	sedge wren
long-billed marsh wren	marsh wren
Sennet's titmouse	tufted titmouse (black-crested form)
Rocky Mountain pipit	American pipit
myrtle warbler	a subspecies of yellow-rumped warbler
summer warbler	yellow warbler
Maryland yellowthroat	common yellowthroat
pink-sided junco	dark-eyed junco
slate-colored junco	dark-eyed junco

SUBJECT INDEX

INDEX OF BIRD NAMES

scoter: black, 82; surf, 82; white-winged, 82
seedeater, white-collared, 95
shearwater: Audubon's, 212; sooty, 64, 68, 206
shoveler, northern, 96
shrike: loggerhead, 69, 79 90, 92, 101, 278; northern, 243
siskin, pine, 189, 235
skimmer, black, 42, 63, 77, 83, 105, 129, 139, 150, 167, 184, 188, 210, 250, 254
skylark, 96
snipe, common, 129, 155
sora, 35, 190, 236
sparrow: Bachman's, 169, 192; black-throated, 167, 169–70, 209; Botteri's, 166; Cassin's, 92–93, 105, 110, 133, 190–91, 205 222; chipping, 54, 73; clay-colored, 141, 143; field, 54, 73, 82, 90, 97; fox, 97; grasshopper, 118, 230, 259; Harris', 201, 204, 207, 223, 257; Henslow's, 73, 259; house, 259, 280; lark, 54, 62, 82, 93–94, 97, 181, 185; Le Conte's, 73, 154; Lincoln's, 73, 103; olive, 137, 191–92; savannah, 54, 73, 97, 118–19; seaside, 63, 90, 118, 135, 240, 280; sharp-tailed, 73, 118, 145; song, 54, 73; swamp, 42; vesper, 54, 73, 97; white-crowned, 90, 97, 137, 189, 201; white-throated, 30, 35, 82, 97, 201, 227
spoonbill: roseate, 44, 52, 60, 69, 83, 91, 96, 105, 126, 129–31, 135–36, 145, 158, 185, 193, 200, 226, 232, 264, 277
starling, European, 101, 155–56
stilt, black-necked, 52, 54, 63, 69, 110, 157, 210
stork, wood, 59, 153, 178, 193, 200, 226, 231, 238–39, 281
surfbird, 190
swallow, 163–64; bank, 106; barn, 69, 106, 184; cliff, 106, 137, 184, 190; rough-winged, 106, 137; tree, 102, 106, 117, 170, 240
swan, tundra, 173–74, 215, 243–44
swift, chimney, 184, 239; white-throated, 259

tanager: hepatic, 151, 176, 192; scarlet, 103, 204; summer, 103; western, 248
teal, cinnamon, 151, 169

tern: black, 49, 58, 69, 103, 132, 158, 199, 214, 239; Caspian, 71, 83, 113, 129, 146, 238; Forster's, 71, 105; gull-billed, 110, 135, 146, 210, 237; least, 17, 42, 63, 104, 130, 146, 177, 185, 210, 250, 279; royal, 71, 83, 129–30, 146, 238; Sandwich, 129–30, 146, 185; sooty, 81, 198–99
thrasher: brown, 102, 146, 277; long-billed, 95; sage, 188, 194, 207
thrush, hermit, 29, 30, 32, 55, 97, 236
titmouse, tufted, 35, 62, 69, 78, 169, 181
towee: green-tailed, 73, 151, 188, 201; rufous-sided, 34, 151, 169
tropicbird, white-tailed, 145
turkey, wild, 88

veery, 55
verdin, 37, 63, 73, 165–66, 168–70, 188, 222, 227, 280
vireo: Bell's, 29, 37, 63, 93, 198, 210; black-capped, 171, 191; Philadelphia, 103, 190; red-eyed, 103, 190; solitary, 155, 190, 235; warbling, 63, 69, 190; white-eyed, 185, 190; yellow-throated, 55
vulture, black, 131, 173

warbler: Audubon's, 204, 207; bay-breasted, 55, 76–77, 103, 104, 192; black-and-white, 55, 61, 69, 72, 102–103, 180, 256; Blackburnian, 55, 61, 103; blackpoll, 102, 156, 222; black-throated blue, 74; black-throated gray, 204, 227; black-throated green, 55, 102; blue-winged, 102; Brewster's, 84, 141; Canada, 55; Cape May, 84, 103, 156, 222; cerulean, 55, 103, 152, 156, 222; chestnut-sided, 55, 102, 103; Connecti-cut, 76–77, 156, 227; golden-cheeked, 150, 170–71, 191; golden-winged, 103, 152; hooded, 55, 102; Kentucky, 55, 61, 102; Lucy's, 34; magnolia, 55, 103; mourning, 76–77, 156, 256; myrtle, 30, 204, 207; Nashville, 102; orange-crowned, 55, 90, 97, 102, 150, 228, 235, 245; palm, 104, 207; pine, 90, 102, 168, 179, 189, 207, 237; prairie, 240; prothonotary, 55, 102–103, 243; Swainson's, 72, 190; Tennessee, 55,

ISBN 1-58544-164-3

90000

9 781585 441648